D1233079

Regional Econometric Modeling

International Series in Economic Modeling

Editor:

M. Ray Perryman
  Herman Brown Professor of Economics
  Center for the Advancement of Economic
     Analysis
  Hankamer School of Business
  Baylor University
  Waco, Texas 76798

Advisory Board:

Estelle Bee Dagum
  Statistics Canada
Jan Tinbergen
  Erasmus University
M. Aoki
  Osaka University
Edgar Ortiz
  Universidad Nacional Automatica de Mexico
Houston Stokes
  University of Illinois—Chicago Circle

Regional Econometric Modeling

edited by

M. Ray Perryman
Baylor University
Waco, Texas

James R. Schmidt
University of Nebraska
Lincoln, Nebraska

Kluwer•Nijhoff Publishing
a member of the Kluwer Academic Publishers Group
Boston/Dordrecht/Lancaster

Distributors

for the United States and Canada: Kluwer Academic Publishers, 101 Philip Drive, Assinippi Park, Norwell, Massachusetts 02061, USA

for the UK and Ireland: Kluwer Academic Publishers, MTP Press Limited, Falcon House, Queen Square, Lancaster LA1 1RN, UNITED KINGDOM

for all other countries: Kluwer Academic Publishers Group, Distribution Centre, Post Office Box 322, 3300 AH Dordrecht, THE NETHERLANDS

Library of Congress Cataloging-in-Publication Data

Regional econometric modeling

    (International series in economic modeling)
    Bibliography: p.
    Includes index.
    1. Regional economics—Econometric models.
2. Regional planning—United States—Econometric models.
3. United States—Economic conditions—1945- —Econometric models.   I. Perryman, M. Ray (Marlin Ray), 1952–
II. Schmidt, James R.   III. Series.
HT391.3.R44   1986   330′.028   86-5441
ISBN 0-89838-216-5

Copyright

Contents

Contributing Authors

Jerald R. Barnard, Institute for Economic Research, The University of Iowa, 475 Phillips Hall, Iowa City, Iowa 52242

Richard M. Beemiller, Regional Economist, Bureau of Economic Analysis (BE-61), U.S. Department of Commerce, 1401 K Street NW, Washington, D.C. 20230

Carl G. Brooking, School of Management, Millsaps College, Station A, Jackson, Mississippi 39210

Joseph V. Cartwright, Regional Economist, Bureau of Economic Analysis (BE-61), U.S. Department of Commerce, 1401 K Street NW, Washington, D.C. 20230

Alberta H. Charney, Research Specialist, Division of Economic and Business Research, University of Arizona, Tucson, Arizona 85721

David F. Findley, Statistical Research Division, Bureau of the Census, U.S. Department of Commerce, Washington, D.C. 20233

James E. Kennedy, Board of Governors of the Federal Reserve System, 20th & C Street NW, Washington, D.C. 20551

John R. Kort, Regional Economist, Bureau of Economic Analysis (BE-61), U.S. Department of Commerce, 1401 K Street NW, Washington, D.C. 20230

Brian C. Monsell, Statistical Research Division, Bureau of the Census, U.S. Department of Commerce, Washington, D.C. 20233

M. Ray Perryman, Center for the Advancement of Economic Analysis, Suite 212, Hankamer School of Business, Baylor University, Waco, Texas 76798

Nancy S. Perryman, Center for the Advancement of Economic Analysis, Suite 212, Hankamer School of Business, Baylor University, Waco, Texas 76798

James R. Schmidt, Associate Professor of Economics, University of Nebraska–Lincoln, 342 College of Business Administration, Lincoln, Nebraska 68588-0489

Carol A. Taylor, Program Director for Forecasting, Bureau of Economic and Business Research, University of Florida, 221 Matherly Hall, Gainesville, Florida 32611

Jan Tinbergen, Haviklaan 31, 2566XD The Hague, THE NETHERLANDS

Richard E. Weber, Monmouth College, School of Business, Cedar Avenue, West Long Branch, New Jersey 07764

List of Tables

List of Figures

Preface

This book is the first volume of the *International Series in Economic Modeling*, a series designed to summarize current issues and procedures in applied modeling within various fields of economics and to offer new or alternative approaches to prevailing problems. In selecting the subject area for the first volume, we were attracted by the area to which applied modeling efforts are increasingly being drawn, regional economics and its associated subfields. Applied modeling is a broad rubric even when the focus is restricted to econometric modeling issues. Regional econometric modeling has posted a record of rapid growth during the last two decades and has become an established field of research and application. Econometric models of states and large urban areas have become commonplace, but the existence of such models does not signal an end to further development of regional econometric methods and models. Many issues such as structural specification, level of geographic detail, data constraints, forecasting integrity, and synthesis with other regional modeling techniques will continue to be sources of concern and will prompt further research efforts. The chapters of this volume reflect many of these issues. A brief synopsis of each contribution is provided below:

Richard Weber offers an overview of regional econometric models by discussing theoretical specification, nature of variables, and ultimate usefulness of such models. For an illustration, Weber describes the specification of the econometric model of New Jersey. His chapter serves as a useful example of a state econometric model and the details that surround a state model.

Carl Brooking conducts an analysis of the forecasting accuracy of econometric models for six states in the southeastern region of the United States. Analysis of forecasting performance is an integral part of developing a regional econometric model and Brooking utilizes several standard measures of forecast accuracy in his assessment.

M. Ray and Nancy S. Perryman examine the dynamics of the regional business cycle. In particular, a measure of the cyclical sensitivity of regional economies to national fluctuations is developed and applied to several regions of the United States. The results are easily generalized and provide an index that is independent of the current position in the cyclical pattern.

James R. Schmidt presents a general method of estimating data series at frequencies that are higher than the official reporting frequency. Thus, the method represents an approach to the common problem of having only a few data series available at high reporting frequencies for substate geographic areas. The method is general in the sense that the reporting frequency of a variable need only be an integer multiple of the desired frequency. As an illustration, quarterly personal income series for counties are estimated from the reported annual series.

David F. Findley and Brian C. Monsell introduce new measures for determining whether a time series can be seasonally adjusted in a reliable manner or whether it should remain in unadjusted form. This issue has particular relevance to econometric modeling efforts at substate geographic levels where time series can behave quite erratically and efforts to seasonally adjust them can yield puzzling results.

Alberta H. Charney and Carol A. Taylor consider the problem of integrating state and substate econometric models. Specifications of a relatively large and integrated modeling system for the state of Arizona and its SMSAs are described in detail. Careful attention is given to the role of the government sector within the model. Various fiscal policy changes are simulated to illustrate the applicability of this modeling approach.

John R. Kort, Joseph V. Cartwright, and Richard M. Beemiller discuss the separate characteristics of, and linkage between, two regional modeling systems: the National-Regional Impact Evaluation System (NRIES II) and the Regional Input-Output Modeling System (RIMS II). The NRIES II model is a large multiregional econometric model consisting of models for each state. Powerful capabilities of impact and policy analysis are achieved by linking the two modeling systems.

Jerald R. Barnard and James E. Kennedy present a method of analysis for determining the strength and pattern of regional responses to national business cycles. Their method is based on vector autoregressive models that contain key regional and national economic variables. Thus, the method represents a departure from using traditional structural models of regional economies for assessing sensitivities to national economic movements.

Jan Tinbergen analyzes important issues in the specification and estimation of cross-sectional production functions. This type of analysis has extensive applicability in recent efforts to link regional models into larger systems. The methodology is applied to cross-sectioned data for the states in the United States.

Obviously, we have selected a broad range of issues relevant to the contemporary frontiers of regional economic modeling. Our authors, ranging from the Nobel laureate who developed the first econometric model to young scholars engaged in pioneering efforts, are highly regarded for their innovation and expertise. It is the hope of the editors that the papers in this volume will serve to stimulate additional efforts directed toward the advancement of the exciting and rapidly growing field.

I METHODOLOGICAL ISSUES

1 SOME EXTENSIONS AND REFINEMENTS OF GOTTSCHALK'S ESTIMATION OF PRODUCTION FUNCTIONS

Jan Tinbergen

I. The Use of Production Functions with Multiple Inputs

It goes without saying that *production functions* constitute one of the central concepts in economic science, comparable in importance with utility functions. They are the concept from which supply of products and demand for production factors are derived, whereas utility functions are at the origin of the demand for products and the supply of production factors.

The importance of production functions explains why extensive and diversified research on their structure has developed. A great variety of mathematical functions have been tested and a large degree of ingenuity has been devoted to what forms of such functions bring about satisfactory results. In fact, more creativity and effort has been devoted to this aspect of the productive process than to the question of the number of factors involved. In virtually all of the well-known literature, the number of factors is presumed to be small, i.e., at most four inputs. There are, however, also situations in which a large number of inputs is essential. This scenario occurs, for example, in productive processes in which raw materials are considered as (alternative) inputs, i.e., where gross output is treated as a measure of production rather than value added. It also applies if a distinction between

3

many types of labor must be made, as when differences in earnings across a large number of occupational groups are studied. The examination of income distribution patterns serves as an illustration of this type of analysis.

II. Gottschalk's Imaginative Method and Remarkable Results

Professor Peter T. Gottschalk (1978) is one of the few scholars to systematically pursue the problem of estimating a multiple input production function. The main difficulty to be expected when the number of productive factors—and, hence, independent variables for medium- or long-term production functions—is large is the occurrence of *multicollinearity*. Gottschalk proposed and applied an imaginative method by assuming that the production process could be treated as a *combination of two subprocesses*. A very simple example he gives is the dual functions of shaping a piece of pottery and painting it. A more general example used in his application draws the distinction between *technical production* and *administration*. His additional assumption is that *one* of the production factors (whose quantity is denoted by j) is used in both subprocesses in quantities j_1, and j_2, respectively. All other production factors are employed in only one of the subprocesses with the relevant quantities being indicated by m_h ($h = 1, 2, \ldots, H$) for subprocess 1 and by n_k ($k = 1, 2, \ldots, K$) for subprocess 2. Thus, the number of inputs is $1 + H$ for subprocess 1, $1 + K$ for subprocess 2, and $1 + H + K$ for the complete process.

The method presented here is designed for a set of observations among which the quantities of each single factor do not differ substantially. This case is often applicable to cross-sectional studies across geographical areas, e.g., American states or Japanese prefectures. The variables are expressed as *deviations from their averages* and, consequently, the observations of each variable must, by definition, sum to zero. The equations for the subprocesses will be written

$$y = f_1^0 j_1 + \sum_{h=1}^{H} f_h^1 m_h \tag{1.1}$$

and

$$y = f_2^0 j_2 + \sum_{k=1}^{K} f_k^2 n_k \tag{1.2}$$

where $j = j_1 + j_2$ (1.3)

In these expressions, y denotes product and the f values represent marginal productivity. In the superscript index, 0 refers to factor j or its components, 1 to the other inputs to subprocess 1, and 2 to the other inputs to subprocess 2. Similarly, the subscripts 1 and 2 in the first right-side term refer to j_1 and j_2, h denotes the factors used in subprocess 1, and k indicates those used in subprocess 2.

The economic problem under consideration (as distinct from the estimation problem) is the determination of values for y, j_1, and j_2, given quantities j, m_h, and n_k. The solutions can be generated from equations 1.1, 1.2, and 1.3 as follows:

$$j_1 = \frac{y - \sum_h f_h^1 m_h}{f_1^0} = b_1(y - \sum_h f_h^1 m_h) = b_1(y - m) \tag{1.4}$$

$$j_2 = \frac{y - \sum_k f_k^2 n_k}{f_2^0} = b_2(y - \sum_k f_k^2 n_k) = b_2(y - n) \tag{1.5}$$

where $b_i = 1/f_i^0 (i = 1, 2)$, $m = \sum_h f_h^1 m_h$, and $n = \sum_k f_k^2 n_k$. Addition of equations 1.4 and 1.5 yields

$$j = by - b_1 m - b_2 n \tag{1.6}$$

where $b = b_1 + b_2$. From this expression we derive

$$y = \frac{j + b_1 m + b_2 n}{b} \tag{1.7}$$

Substituting 1.7 into equations 1.4 and 1.5, we obtain

$$j_1 = b_1(j - b_2 m + b_2 n)/b \tag{1.8}$$

$$j_2 = b_2(j + b_1 m - b_1 n)/b \tag{1.9}$$

For a discussion of these results it is preferable to return to the marginal productivity notation, i.e.,

$$y = \frac{f_1^0 f_2^0}{f_1^0 + f_2^0} j + \sum_h \frac{f_h^1 f_2^0}{f_1^0 + f_2^0} m_h + \sum_k \frac{f_k^2 f_1^0}{f_1^0 + f_2^0} n_k \tag{1.10}$$

Although the notation conventions differ, this formula is identical to that derived by Professor Gottschalk (1978).

In the Gottschalk analysis, equation 1.1 is applied to data on *manufacturing in the United States*. The estimation utilizes 1959 *Census of Population* data, as well as information from the 1958 *Census of Manufactures*. Six types of labor were used, i.e., professionals, managers, sales workers, operatives, craftsmen, and "supporting workers" (clerical workers, service workers, and laborers). Additionally, an estimate of the quantity of capital utilized in the production process is included.

The remarkable findings from this analysis consist of two classes of results. *Statistically*, Gottschalk succeeds in obtaining clearly *more reliable* regression coefficients than previous authors. Substantively, his conclusions are of considerable economic and perhaps even political interest. He finds clear *deviations* between median *incomes* of the types of labor considered and their *marginal productivities*. This result may be explained in two different ways—either the labor market compartments involved show deviations from free competition or the way in which marginal productivity is estimated must be rejected. These possibilities have been explored elsewhere (see Tinbergen, 1981; 1982) and the interested reader is referred to these sources. It is the objective of this chapter to discuss a correction of Gottschalk's method and its application, which seems necessary, but which invalidates neither the method's originality nor the main results.

III. The Need for a Correction and Alternative Methods of Correction

The requisite correction lies in the fact that Gottschalk estimates the marginal productivities in the subprocesses 1.1 and 1.2 by replacing both j_1 in equation 1.1 and j_2 in equation 1.2 by j.

Two methods of correction seem to be possible. We will refer to them, respectively, as a *restrictive version* and a *general-validity version*. In the former case, we will consider an approach characterized by an *additional assumption* that evidently implies that while the results (slightly modified) remain valid, they are *subject to a restriction*. Secondly, we present a (general-validity) process which provides a correction method that is not subject to a limitation (but differs, of course, from the original formulation).

IV. The Correction in Its Restrictive Version

The replacement of j_1 and j_2 by j may be accepted if we add a restriction of the form

$$j_1 = \alpha_j \tag{1.11}$$

This constraint will be termed the *proportionality hypothesis* (recall that equation 1.11 only applies to the deviations j_1 and j_2 from their respective averages). In addition to restricting the model of equations 1.1–1.3, this hypothesis also introduces an additional *degree of freedom* provided that we do not prescribe a specific value for α. We will consider two cases, one in which α is given an a priori value of 0.5 and the other in which α is treated as a parameter to be determined in accordance with some predefined criterion. This criterion may be either statistical—e.g., the maximum $\bar{R}^2$ for an expression equivalent to equation 1.10—or economic. We elect the latter option and require that the total income shares of the factors of production add up to unity, i.e., the case of *no returns to scale* for the economy as a whole.

It can be easily shown that equation 1.1 must be replaced by

$$
y = \frac{\dfrac{f_1^0 f_2^0}{\alpha(1-\alpha)}}{\dfrac{f_1^0}{\alpha} + \dfrac{f_2^0}{1-\alpha}} j + \sum_h \frac{\dfrac{f_h^1 f_2^0}{1-\alpha}}{\dfrac{f_1^0}{\alpha} + \dfrac{f_2^0}{1-\alpha}} m_h + \sum_k \frac{\dfrac{f_k^2 f_1^0}{\alpha}}{\dfrac{f_1^0}{\alpha} + \dfrac{f_2^0}{1-\alpha}} n_k \tag{1.12}
$$

Some numerical examples will be shown in section VI, after the other version has been examined.

V. The Correction in Its General-Validity Version ("A" Method)

If we do not find the restrictive version of the first correction to be satisfactory, we are faced with a more complex situation. It can be seen from equations 1.8 and 1.9 that j_1 or j_2 cannot be replaced by j and only one of the other input combinations m or n. This approach was adapted by Gottschalk (1978) when, in his estimation process, he estimates equations 1.1 and 1.2 while replacing j_1 and j_2, respectively, by j. If j_1 and, hence, j_2 are not proportional to j, then they must be replaced by a linear combination of j, m, and n, as per equations 1.8 and 1.9. I have discussed this estimation process elsewhere (see Tinbergen, 1982b) and will only summarize my general-validity version in the present section. My choice of the linear combinations just mentioned was to express n and m as follows:

$$
n = \sum_k f_k^2 n_k = A_{20} j + \frac{b_1}{b_2} A_{21} \sum_h f_h^1 m_h \tag{1.13}
$$

$$
m = \sum_h f_h^1 m_h = A_{10} j + \frac{b_2}{b_1} A_{12} \sum_h f_k^2 n_k \tag{1.14}
$$

Substituting 1.13 into 1.8 and the resulting expression into 1.1 yields

$$y = \frac{1 + b_2 A_{20}}{b} j + \frac{b_1(1 + A_{21})}{b} \sum_h f_h^1 m_h \tag{1.1'}$$

Similarly, substitution of 1.14 into 1.9 and the result into 1.2 gives an expression of the form

$$y = \frac{1 + b_1 A_{10}}{b} j + \frac{b_2(1 + A_{12})}{b} \sum_k f_k^2 n_k \tag{1.2'}$$

Note that the A's are purely *empirically determined regression coefficients* which register the optimal means of eliminating the n and m from equations 1.1 and 1.2.

Thus far, we have confined our analysis to the algebraic side of the problem. We will now, however, proceed to the estimation procedures. The coefficients to be *estimated* will be denoted by B in order to strictly distinguish them from the preceding coefficients. Specifically, estimate the B's of the following four regression equations:

$$y = B_1^0 j + \sum_h B_h^1 m_h \tag{1.15}$$

$$y = B_2^0 j + \sum_k B_k^2 n_k \tag{1.16}$$

$$\sum_k B_k^2 n_k = B_{20} j + B_{21} \sum_h B_h^1 m_h \tag{1.17}$$

$$\sum_h B_h^1 m_h = B_{10} j + B_{12} \sum_k B_k^2 n_k \tag{1.18}$$

It is apparent that equations 1.15 and 1.16 have to be estimated initially in order to know the values of B_h^1 and B_k^2 in 1.17 and 1.18. These coefficients then supply us with the B_{10}, B_{12}, B_{20}, and B_{21}.

Confrontation of equations 1.15 through 1.18 with equations 1.1', 1.2', 1.13, and 1.14 then yields the following set of results:

$$B_1^0 = \frac{1 + b_2 A_{20}}{b} \tag{1.19}$$

$$B_2^0 = \frac{1 + b_1 A_{10}}{b} \tag{1.20}$$

$$B_h^1 = \frac{b_2(1 + A_{21})}{b} f_h^1 \tag{1.21}$$

$$B_k^2 = \frac{b_2(1 + A_{12})}{b} f_k^2 \tag{1.22}$$

$$B_{20} = \frac{b_2}{b}(1 + A_{12}) A_{20} \tag{1.23}$$

$$B_{10} = \frac{b_1}{b}(1 + A_{21})A_{10} \qquad (1.24)$$

$$B_{21} = \frac{1 + A_{12}}{(1 + A_{21})^2} \frac{bA_{21}}{b_1} \qquad (1.25)$$

$$B_{12} = \frac{1 + A_{21}}{(1 + A_{12})^2} \frac{bA_{12}}{b_1} \qquad (1.26)$$

The unknowns of our problem are now the f_h^1, f_k^2, b_1, b_2, b ($= b_1 + b_2$); and four A's, numbering $H + K + 6$. We thus have a system of eight equations and eight unknowns, i.e., a solvable model. A numerical example is elaborated in Tinbergen (1982a), a portion of which will be shown in section VI.

VI. Some Numerical Results for the USA 1959

In the present section we will show some results illustrating Gottschalk's method and our proposed corrections in order to compare them with a direct estimation of the production function for the United States in 1959. Since Gottschalk's data are not at our disposal, we use the information from Kol and Tinbergen (1980). The cross-sectional observations in the sample refer to the fifty states in the United States. In the estimated expression, production is measured by annual income in dollars per capita (y) and the quantities of five types of labor are expressed in millions of persons employed. With regard to the specific types of workers, x_1 refers to technicians, professionals, etc., x_2 to managers etc., x_3 to white collar workers (sales workers and clerical workers), x_4 to blue collar workers (service workers, laborers, operatives, and craftsmen), and x_5 to farm managers and workers. A linear function of the proportion of workers (all types) employed in capital-intensive industries (transportation, public utilities, mining, and production of durable consumer goods) was utilized as a proxy x_6 for the capital stock. Five sets of results are enumerated in table 1-1. Specifically, case 1 expresses ln y as a linear function of the ln of x_1 through x_6. Similarly, case 2 expresses y as a linear function of x_1 through x_6 and cases 1 and 2 are estimated directly, i.e., in a single regression equation. Cases 3 through 5 are estimated with the aid of Gottschalk's method. In subprocess 1 (technical production) x_1, x_4, x_5, and x_6 are used as independent variables, while subprocess 2 (administration) employs x_1, x_2, and x_3. Case 3 uses his method without correction. Cases 4 and 5 utilize the method of correction, with α being assigned values of 0.5 and 0.25, respectively.

Table 1-1. Regression Coefficients and Shares of Six Production Factors, Obtained in Seven Cases, for Direct Method, Gottschalk Method, and Corrected Gottschalk Method

Case	Method	Variables	x_1	x_2	x_3	x_4	x_5	x_6	
1	Direct	logs	0.237	0.006	0.741	−0.305	−0.0072	0.098	
2	Direct	abs.	6.47	−0.06	7.69	−0.57	−0.89	0.55	
3	G uncorr.	abs.	5.37	−3.16	4.98	0.031	−0.285	0.566	
4	G corr.	$\alpha = 0.5$	10.74	−3.16	4.98	0.031	−0.285	0.566	
5	G corr.	$\alpha = 0.25$	9.32	−4.11	6.48	0.014	−0.124	0.246	
									Sum of Shares
			Shares in Total Product (in promilles)						
1	Direct	logs	237	6	741	−305	−72	98	705
2	Direct	abs.	354	−3	765	−133	−39	56	1000
3	G uncorr.	abs.	294	−135	496	7	−12	57	707
4	G corr.	$\alpha = 0.5$	587	−135	496	7	−12	57	1000
5	G corr.	$\alpha = 0.25$	510	−176	645	3	−5	25	1002

x_1 professions, technicians, etc. x_4 blue collar   abs.: absolute value
x_2 managers, etc. x_5 farm   uncorr.: uncorrected
x_3 white collar x_6 capital   corr.: corrected

VII. Some Comments

As disscussed in previous publications (Kol and Tinbergen, 1980; Tinbergen, 1981, 1982a, b), negative marginal utilities are less rare than is often thought. For blue-collar workers, the phenomenon may occur as a consequence of keeping in reserve a number of laborers when an economic recovery is anticipated. For farmers, it may be explained by an underestimate of labor costs associated with small farmers and their family members or, alternatively, by a maximum level of production rather than maximum profit. For managers, seeking it may be the result of counterproductivity when the marginal production figure is estimated from industry data as opposed to single-firm information.

In the publications previously referred to it was also demonstrated that the t values of the results obtained by Gottschalk are considerably higher than those generated via the direct method of estimation.[1] The principal conclusion justified by table 1-1 is that negative or very small marginal utilities are obtained for the same production factors in both the uncorrected approach and the corrected Gottschalk methods. Although the modifications seem to be desirable, they do not affect the originality and the usefulness of Gottschalk's method. Moreover, the latter technique admits generalizations and variations that make it an attractive avenue for further investigation. These extensive areas will be discussed in subsequent work.

Note

[1] This finding may be illustrated by the following regression equations, obtained by Jacob Kol, whom I wish to thank for his computing assistance. Direct regression using absolute values of the variables (t-values in parentheses):

$$y = 6.74x_1 - 0.06x_2 + 7.69x_3 - 0.57x_4 - 0.89x_5 + 0.55x_6 \qquad \bar{R}^2 = 0.66$$
$$\quad (2.02) \quad (0.02) \quad (3.83) \quad (1.17) \quad (1.61) \quad (0.74)$$

Regressions for the two subprocesses:

$$y = 15.48x_1 \qquad\qquad + 0.10x_4 - 0.82x_5 + 1.63x_6 \qquad \bar{R}^2 = 0.57$$
$$\quad (9.31) \qquad\qquad\qquad (0.20) \quad (1.45) \quad (2.22)$$

$$y = 8.23x_1 - 4.84x_2 + 7.63x_3 \qquad \bar{R}^2 = 0.65$$
$$\quad (2.65) \quad (1.83) \quad (5.08)$$

The general pattern of higher t-values in the latter case should be noted.

References

Gottschalk, P. T. 1978. A comparison of marginal productivity and earnings by occupation. *Industrial and Labor Relations Review* 31:368–378.

Kol, J., and J. Tinbergen. 1980. Market-determined and residual incomes—some dilemmas. *Economie Appliquée* 33:285–301.

Tinbergen, J. 1981. Contraproduktie. In P. J. Eygelshoven and L. J. van Gemerden (Eds.), *Inkomensverdeling en openbare financiën*. Utrecht/Antwerpen: Opstellen voor Jan Pen, Het Spectrum (Dutch).

Tinbergen, J. 1982a. Deviations between earnings and marginal productivity: Two studies compared. In G. R. Feiwel (Ed.), *Samuelson and Neoclassical Economics*. Boston/The Hague/London: Kluwer-Nijhoff.

Tinbergen, J. 1982b. Fonctions de production à plusieurs facteurs: une seconde correction. Cahiers du Département d'Econométrie, Faculté des Sciences Economiques et Sociales, Université de Genève, Cahier 82.04.

2 REGIONAL ECONOMETRIC MODELING AND THE NEW JERSEY STATE MODEL

Richard E. Weber

I. Introduction

Beginning with the widespread availability of computers in the 1960s and following the rash of activity in building and using multiequation econometric models of the national economy, there began the application of these techniques to modeling regional economies.

Econometric models have two major purposes: (1) to provide forecasts of economic activity and (2) to provide estimates of economic impacts. Forecasts and impact analysis are used by government and business to select and implement policies and to infer reactions from such policies and from other exogenous shocks such as the energy crisis of the early 1970s. The major factors leading to the widespread development of regional economic models include: (1) widespread acceptance and use of national models; (2) major improvements in the quality and extent of regional data; (3) significant advances in the size, cost reduction, and availability of computers; (4) a more active and sophisticated approach to planning by government and business; and (5) the rapid growth of statistical and econometric theory and the technology of model building—i.e., more growth yields more growth.

The bibliography to this chapter lists articles and papers describing many

13

of these models. A summary of models and modeling approaches used at the time is given by J. L. Knapp, et al. (1976); and what one might call an update on the state of the art is given by Kort (1982).

II. Regional Modeling

Regional economic models may be thought of as either input-output (I-O) or econometric, although several econometric models incorporate I-O subsectors. Examples of the latter may be found in Dresch and Goldberg (1973), d'Amours (1979; d'Amours et al., 1975), L'Esperance (1977), Bourque, et al. (1977), Glickman (1977), Treyz (1980), and Kort and Cartwright (1982). I-O models are generally used for regional impact analysis, where detailed interindustry effects are of importance. It has been difficult to make the technical coefficients dynamic, which limits their usefulness for continuing impact analysis and in general precludes their use as forecasting tools.

While econometric models are used for both forecasting and impact analysis, most designs are clearly more attuned to forecasting. The major problem in using econometric models for impact analysis is that the changing of a major policy variable explicitly invalidates major assumption utilized in estimating the parameters, i.e., that future interactions among variables will be the same as in the past. Additionally, the heavy reliance on chosen values for the "add factors" used to adjust the outcome of simulations calls into question the validity of impacts implied by the model.

Regional econometric modeling differs considerably from national modeling. First, economic theory is an excellent guide to the construction of national models in that the assmption of a closed system is supportable. The basis for national models is the theory of income and employment determination simply expressed by the equations

$$Y = C + I + G + (X - M)$$
$$C = a + bY$$
$$I = c + dP + eY$$

with P, G, X, and M exogenous

where

Y = gross national product
C = consumption expenditures
I = investment expenditures

P = profit expectations
G = government expenditures
X = exports
M = imports

Given small values for X and M, and understanding that policy actions dictate G, the above system becomes completely closed. Alternatively, regional models deal with an open system in which external economic impacts are far more important than endogenous factors, i.e., the X and M values are not insignificant.

Second, in most developed nations there are abundant data for use by the national model builder. But in the case of regions within those nations, there is a paucity of data, and what data are available are rarely from a unified source.[1] Five approaches to regional model building have been identified: (1) satellite single-region, (2) top-down single-region, (3) top-down multiregion, (4) bottom-up multiregion, and (5) hybrid multiregion.[2] The first of these, of which the model presented herein is an example, will be discussed shortly.

In the top-down approach, as in the satellite single-region approach, regional economic activity is determined by exogenous national variables and the result is then distributed to local areas within the region. The top-down multiregional approach is similar in that economic activity is determined at the national level and then distributed to regions with the constraint that the share coefficients sum to 1 across all regions. In a variation on this theme, economic activity is estimated at the regional level and summed across regions to get the national values, with any discrepancy between the summed values and those generated by a national model removed by adjustment of the regional values. The bottom-up multiregional approach carries this last step to its logical extension by eliminating the national model altogether and simply using the combined regional values as the national estimates, without adjustment. Finally, in the hybrid multiregion approach all regional activity is not forced to national control totals; rather, certain variables are designated as determinants of regional activity and certain other variables are aggregated, without adjustment, to national totals. The National Regional Impact Evaluation System (NRIES), developed by the U.S. Department of Commerce, Bureau of Economic Analysis (BEA) is such a model.

Satellite Single-Region Models

In the satellite single-region approach, as suggested by Klein (1969), the regional endogenous variables are determined as functions of one another and by a number of regional exogenous variables, while the whole system is driven by national exogenous variables. It is assumed that there is no impact on the national variables by changes in the region. For most regions any such impact would be quite small and thus, it is thought, can be ignored. In matrix notation the system would be

$$Y_r = A \cdot X_r + B \cdot X_n$$

where A and B are coefficient matrices and Y and X are endogenous and exogenous variable vectors identified by the subscripts (r) regional, and (n) national.

Examples of such models for states are Ohio (L'Esperance et al., 1969), Georgia (Grimes, 1973), Mississippi (Brooking, 1974), Pennsylvania (Klein and Glickman, 1974), New Jersey (Weber, 1976), and Tennessee (Chang, 1976; Gustely, 1978). Examples of local models are Philadelphia SMSA (Glickman, 1971, 1977), Boston SMSA (Engle et al., 1972), Buffalo SMSA (Crow, 1973), Los Angeles SMSA (Hall and Licari, 1974), Milwaukee SMSA (Rubin and Erickson, 1980), and Chicago SMSA (Duobinis, 1981).

Theoretical Design

As indicated above, designers of regional models do not have the luxury of working with a complete economic theory in developing their model. The concept of structural modeling is that endogenous variables are related to one another and to a set of exogenous variables. At the national level this concept can be implemented, as it is possible to design a closed system of simultaneous equations through which the model can account for virtually all economic activity. At the regional level the system is so open, with a major part of the economic activity spilling over to nearby regions and to the national economy, that a structurally sound system of simultaneous equations is not possible. Moreover, were such an approach theoretically achieved, lack of sufficient data for estimation of equations would prohibit use of the theoretical model. Thus, the designer of the regional model is forced to rely on economic theory for the basic design, but must modify that design as dictated by the realities of the open system and data limitations.

Methods of design have included: informal judgmental methods, leading indicators, trend extrapolation, (semi) structural econometric models, reduced-form econometric models, and advanced methods of time series analysis (Kinal and Ratner, 1982). Usually, the selection of determinant variables is based on economic theory.[4] For example, income/output variables are modeled on the basis of demand theory and employment/wage variables on the basis of derived demand theory. Final selection of independent variables and model structure depends on statistical tests such as R^2, Students' t, and Durbin-Watson. Completed models usually contain both simultaneous and recursive sectors.

Nature of Variables

Typically, regional econometric models are either income or output based, although the latter designation is really a misnomer. The model to be described herein would be designated an output-based model. However, a reading of the author's works on estimating GSP (Weber, 1979, 1980, 1982) would quickly reveal that the so called output data are in reality estimates of output based on income data. Thus, any such models, though called output models, are in reality income-based models.

Using that designation, most single-region models are of the income type, probably because of the simple reason that the most complete set of reliable economic data for regions is published by BEA and consists of total personal income (either by place of work or by origin) and its components. These data are available annually for every county in the United States, and both annually and quarterly for every state. A more complete discussion of these data can be found in Weber (1979, 1980, 1982). A particular advantage of this data set to the regional modeler is that the data are benchmarked to the National Income and Product Accounts. The latter form the basis for most of the national models from which many of the exogenous variables used to drive the regional model are selected. They are also the variables most used to describe and analyze the national economy and thus provide a useful framework for the regional model.

Regional models also are likely to include employment and wage variables because these variables are of major importance in describing and analyzing the economy, and a reliable set of data is available from the U.S. Department of Labor Bureau of Labor Statistics (BLS). Like the income data, these data are available on an annual basis for states and counties. Moreover, they are both temporally and spatially consistent with the BEA income data. An added attraction is that labor force and unemployment data, both important descriptive and analytic variables, are available from BLS on a basis compatible with the employment and wage information.

Unfortunately, for most areas these data are lacking in spatial consistency and accuracy due to deficiencies in estimation methods (Kort, 1982). This does not hold, however, for the regional modeler in the ten most populated states in which the BLS uses the Current Population Surveys as the basis for their estimates of employment and unemployment data. In this case, the accuracy and spatial conformance is quite good.[5]

Other national sources of data for the regional modeler include the population data from the decennial census augmented by the Current Population Reports and data on manufacturing from the Census of and Annual Survey of Manufactures, both provided by the Bureau of the Census. For those interested in states with major farming sectors, the U.S. Department of Agriculture provides ample data for model building. Some modelers also are tapping the Social Security Administration's Continuous Work History Sample for labor force and migration estimates and the Internal Revenue Service's Statistics on Income, both annual series disaggregated by state. Beyond these sources, national data become spotty in that, where spatially complete, they are given only for selected years, leaving the modeler to wonder how to develop reliable parameter estimates from such data.

Recent Directions

Recent work in regional modeling seems to be taking two directions: (1) technological improvement and (2) expansion. The first of these is exemplified by the variety of national-regional approaches such as the NRIES mentioned above and by extensions thereof. For example, Perryman (1981) has discussed the extension of the Texas model to include geographical and sectoral subsectors. Another theoretical direction being taken is the development of quarterly models (Doti, 1982), although some work seems to have been done in that direction earlier (Burton and Dyckman, 1965). And finally, there is the development of new methods of parameter estimation represented by the use of ARIMA methods for estimating complete model parameters (Kinal and Ratner, 1982). In the latter case, the focus is strictly on forecasting since the models are not suitable for impact assessment.

The second direction of change is a beginning of the process of including interregional variables. This has taken the form of economic-demographic modeling exemplified by Isserman (1982), Plaut (1981), and Greenberg and Renfro (1982), in which migration to and from the "rest of the world" is implied. Another example is Polenske (1980), in which interregional trade flows are modeled.

Usefulness

The "test of the market" clearly indicates that both national and regional models are useful, since there is a proliferation of both. We do not buy what we cannot use. (Although in this respect there may be a pseudo-Gresham's-law effect, in which "bad-models" drive out "good-models," caused by the emphasis on marketing by makers of the former and on design by makers of the latter). Part of this success is attributable to a *prestige effect* in that a forecast that can be referred back to a nationally recognized model is considerably more acceptable to policy makers in business and government—the appeal-to-authority argument. In this connection it is particularly interesting to note that virtually all models contain some equations that have been adjusted by so called "add factors" based on expert judgment as to what would be an acceptable forecast, actually improving accuracy in the long run. Additionally, even when pure mechanical forecasts are developed using these models, an economic forecaster will edit and interpret the forecast for the decision maker (Zarnowitz, 1974). One might question just how much better forecasts from such models would be when compared to simple judgmental forecasts. That is, as Paul Samuelson is alleged to have remarked, "The secret of the Wharton [econometric] model is that Larry Klein is inside" (Kinal and Ratner, 1982). However, if the forecasts resulting from the use of these models failed to provide generally useful and accurate results, this appeal-to-authority argument would not be sufficient.

Studies have shown national models to improve on our ability to forecast the level and direction of the economy. In one study, with a sample of well-regarded forecasters using structural econometric models, real GNP was predicted one year ahead during the period 1959–1976 with an average error of 1 to 1.5 percentage points. The inflation rate was predicted with an average absolute error of about 1.4 percentage points. The forecasts outperform a naive extrapolation of last year's change—though only the real GNP forecasts do so by a wide margin (Zarnowitz, 1978). In another study, when the record of five major econometric models is studied, over half of the median forecasts of real GNP (for four quarters ahead) were within 0.5 percent of the actual value (McNees, 1979). In an earlier study of seven models, McNees (1974) reported that accuracy in forecasting inflation one to four quarters ahead ranged from 1.3 to 2.1 percent.

The success of national models does not prove that regional models will also be successful. However, it certainly is a good indication that if the same methods of development are used in constructing regional models as was used in making national models (and this actually is the case) regional models will give similar results. Some evidence for this conclusion does exist. Brooking and Hake (1980) report that three econometric models of the southeastern states had average errors of 2 to 2.7 percent in forecasting state employment and personal income.

In any case, the major utility of either national or regional models is not the actual forecast resulting from a purely mechanical simulation of the model. Rather, the utility of these models is threefold:

1. They provide a useful starting place for the development of the forecast to be used.
2. They identify those variables for which judgmental decisions are to be made and the relative impact of changes in these judgmental variables.
3. Finally, and perhaps most importantly, they force a consistency among the values of a variables appearing in final results, i.e., the forecast is forced to be internally consistent (Zarnowitz, 1974).

Of course, as we learn in economics, there is no unmitigated good. One major limitation of satellite single-region models is the lack of interregional feedbacks among contiguous areas. As presently designed, while economic effects follow *economic* boundaries the models usually follow *political* boundaries, thus missing important economic feedbacks within the region. The multiregional models and extensions of single regional models discussed above are attempts to resolve this problem.

III. Gross State Product

The next section will present a detailed description of the design and testing of an econometric model of New Jersey. The fundamental purpose of the model is to provide forecasts of the various components of gross state product (GSP). For that reason GSP forms the central part of the model. In order to assist the reader in understanding the description of the model to follow, a description of the nature and concept of the GSP accounts is presented first.

The estimates of GSP used in developing the model follow the same framework as the GNP accounts provided by the U.S. Department of Commerce. A system of regional accounts can be expressed in any one of three equivalent sets of aggregate measures of economic activity: gross expenditures by class (GSE), gross income by type (GSI), and gross product by sector (GSP).

This equivalence is demonstrated in figure 2-1, which shows an abstract view of a typical economy, and table 2-1, which lists the various categories of figure 2-1 by type of measurement. GSE is equal to the sum of the categories

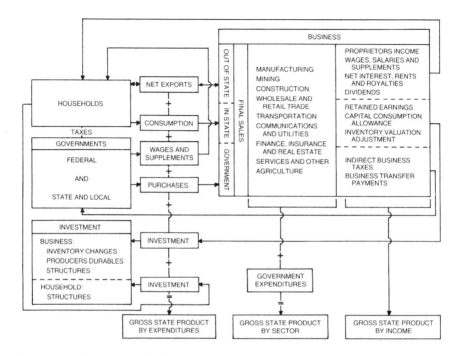

Figure 2-1. Flow Chart of Regional Economic Activity

in the left-hand column of both figure 2-1 and table 2-1. GSI is equal to the sum of the center columns and GSP is equal to the sum of the right-hand columns. The circular flow of activity depicted in figure 2-1 clearly indicates the equivalence of the three measures, as inflows from one stage are necessarily outflows from another. For example, the receipts of households are the source of expenditures for that sector and are at the same time the result of expenditures of the business sector. Because of this equivalence GSP can be measured at any of the three stages, theoretically always resulting in the same total.

Complete data are not gathered at anything less than the national level by any governmental agency for any one of the three accounts (nor, to our knowledge, by any private agency). It is quite difficult, if not impossible, to adequately estimate the import and export components of regional expenditures, thus making it impractical at this time to attempt a model based on

Table 2-1. Gross Regional Product of Alternative Concepts

Gross Regional Expenditure (GRE)	Gross Regional Income by Type Originating in Region (GRI)	Gross Regional Product by Sector and Industry (GRP)
Personal consumption expenditure	Labor compensations	Government
Gross private business investment	Wages and salaries	Private industry
Residential Construction	Supplements	Farm
Plant and equipment	Proprietors' income	Nonfarm
Inventory change	Net interest, rents, and royalties	Mining
Net exports of goods and services	Corporate profits and inventory	Manufacturing
Other regions	valuation adjustment	Trade
Rest-of-world	Total factor income	Finance, insurance, and real estate
Government purchases	Indirect business taxes	Transportation, communications,
Federal (in region)	Business transfer payments	and public utilities
State and local	Less: Net subsidies	Services and other
	Capital consumption allowance	
Total regional expenditure	Total regional income	Total regional product

GSE.[6] However, some of the components important to an understanding of the state economy are available from published data and are included in this system of accounts. Methods have been developed for estimating both GSI and GSP (Weber, 1979, 1982).

Estimating GSP

Because of the major importance of commercial and industrial development in a region, the GSP accounts have been given the most elaborate treatment in this model. Estimates of income by place of work and by industrial sector for each state and for the United States, along with estimates of GNP originating in each industrial sector, are published in the U.S. Department of Commerce *Survey of Current Business*. The reader interested in the methodology used to convert these data into estimates of GSP is referred to the previously mentioned articles by the author. In general, the method consists of multiplying income received in the state in each sector by the ratio for the United States as a whole in that sector of GNP Originating to Income Received. This provides an estimate of GSP in that sector based on the assumption that the national and regional ratios for that sector are the same. The effect is to add a correction to the "income by place of work data" for the absence in those data of rental and net interest incomes, corporate profits, inventory valuation adjustments, capital consumption allowances, and indirect activities of government such as business subsidies. Since the true value of GSP in any region is never known, it is not possible to evaluate the accuracy of this method. However, the estimates are generally thought to be quite good (Weber, 1979, 1982).

In any case, the essence of this method is that it uses knowledge about the differences in relative importance among the various sectors in the state to estimate GSP for those sectors. Thus, even if the accuracy of the *absolute level* estimates were not good, the accuracy of *relative changes* in those levels is likely to be quite good. The result is an estimate of GSP by sector that can be used to describe, analyze, and develop models of the regional economy.

IV. Econometric Model

The econometric model is designed to explain and forecast the behavior of forty-two endogenous variables for the state of New Jersey. The approach has been to use OLS regression analysis to determine parameter estimates for various sets of hypothesized determinants of individual endogenous variables. As a result of the common secular trend in economic time series data, econometricians suspect the existence of the statistical problems of autocorrelation, heteroscedasticity, and multicollinearity. This would suggest the use of some other estimating technique such as GLS, TSLS, or LISE to avoid bias in the estimated parameters. However, as Glickman noted (1971) and as has been the experience of the author, OLS estimates give as good results as these others when judged by MAPE tests. Further evidence to this effect can be obtained by a cursory examination of the sets of OLS and TSLS estimated equations published by L'Esperance et al. (1969) which show very little difference between the estimated coefficients. Moreover, since this model is primarily intended for use in forecasting, it is not as essential that each coefficient be unbiased as it is that the collection of coefficients in each equation set be unbiased. Only in the case of the exogenous variables is the particular coefficient required to be unbiased, and in such cases the direction of causation is so clearly one-sided that there is little likelihood of multicollinearity, the major statistical problem expected. Finally, it should be noted that in order to limit as far as possible the effects of multicollinearity, the specification of each equation was limited to as few variables as was absolutely necessary to the provision of a reasonably high level of explanatory power, rather than try to include all variables that theory would suggest as determinants of a particular sector.

Model Testing

The relevant statistical measures—such as R^2 and t statistics, a priori notions about the signs and magnitudes of variable coefficients, and the Durbin-Watson statistic—were examined to determine which equations showed the most promise for accurate results. Equations thus selected were written into a combination recursive-simultaneous–solution model of the total state economy.

A final check of the ability of the model was to simulate the last ten years and use two tests to evaluate the suitability of the total model. These are not rigorous statistical tests, rather they are intended only as descriptive summaries of the behavior of the model as a whole. By using solution values

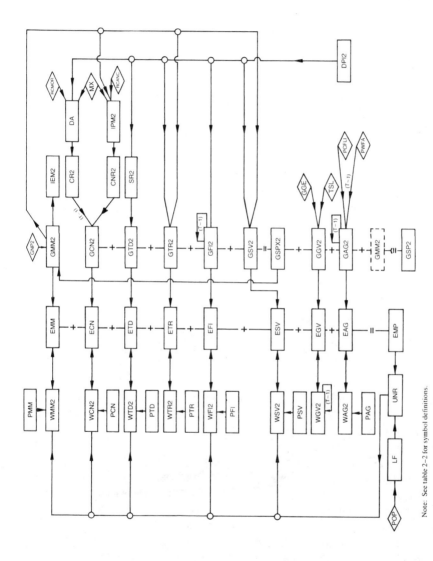

Note: See table 2–2 for symbol definitions.

Figure 2-2. Functional Diagram of Regional Econometric Model

rather than actual values wherever lagged endogenous variables entered the equations, the tests become dynamic in nature and represent quite severe tests, since any errors would be cumulative throughout the test period.

One test consisted of an examination of the differences between the simulated and the actual value of each endogenous variable for each period as to any indication of consistently positive, negative, or cyclical behavior, i.e., the equivalent of autoregressive residuals in a single equation. If any such evidence was found, additional work on the model was required until all traces disappeared.

The second test was to calculate Ball's Q^2. This test value is similar to the multiple R^2 test for single equations. The calculation to be made is

$$Q^2 = 1 - \frac{(\hat{y}_{tc} - y_t)^2}{(\bar{y} - y_t)^2}$$

A Q^2 equal to 1.0 indicates the model to be forecasting the actual values of the test period exactly, and a value of 0 indicates that the naive prediction that each value is equal to the mean value of the test period would have done just as well.

Theoretical Model

A functional diagram of the final model is given in figure 2-2, a list of symbols for which is given in table 2-2. The model contains elements of both Keynesian macroeconomics and neoclassical microeconomics. Total receipts of business, i.e., GSP by sector, represent consumption expenditures (C) in the simple Keynesian model listed in section II above. Business expenditures for investment goods represent investment expenditures (I)—except for that part of investment classified as inventory, which is not accounted for in the model. Expenditures by the federal, state, and local sectors represent government expenditures (G)—with the exception of that part of government expenditures for goods, which is included in the sales of the business GSP sector. Exports and imports (X,M), which in this case are interpreted as transfers between the state and the national economy, are accounted for by the introduction of GNP and New Jersey personal income, the latter of which contains elements of income both from within the state and from without. The advantage of formulating this part of the model in macroeconomic terms is that the effects of changes in government policy, expenditures, and other major exogenous factors on the state economy can be estimated through model simulations.

Table 2-2. Key to Symbols

Suffixes used for the various sectors of the economy are:

Symbol	Description
MM	Manufacturing, mining
CN	Construction
TD	Trade (wholesale and retail)
TR	Transportation, communications, and utilities
FI	Finance, insurance, and real estate
SV	Service
GV	Government (state and local)
AG	Agriculture
SP	Total output
SPX	Nonfarm, nongovernment output
CM	Nonmanufacturing output

For use with these suffixes are four prefixes:

G representing gross output
E representing employment
W representing wage
P representing productivity

For example GMM represents gross output for the Manufacturing, mining sector, and EMM represents employment in the Manufacturing, mining sector.

Other endogenous variables are:

Symbol	Description
EMP	Total employment
LF	Labor force
UNR	Unemployment rate
DPI	Disposable personal income
IEM	Investment in equipment and machinery
IPM	Investment in manufacturing plant
CR	Residential construction
DA	Dwelling units authorized
CNR	Nonresidential construction
SR	Retail sales

And the exogenous variables are:

Symbol	Description
GNP	Gross national product
POP	Population
RCMOR	Mortgage interest rates
RCANC	Corporate bond rate
MX	Money supply
GGE	Government spending on goods and services
TSL	State and local taxes
PCFLI	Prices paid by farmers
PWFA	Prices paid to farmers

(All variables followed by the number 2 are in 1972 dollars.)

The microeconomic element is observed in the various wage-employment determination equations. Each sector has associated supply-demand equations of the form

$$E_d = f(W, Z_i)$$
$$E_s = f(W, Z_i)$$
$$E_d = E_s$$

where

E = number employed
W = wage rate
Z = series of determinants
and s and d are supply and demand subscripts

The advantage of including these microeconomic elements is that the important effects of changes in demography on the economy, which can be ignored in the Keynesian description of a national economy, are made explicit in the regional economy where they are far more important, largely due to migration. This linkage between demographic and economic factors is made through the impacts on the labor force and the unemployment rate, which appear as supply factors in the employment determination equations.

The following is a detailed description of the model equations. The model can be divided conveniently into three sections: GSP, employment, and income. The equations in each section will be discussed in turn.

GSP Section

Manufacturing:

$$\Delta GM = f(\Delta GNP, \Delta GSPX) \tag{2.1}$$

Where Δ is the first-difference operator. Manufacturing presently accounts for about one-quarter of state output, down from one-third ten years ago, and continuing to fall. In this equation the output of the manufacturing sector (GM) is determined by the needs of the nation as a whole, represented by GNP which accounts for final demand in and out of the state, and the rest of the industrial sector of the state, represented by $GSPX$ which accounts for most intermediate demands, the balance of which are accounted for by the GNP variable. The use of first-differenced variables in this equation is to simulate Keynesian theory in which it is the *change* in exogenous variables, not the *level*, that causes changes in the equilibrium value of total output.

Trade:

$$GTD = f(SR) \qquad (2.2a)$$

$$SR \ \ = f(DPI) \qquad (2.2b)$$

The trade sector (GTD) accounts for 18 percent of state output, equally divided between retail and wholesale activity. Trade is found to be determined by retail sales in the state (SR), thus including the wholesale component. Retail sales, in turn, is determined by final demand represented by disposable personal income (DPI). Thus, the combination of equations accounts for both wholesale and retail trade.

Finance, Insurance, and Real Estate:

$$GFI = f(DPI, GFI_{t-1}) \qquad (2.3)$$

Finance, insurance, and real estate (GFI) is another important component of the New Jersey economy, accounting for 15 percent of output and growing. With its close link to both the flow and stock of wealth in the community, output in this sector is determined by disposable personal income representing the flow, and the lagged value of GFI acting as a proxy for the stock of wealth.

Transportation, Utilities, and Communication:

$$GTR = f(GM, DPI) \qquad (2.4)$$

Transportation, utilities, and communications (GTR) represents approximately 10 percent of state output. Considering the link between the various forms of transportation and the manufacturing output of the state along with the ability of persons to afford travel, it seems appropriate that the output of this sector is determined by GM, representing the former, and DPI, representing the latter. The close link between communications and utilities and the manufacturing sector, exemplified by the inclusion of GM, is also evident in this equation.

Service:

$$GSV = f(GM, DPI, \Delta DPI) \qquad (2.5)$$

The service sector (GSV) of the economy currently represents 15 percent of output and is growing rapidly, up from 10 percent ten years ago. In this equation the relationship between disposable personal income and some of its components—such as hotel, personal services, and amusements—and between the manufacturing sector and other components—such as business and professional services—suggests the use of DPI and GM as independent variables. In addition, a first-differenced DPI variable is added to the equation to account for some of the curvature expected in the income related portion of the service sector resulting from an increasing propensity to consume services as incomes grow (e.g., the increase in leisure activities evidenced in the state as income has grown).

Government:

$$GGV = f(GGE, TSL) \tag{2.6}$$

Government output in the state (GGV) accounts for a stable 11 percent of output. It is determined by federal and state and local governmental activity. Federal activity is included as the total purchase of goods and services by the federal government (GGE), while state and local taxes (TSL) is used as a proxy for the ability of government at those levels to support various expenditures.

Construction and Investment:

$$GCN = f(CR_{t-1}, CNR) \tag{2.7a}$$

$$CR = f(DA) \tag{2.7b}$$

$$DA = f(RCMOR, MX, DPI) \tag{2.7c}$$

$$CNR = f(IPM) \tag{2.7d}$$

$$IEM = f(IPM, GM, TSL) \tag{2.7e}$$

$$IPM = f(GM, RCANC, MX) \tag{2.7f}$$

Excepting the agricultural sector of the economy, which is miniscule, and the catch-all "other" sector, the construction sector of the economy is the smallest party of the New Jersey economy, representing only 3 percent of output and generally falling in importance. Because most of the mining activity in the state is allied with construction, mining and construction have been combined into a single variable (GCN). Despite its minor importance as a part of output, construction receives somewhat elaborate treatment in the model because of its importance as an indicator of future economic activity. Moreover, since investment plays such a pivotal role in Keynesian macroeconomics, it is desirable that investment be given explicit treatment in the model. Clearly, there is an economic link between investment and construction and so both are treated in this part of the model.

In the first equation (2.7a), total construction (and mining) in the state (GCN) is determined by its components, residential (CR) and nonresidential construction (CNR). The dollar volume of residential units (CR) is determined by the number of dwelling units authorized (DA), which in turn is determined by mortgage rates $(RCMOR)$, the availability of money (MX), and the demand for housing represented by DPI. The value of nonresidential construction (CNR) is determined in the next equation by investment in plant and equipment (IPM). In equation 2.7e, investment in new machinery and equipment (IEM) is determined by the needs of construction as represented by industrial investment in plant and equipment (IPM), the needs of the manufacturing sector (GM), and the needs of government as represented by state and local taxes (TSL). Finally, investment in plant and equipment (IPM) is determined by the needs of the manufacturing sector GM, along with the cost and availability of money represented by the corporate bond rate $(RCANC)$ and the mortgage credit money supply (MX).

Agriculture:

$$GAG = f(PCFLI, PWFA_{t-1}, GAG_{t-1}) \qquad (2.8)$$

The agriculture sector (GAG) represents only 0.4 percent of state output. Were it not for the importance of this sector in certain parts of the state and the availability of significant amounts of data, it would hardly be worth estimating separately. Agricultural output depends on the prices paid by farmers $(PCFLI)$ and the prices paid to farmers $(PWFA)$ as well as the volume of agricultural output represented by the lagged dependent variable. The lagging of both $PWFA$ and GAG is done to capture well-known lag effects in agricultural decision making.

Identities:

$$GSP = GAG + GCN + GM + GTR + GTD + GFI + GSV + GGV \qquad (2.9)$$

$$GCM = GSP - GM \qquad (2.10)$$

These are identities which simply sum the various sectors to arrive at Gross State Product and a derivative, Gross State Product-Commercial (non-manufacturing output, GCM), the latter being a useful measure for certain types of government and business policy decisions.

Simultaniety in the GSP section takes the form of feedback from the total of the industrial sector (GX) into the manufacturing sector (GM), and from the manufacturing sector (GM) into the transportation (GTR), service (GSV), and investment $(IEM$ and $IPM)$ sectors. Only the government (GGV) and agricultural (GAG) sectors are independently determined. Decisions in the government sector are held to be exogenous in the region and agriculture is a very minor part of the total.

Employment Section

In neoclassical economic theory, labor employment is considered to be a derived demand, i.e., the demand for a productive input is derived from the demand for the output of the industry. Derived demands are essentially a function of the marginal revenue product of the particular input. Thus, the demand for labor would be a function of (1) the price of the input, in this case the wage rate; (2) the quantity of complimentary inputs; (3) the price of the product produced; and (4) the state of technology. The unavailability of data and mathematical problems of multicollinearity prohibit the estimation of equations using these variables. Therefore, in the present case the output of each sector is taken as a proxy for both the price of the output and the quantity of complimentary inputs. The wage level is used as the price of labor input. Any changes in technology over the estimation period are assumed to be of minor importance, or to be embodied in the final output variable. The equations for the employment section are:

$$EM \ =f(GM,WM) \qquad \text{Manufacturing} \qquad (2.11)$$

$$ETD =f(GTD,WTD) \qquad \text{Trade} \qquad (2.12)$$

$$EFI \ =f(GFI,WFI) \qquad \text{F.I.R.E.} \qquad (2.13)$$

$$ETR =f(GTR,WTR) \qquad \text{Transportation} \qquad (2.14)$$

$$ESV \ =f(GSV,WSV) \qquad \text{Services} \qquad (2.15)$$

$$EGV =f(GGV,WGV) \qquad \text{Government} \qquad (2.16)$$

$$ECN =f(GCN,WCN) \qquad \text{Construction} \qquad (2.17)$$

$$EAG =f(GAG,WAG) \qquad \text{Agriculture} \qquad (2.18)$$

The simultaneous-recursive nature of the model is evident in this series of equations. While the GSP sector is determined simultaneously within itself, none of its components are dependent upon variables in the employment section of the model. Instead, each sector of the Employment section is dependent upon its counterpart in the GSP section. Thus, the GSP section is simultaneous and the employment section is recursively linked to it.

Income Section

Given the demand functions of labor inputs as specified above, neoclassical economic theory requires that the wage level be simultaneously determined along with the quantity of labor, using a market supply function of the form

$$N_s = N_s(W_o, W_a, R)$$

in which

N_s is the quantity of labor supplied
W_o is the wage rate
W_a is the price of competitive inputs
R is the availability of labor, i.e., a variable to represent the age-education composition of the population

Suitable proxies for W_a and R are not available. However, since the model is of a region the availability of the input—and thus the determinants of labor supply—can be ignored, since labor is readily available from neighboring regions and may be assumed to be infinitely elastic. Another approach has been taken for the price of competitive inputs. The productivity of labor as measured by the ratio of dollar output (in constant dollars) to the number employed in the industry is used as a proxy for the wage rate of competitive inputs. Then, the average annual wage in the industry represents the wage rate for labor supplied. The use of this variable does not allow for the variation in hours worked per laborer, but data limitations prevent taking this factor into account. Considering the near universality of the forty-hour week, this shortcoming is not expected to compromise the resulting model. The wage equations of the model are

$$WM = f(PM, UNR, EM) \tag{2.19}$$

$$WTD = f(PTD, ETD) \tag{2.20}$$

$$WFI = f(PFI, EFI) \tag{2.21}$$

$$WTR = f(PTR, ETR) \tag{2.22}$$

$$WSV = f(PSV, ESV) \tag{2.23}$$

$$WGV = f(PGV, EGV) \tag{2.24}$$

$$WCN = f(PCN,ECN) \tag{2.25}$$

$$WAG = f(PAG,EAG) \tag{2.26}$$

In the manufacturing sector the variable UNR is being used as a proxy for the availability of supply of labor, since it is felt that as the national economy ebbs and flows nearby regions might draw on this part of the state's trained work force.

V. The Output

Table 2-3 provides an example of a typical output of a model simulation. The results are divided into the major categories of interest: (1) demography and construction, (2) income, (3) employment, and (4) output. Within each category are listed the industry sectors described above. Although the example only shows three years of data, simulations can be done for any number of years desired.

VI. Future Directions

Plans are to include the following identity for total labor in the employment section of the model.

$$EMP = EM + ECN + ETD + ETR = EFI = ESV + EGV + EAG \tag{2.27}$$

and a pair of feedback equations through the unemployment rate (UNR).

$$UNR = f(LF,EMP) \tag{2.28}$$

$$LF = f(POP) \tag{2.29}$$

The addition of these equations will have the same effect of making the section internally simultaneously as does the GX variable in the GSP section.

Next, recent availability of quarterly data on "income received by place of work" and techniques developed for estimating gross regional product from these data suggest the possibility of a quarterly model similar to that described. In addition, the model could be expanded by disaggregating the manufacturing sector into durables and nondurables components and the trade sector into wholesale and retail components. Finally, an attempt to respecify the whole model in terms of income originating by sector instead of by gross product originating by sector may provide an improved model. If

Table 2-3.   Typical Output of New Jersey State Econometric Model[a]

	1981	1982	1983
N.J. Demography and Construction			
Population (# millions)	8.10	8.20	8.30
Number of households (# millions)	2.00	2.05	2.10
Dwelling units authorized (monthly—thousands)	4.10	4.15	4.20
Residential construction contracts ($ billion)	1.00	1.10	1.15
New structures and addition to plant ($ billion)	.10	.15	.15
Nonresidential construction contracts ($ billion)	.65	.75	.85
New machinery and equipment ($)	.70	.71	.72
N.J. Income ($ billion)			
Personal income	90.70	97.60	104.50
Per capita income ($ thousand)	12.25	13.25	14.25
Disposable personal income	72.00	77.50	83.00
Total wages	63.00	68.50	73.00
Manufacturing	20.00	20.50	21.00
Nonmanufacturing	43.00	48.00	52.00
Wholesale and retail trade	10.50	11.50	12.00
Finance, insurance, and real estate	5.30	5.50	6.00
Services and miscellaneous	13.50	15.00	16.30
Transportation	2.00	2.50	3.00
Contract construction	3.00	3.70	4.50
Agriculture	.20	.20	.20
Government	8.50	9.60	10.00
N.J. Employment (# million)			
Labor force	3.65	3.70	3.75
Unemployment rate (%)	7.3	9.0	7.8
Total employment	3.10	3.15	3.20
Manufacturing	.70	.72	.74
Nonmanufacturing	2.33	2.35	2.37
Wholesale and retail trade	.69	.70	.71
Finance, insurance, and real estate	.16	.16	.17
Services and miscellaneous	.64	.66	.68
Transportation	.18	.18	.19
Contract construction	.10	.10	.10
Agriculture	.20	.20	.20
Government	.53	.52	.53

Table 2-3   (*Contd.*)

N.J. Gross State Product ($ billion)			
Gross state product			
Manufacturing	22.50	24.00	25.50
Nonmanufacturing	72.00	76.00	80.00
Wholesale and retail trade	17.00	19.00	21.00
Finance, insurance, and real estate	13.00	14.00	15.00
Services and miscellaneous	14.00	15.00	16.00
Transportation	10.50	11.00	11.50
Contract construction	5.50	6.00	6.50
Agriculture	.32	.33	.34
Government	10.00	10.50	11.00

[a] Figures given are for demonstration purpose only.

so, then the present technique used to estimate GSP by sector prior to entry into the model could become the last stage of model simulations. Clearly, there is a trade-off here between simplicity and efficiency in the model and quality of results. The superior method remains to be determined.

Notes

[1] This, incidentally, is also the case for the less developed nations.

[2] This classification and the associated descriptions are found in Kort (1982).

[3] An interesting sidelight to this model is the BEA practice of sending copies of Baseline Economic Projections to those having regional models for mutual comparison, thus achieving a kind of "theoretical feedback" for future model improvement.

[4] Though there does seem to be far too much use of lagged dependent variables without any theoretical justification.

[5] However, even this may be in question. For example, there has been ongoing litigation between the state of New Jersey and the federal government as to the accuracy of these figures.

[6] Although some work has been done in the way of developing complete regional accounts by Armstrong (1980).

References

Armstrong, R. B., et al. 1980. *Regional Accounts: Structure and Performance of the New York Region's Economy in the Seventies*. Bloomington: Indiana University Press.

Bourque, P., Conway, R.; and Howard, C. 1977. *The Washington Projection and Simulation Model*. Seattle, WA: University of Washington.

Brooking, C. 1974. A Farm-oriented econometric model of Mississippi. Unpublished PhD dissertation, University of Pennsylvania, Philadelphia, PA.

Brooking, C. G., and Hake, D. A. 1980. The impact of the regional econometric model on the policy formation decision process. In F. G. Adams and N. J. Glickman (Eds), *Modeling the Multi-regional Economic System*. Lexington, MA: Heath (Lexington Books).

Burton, R. P., and Dyckman, J. W. 1965. *A Quarterly Economic Forecasting Model for the State of California*. Berkeley: University of California.

Chang, H. S. 1976. *Tennessee Econometric Model: Phase 1*. Knoxville: University of Tennessee.

Crossman, P. J. 1981. The Gross State Product and an econometric model of the state of Queensland. PhD dissertation, James Cook University of North Queensland, Australia.

Crow, R. T., et. al. 1973. An econometric model of the Buffalo SMSA: a progress report. Working Paper No. 161. Buffalo: SUNY.

Doti, J. 1982. A quarterly econometric model for an SMSA. Orange, CA: Chapman College (mimeo).

Dresch, S., and Goldberg, R. 1973. IDIOM: an interindustry, national-regional policy evaluation model. *Annals of Economic and Social Measurement* 2:323–356.

d'Amours, E. 1979. Salaires prix et chomage: une approche regionale. *L'Actualite Economique* 51:603–633.

d'Amours, E., Simard, G., and Chabot-Plaute, F. 1975. Candide-r. *L'Actualite Economique* 47:587–620.

Duobinis, S. F. 1981. An econometric model of the Chicago Standard Metropolitan Statistical Area. *Journal of Regional Science* 21:293–318.

Engle, R. F., Fisher, F. M., Harris, J. R., and Rothenberg, J. 1972. An econometric simulation model of intra-metropolitan housing location: housing, business, transportation, and local government. *American Economic Review* 62:89–97.

Ghali, M., and Renaud, B. 1978. *The Structure and Dynamic Properties of a Regional Economy, an Econometric Model for Hawaii*. Toronto: Heath (Lexington Books).

Glickman, N. J. 1971. An econometric forecasting model for the Philadelphia region. *Journal of Regional Science* 11:15–32.

Glickman, N. J. 1977. *Econometric Analysis of Regional Systems*. New York: Academic Press.

Glickman, N. J. 1974. Son of "The specification of regional econometric models." *Papers of the Regional Science Association* 32:155–177.

Greenberg, C., and Renfro, C. 1982. An econometric-demographic model of New York State. Paper at the American Statistical Association/U.S. Bureau of Census International Conference on Forecasting Regional Population Change and Its Economic Determinants and Consequences. Airlie, Virginia.

Grimes, A. R. 1973. A satellite econometric model for Georgia. Athens: University of Georgia (mimeo).

Gusteley, R. D. 1980. *Forecasting Regional Economic Activity: The Tennessee Econometric Model (TEMII)*. Knoxville: University of Tennessee.

Hall, O. P., and Licari, J. A. 1974. Building small region econometric models: extension of Glickman's structure to Los Angeles. *Journal of Regional Science* 14:337–353.

Hawaii Department of Planning and Economic Development. 1980. An econometric model of the Hawaii construction industry. Honolulu: State of Hawaii.

Isserman, A. M. 1982. Multiregional demoeconomic modeling with endogenously determined birth and migration rates: theory and prospects. Paper at the American Statistical Association/U.S. Bureau of the Census International Conference on Forecasting Regional Population Change and Its Economic Determinants and Consequences. Airlie, Virginia.

Kinal, T., and Ratner, J. B. 1982. Regional forecasting with vector autoregression: the case of New York state. Working Paper No. 155. Albany: SUNY Albany.

Klein, L. R. 1969. The specification of regional econometric models. *Papers of the Regional Science Association* 23:105–115.

Klein, L. R., and Glickman, N. J. 1974. An econometric model of Pennsylvania. Discussion Paper no. 295. Philadelphia: University of Pennsylvania.

Knapp, J. L., Fields, T. W., and Jerome, R. T. 1976. A survey of state and regional econometric models. Working paper, Taylor Murphy Institute, Charlottesville, NC.

Kort, J. R. 1982. An overview of regional modeling methodology and data requirements. Washington, DC: BEA, U.S. Department of Commerce.

Kort, J. R., and Cartwright, J. V. 1982. Modeling the multiregional economy: integrating econometric and input-output models, *Review of Regional Studies*.

Lathan, W. R., Lewis, K. A., and Landon, J. H. 1979. Regional econometric models: specification and simulation of a quarterly alternative for small regions. *Journal of Regional Science* 19:1–13.

L'Esperance, W., Nestle, G., and Fromm, D. 1969. Gross state product and an econometric model of a state. *Journal of the American Statistical Association* 64:787–807.

L'Esperance, W. 1977. Conjoining and input-output with an econometric model of Ohio. *Regional Science Perspectives* 2:54–77.

McNees, S. K. 1974. How accurate are economic forecasts? *New England Economic Review* November/December.

McNees, S. K. 1979. The forecasting record for the 1970's. *New England Economic Review* (September/October):33–53.

Perryman, M. R. 1981. Geographical and sectoral linkages in large regional econometric models. *Atlantic Economic Society*.

Plaut, T. R. 1981. An econometric model for forecasting regional population growth. *International Regional Science Review* 6:53–70.

Polenske, Karen R. 1980. *The U.S. Multiregional Input-Output Accounts and Model*, Lexington, MA: Heath (Lexington Books).

Rubin, B. M., and Erickson, R. A. 1980. Specification and performance improvements in regional econometric forecasting models: a model for the Milwaukee metropolitan area. *Journal of Regional Science* 20:11–35.

Treyz, G. 1980. Design of multiregional policy analysis model. *Journal of Regional Science* 20:191–206.

Treyz, G., et al. 1980. An overview of the Massachusetts economic policy analysis (MEPA) model. Paper presented at the Harvard/MIT Joint Center for Urban Studies Conference on An Assessment of the State of the Art in Regional Modeling, Cambridge, MA.

Weber, R. E. 1976. New Jersey state econometric model. In *Demand for Electricity*, PSE&G, Newark, New Jersey, sec. 27.

Weber, R. E. 1979. A synthesis of methods proposed for estimating gross state product. *Journal of Regional Science* 19:217–230.

Weber, R. E. 1979. Estimating quarterly gross state product. *Business Economics* 14(1):38–43.

Weber, R. E. 1980. Estimating gross manufacturing product at the sub-national level, a reply. *Journal of Regional Science* 20(4):521–522.

Weber, R. E. 1982. A gross regional product algorithm and a method for constructing a matrix of regional sectoral deflator. *Journal of Regional Science* 22(2):241–250.

Zarnowitz, V. 1974. How accurate have the forecasts been? *Methods and Techniques of Business Forecasting*. Englewood Cliffs, NJ: Prentice-Hall. Pp. 565–596.

Zarnowitz, V. 1978. On the accuracy and properties of recent macroeconomic forecasts. *American Economic Review, Papers and Proceedings* 68(2):213–319.

II EXTERNAL LINKAGE ISSUES

3 INTEGRATED STATE-SUBSTATE ECONOMETRIC MODELING: DESIGN AND UTILIZATION FOR LONG-RUN ECONOMIC ANALYSIS

Alberta H. Charney
and Carol A. Taylor

I. Introduction

Between 1965 and 1980, nonagricultural employment in the United States rose 50 percent; it rose only 21 percent in Pennsylvania; and it doubled in Texas. It has been estimated that the income multiplier impact of the HUD budget is 3.6 in the United States as a whole, but only 1.3 in Montana and South Dakota and over 6.0 in Indiana (Ballard, Glickman, and Wendling, 1980).

Clearly, major regional differences in multipliers and growth rates exist, and the smaller the area of focus the more exaggerated these differences become. The task of the regional modeler is not only to quantify behavioral relationships, which are similar among many areas, but to appropriately identify and represent critical economic linkages which result in area deviations from a national norm. Central to this latter analysis are:

1. *The role of migration in regional economic development.* The openness of state and local economies results in population shifts which affect and are affected by interregional economic differences. While population change is largely ignored in aggregate U.S. impact analyses,

and the demographic component of national forecasts focuses on natural increase and shifting age cohorts, the state or local model is distinguished from its national counterpart by the significance of the demographic-economic migration link.

2. *Interregional differences in external market linkages.* Production of goods and services for a national market is a major channel through which a local area reacts to aggregate cyclical and growth phenomena. Interregional differences in the industrial structure of these links determine not only the magnitude and nature of local economic reactions to variations in the national economy, but also influence the extent to which areas participate in broad national economic growth or stagnation.

3. *Variations in state and local economic integration.* While item (2) focuses on regional export structure, an area's propensity to import is of equal significance in state/local impact and growth analysis. A region's economic integration or self-sufficiency in production of goods and services affects multiplier leakage and determines the extent to which change in one sector becomes amplified into general regional economic expansion or decline.

4. *The revenue/expenditure process of regional governments.* While clearly the economic role of state and local governments differs considerably from that of a national government, area development is not unaffected by the fiscal policy of regional governments. Local taxation influences economic choice in the region. Furthermore, differences in the spending patterns of governmental entities compared with individuals and private businesses result in aggregate growth effects of local fiscal policy even though on average the local budgets may be balanced.

Identification of these critical linkages is not new in regional analysis; however, they are not generally systematically represented and evaluated in state and metropolitan econometric models. Simulations with the long-run forecasting and policy impact econometric model developed for Arizona and its major substate regions clearly attests to the importance of structurally embodying these linkages in such regional models. Since the present model is multiarea, deriving state aggregates from summation or averaging of substate variables, its formulation entailed the additional complexity of explicitly specifying inter-substate area economic relationships, both those directly occurring in the private sector and those indirectly induced by the sharing of state revenues back to local governments.

While the model is complex because of its simultaneous determination of population, income, employment, and government revenues and expenditures at the state and substate levels, this complexity is precisely what permits detailed analysis of multiplier effects and growth factors in the regional economies. In particular, the empirical analysis details temporal shifts in industrial composition of employment multipliers, quantifies the relationship between state and substate multipliers, derives the effect of population growth on multipliers, investigates the growth impact of changing levels of economic integration, and traces through the effects of public-private sector interrelationships at the state and local levels on impact analysis and long-run growth patterns.

Understanding of model specification is prerequisite to interpretation of these empirical results. Consequently, following a very broad overview of the Arizona economy in section II, specifications of major model variables—employment, income, population, state/local government revenues and expenditures—are detailed in section III. The discussion particularly focuses on how the critical linkages, broadly outlined in (1)–(4) above, are explicitly incorporated into model structure. The fourth section presents and analyzes simulation results. It is followed by some brief concluding remarks.

II. Overview of the Arizona Economy

Economically and demographically, Arizona is a moderate-size state, ranking thirtieth in population in the 1980 Census count. However, as evidenced in table 3-1, relative to other states, its population has been rapidly increasing. Between 1970 and 1980, its population growth rate was second only to that of Nevada. This high relative growth is not a new phenomenon; Arizona was consistently one of the four fastest growing states for each of the three decades prior to 1970. In terms of rural/urban distribution, it reflects the U.S. average. Three-quarters of the state's population resides in standard metropolitan statistical areas. Although often depicted as a popular retirement state, Arizona's proportion of population 65 + is equal to the national average and its median age is slightly below the national median.

Approximately 55–60 percent of the state's population and employment are in Maricopa County which constitutes the Phoenix Standard Metropolitan Statistical Area (SMSA). The remainder is divided between the Tucson SMSA (Pima County) and the state's thirteen nonmetropolitan counties (denoted "balance of state").

The state is similar to the nation as a whole in having a low proportion of employment in agriculture—2.8 percent of U.S. employment is in agriculture, while 1.9 percent of Arizona employment is in this same industry.

Table 3-1. Comparative Overview of the Arizona Economy

	United States	Arizona	Phoenix SMSA	Tucson SMSA	Balance of State
1980 Population (000s)	226,546	2,718	1,509	531	678
1970–1980 Population growth (%)	11.4	53.1	55.4	51.1	50.0
1980 Total employment (000s)	99,303	1,112	682	204	226
1980 Civilian nonagricultural employment distribution (%)					
Mining	1.1	2.1	<0.1	3.6	7.2
Construction	4.8	7.6	8.0	7.8	5.9
Manufacturing	22.4	15.2	17.9	11.5	9.9
Transportation, communications, public utilities	5.7	5.1	4.8	4.9	6.0
Trade	22.5	24.0	25.5	22.1	20.8
Finance, insurance, real estate	5.7	5.7	7.1	4.6	2.5
Services	19.8	20.5	20.9	21.4	18.3
Government	18.0	19.9	15.8	24.0	29.4
Average unemployment rate 1979–1981 (%)	6.88	5.97	5.13	5.21	9.07
1980 Per capita income ($)	9,511	8,831	9,630	8,649	7,195
1980 Personal income ($ billion)	2,165.3	24.1	14.6	4.6	4.9
1980 Retail sales ($ billion)	958.0	13.9	8.6	2.4	2.9
1980 Total general revenue ($ billion)[a]	—	1.7	1.6	0.6	0.8

[a] Fiscal year July 1, 1979–June 30, 1980. Local revenues include revenues accruing to all local jurisdictions—school districts, municipalities, county governments, and special districts.

However, the state's distribution of civilian nonagricultural employment diverges somewhat from the U.S. average. Arizona's proportion of employment in manufacturing is somewhat less than the U.S. average—15.2 percent in Arizona in 1980 compared with a national proportion of 22.4 percent. The discrepancy has been diminished over time as Arizona's proportion has been rising and that of the United States has been declining—three decades ago, 10.1 percent of Arizona employment was in manufacturing compared with a third of U.S. employment. Over three-quarters of manufacturing employment in the state is durable goods manufacturing, concentrated primarily in defense/electronics goods, construction-related materials, and—in the "balance of state"—metal smelting.

In looking at a goods-producing aggregate, some of Arizona's low share of employment in manufacturing is made up by its relatively higher share of employment in construction and mining. The higher construction share reflects the high average growth of the state and the mining share derives from the significant copper production in the state, which has been declining in relative importance. In the early 1950s, the "balance of state" was industrially dominated by copper production with mining accounting for 20 percent of civilian nonagricultural employment, but the share has dropped to approximately 8 percent in recent years.

Table 3-1 also makes clear the variation among substate regions in Arizona. The state's mining employment is concentrated in the Tucson SMSA and "balance of state" and both these regions also have unusually high proportions of employment in the government sector. In Tucson, the latter reflects the presence of a major state university. In the "balance of state," the high government employment concentration results from an unusually large federal employment sector which administers the vast government-owned lands in Arizona. The regional diversification is further emphasized by the data on unemployment rate and per capita income. On average, Arizona's unemployment rate is below national average, but the statewide figure masks chronic high unemployment rates in the nonmetropolitan portions of the state. Similarly, per capita incomes vary from above national average in Phoenix to well below the national mean in the "balance of state."

Governmental entities in Arizona include the state government, city governments, county governments, school districts, and special districts. The latter are small units organized to provide a specific good or service; fire protection districts and water supply districts are common examples. The county government assists in the formation of these districts and their administrative operation, but exercises little direct control over their actions. While geographic delineations of school districts and special districts are not necessarily contiguous with county boundaries, neither do they overlap counties.

Major sources of revenue to state government include federal government aid, fuel taxes, sales taxes, and corporate and individual income taxes. Local governments primarily derive revenues from shared state taxes, state grants-in-aid, city-levied sales taxes, property taxes, and user fees.

III. Model Specification

It is perhaps simplistic to observe that the results of model simulation are a direct expression of equation specifications and the interactions of those specifications. However, the observation underscores the critical role of equation formulation in the model building process. If particular linkages and economic relationships are not embodied in the structure of individual equations, they will not affect the simulated multipliers and growth paths. Consequently, this section details model specifications, in terms of both theoretical basis and empirical application. Major model sectors are covered—private sector employment, population, income, and government revenues/expenditures (including government employment).

A. Private Sector Employment

1. Aggregation and Model Linkages. Specification and aggregation are inextricably linked in the employment sector of a regional econometric model. Use of the same specification in a four-digit employment category and in an aggregate of one-digit categories would generally result in failure to capture the detailed nuances of the former and/or omission of major economic influences on the latter. Consequently, choice of sectoral detail is an initial and critical phase of employment specification.

Level of disaggregation is logically constrained by sector size and data consistency. Excessive detail, resulting in few firms and/or employees per sector, yields estimation problems of small-sample specification, substantially discrete adjustments as opposed to a smooth continuum of response to shifts in economic conditions, and/or difficulty in allowing for significant, readily achieved intercategory substitutions. Historical changes in standard industrial code classifications have resulted in data inconsistencies even among some large, two-digit employment categories. A cost of disaggregation can be restriction of the time period of estimation to one of consistent definition and this restriction tends to yield imprecise coefficient estimation and/or an equation whose relationships are not stable outside the brief period of empirical analysis.

At the other extreme, level of aggregation is logically constrained by homogeneity in determination of employment. While theoretically many factors could be included in one equation to determine the employment in a large, heterogeneous category, empirically problems of mulitcollinearity and degrees of freedom prohibit this approach. Ad hoc omission of determinants of smaller components in an aggregated category may not clearly affect apparent historical fit of an individual equation, but in the total model, may eliminate the impact of factors that are substantial in the aggregate, but operate through diverse smaller sectors.

The initial phase of specification—choice of sectoral employment detail—necessarily balances these problems of excessive disaggregation and extreme aggregation. The employment detail of the present model, summarized in table 3-2, reflects a balance derived with particular attention to allowing the specification of the critical linkages outlined in the introduction. In particular, the level of disaggregation permits formulation of the following.

a. External State Linkages.   Primary export-base sectors of the Arizona economy are mining, the manufacturing sectors of machinery (electrical and nonelectrical) and defense/scientific instruments, and tourism. The pertinent mining and manufacturing sectors are represented in table 3-2 and the significantly tourist-impacted trade and service sectors are isolated—gasoline stations, restaurants and bars, hotel/motel, and admissions/recreation.

b. Intra-area Industrial Linkages.   Employment in two categories of durable manufacturing, metals (primary and fabricated) and the residual (durable manufacturing net of employment in standard industrial codes [SIC] 19 and 3-2 through 38), are primarily derived from the level of local activity in other manufacturing, mining, and construction sectors. In addition, the construction cycle permeates trade, financial, and utility and communication sectors. Of particular importance are the specific categories of trade in building materials and household furnishings, and the financial sectors of banking and real estate. Furthermore, the most labor intensive aspects of the provision of communications and utilities are line expansions and new hookups, hence new construction is a significant determinant of employment in these sectors.

c. Inter-area Linkages.   Two forms of substate interarea linkages are significant in the Arizona economy. First, in-state tourism—expenditures for business or recreational travel by residents of one region in another region—

Table 3-2. Employment Detail—State and Substate Regions

Descriptive Category	SIC Code Aggregation	State Level of Employment in 1980 (000s)
Total employment	NA[a]	1,112.4
Agriculture	NA	20.8
Nonagricultural, nonwage and salary	NA	77.7
Nonagricultural, wage and salary	NA	1,014.0
Mining	10–14	21.0
Construction	15–17	76.6
Manufacturing	20–39	154.4
Durable goods	24, 25, 32–39	119.6
Stone, clay, glass	32	6.3
Primary and fabricated metals	33–34	17.3
Machinery	35–36	58.6
Defense/scientific instruments	37–38[b]	27.1
Other	24, 25, 39	10.2
Nondurable goods	20–23, 26–31	34.8
Transportation, communication, public utilities	40–49	51.3
Communications	48	14.5
Utilities	49	13.4
Other	40–47	23.5
Trade	50–59	243.0
Wholesale trade	50–51	49.4
Retail trade	52–59	193.6
Building materials/home furnishings	52, 57	17.4
Auto dealers/gas stations	55	24.2
Restaurants and bars	58	62.6
Other	53–56, 59	89.5
Finance, insurance, real estate	60–67	58.2
Banking/credit agencies	60–61	25.3
Real estate	65–66	14.1
Other	62–64, 67	18.8
Services	70–89	207.7
Hotel/motel	70	22.1
Medical	80	53.1
Recreation/amusements	78, 79, 84	11.1
Other	72–76, 81–83, 86–89	121.4
Government	NA	201.8
Federal	NA	39.1
State and local	NA	162.7

[a] NA Not applicable.

[b] "Transportation equipment" manufacturing in Arizona (SIC 37) is essentially all missiles and hence is designated defense.

is a component of the total tourist industry distinguishable from expenditures of out-of-state tourists. A second set of interarea linkages is observed in industries whose critical viable market size is less than the state as a whole but greater than that of particular substate regions. At any point in time, goods and services of these industries tend to be provided by a structure analogous to classical central place theory, with a higher-order city serving a network of lower-order cities and rural areas. However, over time, the trade relationship is not static. As substate regions grow, they can be expected to internalize provision of more of these goods and services which historically have been imported from the central city. The employment disaggregation has isolated the industries particularly subject to this changing rate of substate internalization or economic integration—nondurable manufacturing (which in Arizona predominantly provides goods for in-state consumption), wholesale trade, medical services, and the financial sectors of banking and investment/insurance.

d. Private–public Sector Linkages. State/local government expenditure directly impacts nongovernment employment through public purchases of privately provided goods and services. While a component of these purchases are imported to the state, state/local government expenditures on construction and services directly affect the in-state level of activity in the corresponding private sectors. Within the private service employment sector, public expenditures primarily impact nonmedical, nontourist services.

2. General Private Sector Employment Specifications. The general specification for labor demand is derived from neoclassical firm cost minimization theory. Assume for industry i there are two factors of production L^i (labor) and M^i (all other inputs) with corresponding prices W^i and P^i_m. Letting I^i_p denote the vector of input prices, $I^i_p = (W^i, P^i_m)$, each firm's cost function may be represented by $C_i(Q^i, I^i_p) = \min_{Y^i} \{I^i_p \cdot Y^i | f_i(Y^i) \ge Q^i\}$

where Y^i is the vector of inputs, (L^i, M^i), f_i is the production function, and Q^i is output. It is straightforward to derive that $C_i(Q^i, I^i_p)$ is positively linearly homogeneous of degree one in I^i_p. From Shepherd's lemma, labor demand is

$$L^i = \frac{\delta C_i(Q^i, I^i_p)}{\delta W^i} = h_i(Q^i, I^i_p) \tag{3.1}$$

Since C_i is positively linearly homogeneous of degree one in I^i_p, h_i is a homogeneous function of degree zero in I^i_p. Consequently, L^i may be written

$$L^i = h_i(Q^i, I_p^{i'})$$ (3.2)

where $I_p^{i'} = I_p^i / W^i$. That is, labor demand is a function of output and relative labor cost.

For local firms which are one of many firms producing for a national market, it may be more appropriate to derive their conditional labor demand function within the context of a national industry-wide cost function. Letting Q^x denote national output, and $I_p^x = (W^i, P_m^i, W^x, P_m^x)$ where W^x and P_m^x represent wage and price of M elsewhere, local labor demand may be derived analogously to equation 3.2:

$$L^i = \frac{\delta C_x(Q^x, I_p^x)}{\delta W^i} = \bar{h}(Q^x, I_p^x)$$ (3.3)

where C_x is the aggregate industry cost function. The homogeneity conditions imply that

$$L^i = \bar{h}(Q^x, I_p^{x'})$$ (3.4)

where $I_p^{x'} = I_p^x / W^i$. That is, local labor demand is a function of aggregate industry output, costs in the local area relative to elsewhere, and wage relative to other input prices.

The appropriateness of equation 3.4 does not imply the invalidity of equation 3.2. An alternative employment formulation for industries producing for a national market utilizes equation 3.2 for employment specification and derives Q_i within the context of the national market. For example, Treyz, Friedlaender, and Stevens (1980) utilize an output specification for exporting industries of the form

$$Q_i = f_q(Q^x, p^x/p^i, W^x/W^i)$$ (3.5)

Rather than equation 3.4 directly in specification of L^i, equations 3.2 and 3.5 may be combined in a two-step estimation procedure for L^i. The benefit of the two-step procedure is the separation of probably highly collinear relative price variables in equation 3.4. In the two-step estimation, input costs relative to those elsewhere determine Q_i as a function of Q^x, and labor costs relative to other input costs determine labor intensity of production of Q_i.

The major problem in empirical application of either equation 3.2 directly or 3.2 and 3.5 combined is general lack of data on local output Q^i. Two extreme approaches to the problem appear in the literature. First, these output data may be constructed prior to estimation using the Kendrick-Jaycox (1965) methodology and extensions of it (e.g., L'Esperance, Nestel, and Fromm, 1969; Moody and Puffer, 1969; Glickman, 1971, 1977; Hall and Licari, 1974; Chang, 1979; Rubin and Erickson, 1980; and Duobinis, 1981).

Alternatively, no explicit local output variables may appear in the model, but Q^i in equation 3.2 is replaced by a vector of determinants of Q^i (e.g., Ratajczak, 1974; Friedlaender, Treyz, and Tresch, 1975; and Latham, Lewis, and Landon, 1979). While contruction of Q^i permit more direct presentation of the theoretical derivations, the construction procedure itself introduces errors which affect the accuracy of the primary variables of interest—employment levels. Second, a more practical consideration is that in a model that uses constructed local output data, typically the local sectoral output, which must also be estimated, is a function of only one or two variables which could easily be used directly in the employment equation. However, possibly offsetting these considerations is the recognition that given the multicollinearity among variables, the explicit construction of Q^i and consequent separation of the determinants of output and output per employee may permit more precise estimation of the impact of different variables on final employment.

Rather than rigidly adhere to one approach or the other, the present model combines specifications to take advantage of the strengths of both techniques. Three basic variants of employment equations are used.

i.   direct modeling of Q^i using either collected data (e.g., in mining) or constructed data;

ii.   replacement of Q^i with an indicator of the level of sectoral activity (e.g., deflated sales or expenditures or employment in other industrial categories); and

iii.   replacement of Q^i with primary determinants of output.

Choice of approach reflects both data availability and need to specify the four primary linkages identified in (a)–(d) above.

3. Sectoral Employment Specifications.

Mining and Export-Base Manufacturing.   Most of Arizona's mining sector produces copper for national and international markets, and such external markets also characterize the output distribution of the machinery and defense/scientific instruments manufacturing sectors. For these industries, the two-step employment estimation procedure embodied in equations 3.2 and 3.5 is particularly critical because of collinearity among variables determining the local share of national output and those determining output per employee. Explicit mine output data in tons of copper provide direct measures of the local share of national output. Given similarity of union-bargained regional wages in copper mining, the more variable intermine production factors affecting the share of total industry output are (1) value of by-product metals, (2) copper ore grade variations, and (3) type of mining process (open pit, underground, leach, etc.). Item 1 is directly included by specification of pertinent by-product prices in local output shares. Physical characteristics of the ore body largely determine items 2 and 3, resulting in inherent cost advantages to particular mines so that share systematically varies with strength and weakness of the copper market as specified by deflated price and aggregate national level of production. Output per employee is estimated as a function of cyclical output variations and long-run productivity trends, with employment derived by identity from local output and output per employee. The local employment and output mining model is embodied in a total U.S. and rest-of-world copper industry model.

Measures of local output in the machinery sector are derived by direct multiplication of U.S. output per employee times local employment, with national output measured by an industrial production index. Lack of data on P^i in equation 3.5 results in a specification of local output as a function of national output and relative local to national labor costs. National projections of labor productivity growth in the machinery sector are used to derive local employment by identity from local output and output per employee.

The ordnance/scientific instruments export-base manufacturing sector is a local conglomerate of specific sectors and consequently is not directly analogous to any particular national sector for which output and employment data are available. In this case, attempts to construct local Q^i would undoubtedly introduce errors into the model. Local employment is estimated directly with equation 3.4, with L^i a function of W^x/W^i, and a set of exogenous national defense expenditure and national employment variables pertinent to determination of the level of output and labor productivity in the specific Arizona conglomerate category.

Local-Serving Manufacturing.   Two distinct types of local-serving manufacturing characterize the areas: (i) that which provides inputs to or processes outputs from other goods-producing sectors and (ii) that which provides commodities for local consumption. In Arizona, durable manufacturing sectors, other than the export-base ones described above, comprise set i and nondurable manufacturing sectors are set ii. The indicator of Q^i for empirical estimation of equation 3.2 in set i is employment in the pertinent sectors and/or output levels from the export-base sector analysis (e.g., copper mine production is a determinant of smelter manufacturing production in the nonurban part of the state). Correlation of output per employee across durable manufacturing sectors often results in insignificant coefficients on the relative wage cost variables in equation 3.2 when Q^i is replaced by a set of employment variables.

As noted above, nondurable manufacturing is one of the sectors subject to changing levels of substate area internalization. As the clearly highest-order city in Arizona, Phoenix has been exporting nondurable consumption commodities to the rest of the state. However, as markets outside of Phoenix expand, they reach a viable size to support increased "own production" of nondurables, resulting in a lower proportion of imports to total consumption. The general approach for estimation of area employment in these sectors subject to changing internalization is

i.   determination in each substate area of a hypothetical level of employment reflecting what employment would be if each area just fully internalized its own production needs, neither importing nor exporting;
ii.   for substate areas outside the exporting center, determination of the ratio of hypothetical employment to actual employment;
iii. derivation of actual employment for importing centers by identity,

$$E^n_{A,j} = E^n_{H,j}/R^n_{H/A,j}$$

where $E^n_{A,j}$ = actual employment in industry n in area j, $E^n_{H,j}$ = hypothetical employment in industry n in area j, and $R^n_{H/A,j}$ is the ratio of hypothetical to actual employment $(E^n_{H,j}/E^n_{A,j})$; and
iv.   derivation of employment in the exporting center, k, as

$$E^n_{H,k} + \sum_{j\varepsilon\Omega_k}(E^n_{H,j} - E^n_{A,j})$$

where Ω_k is the set of lower-order centers served by k and it is assumed k produces all commodities needed for its own consumption (reflected in employment component $E^n_{H,k}$).

Step i—determination of hypothetical, fully internalized employment levels in substate centers—is typically based on a statewide equation. In the case of nondurable manufacturing, it was assumed that

$$E^{nd}_{H,j} = f(CN^{nd}_j, PL^{nd}) \tag{3.6}$$

where CN^{nd}_j is real consumer expenditure by area j residents on nondurable goods provided by the nondurable manufacturing sector (i.e., net of consumer nondurable expenditure on items such as gasoline and food away from home, these being provided by the trade sectors; consumer nondurable expenditure on home electricity and gas, these being provided by the utility sector, etc.) and PL^{nd} is a measure of labor productivity in production of commodities CN^{nd}. Since state and substate data on CN^{nd}_j are not available, these were estimated using a national consumption function:

$$CN^{nd}/P = \alpha_0 + \alpha_1 RYD/P + \alpha_2 PCN^{nd}/PC + \alpha_3(CN^{nd}/P)_{-1} \quad (3.7)$$

where CN^{nd}/P is national real per capita consumption expenditure in the pertinent set of aggregated nondurable consumption categories, RYD/P is U.S. real per capita disposable income, and PCN^{nd}/PC is relative price of the nondurable commodities. Given the estimated coefficients of α_i and area-specific population and real per capita disposable income, equation 3.7 may be used to estimate an area-specific series of real nondurable consumption expenditure. State-level consumption and employment were used to quantify the relationship in equation 3.6, which then, together with sub-state-specific estimates of CN^{nd}, was used to determine a hypothetical, full internalized employment level for each area.

For regions outside the exporting center, step ii is the determination of the ratio of hypothetical to actual employment as a function of market size. Since this ratio logically must be greater than or equal to one, the dependent variable was transformed to be $\ln(R^n_{H/A,j} - 1)$, a formulation that assures this logical consistency in projection. The dependent variable is specified as a quadratic function of population, the estimated coefficient on the level of population being positive and that on population squared being negative. This result implies that for small communities, population growth initially increases the ratio of fully internalized employment to actual employment. That is, consumption expands, but it is primarily filled by imported commodities. After population reaches a threshold size, internalization of production increases with market growth, and the ratio of the hypothetical employment to the actual employment falls.

Construction. Construction employment estimation uses the basic formulation 3.2 with Q^i designated by current and lagged deflated construction awards, the latter subdivided into residential and nonresidential. Awards data, as opposed to variables such as housing starts, are used because their value basis permits direct integration of the government expenditure data into the construction sector. In particular, government construction expenditure in the private sector was netted out of total nonresidential awards, the net awards variable was directly estimated, and the government expenditure component was derived as described in section III.D below.

Trade. The availability of taxable sales data in the trade sector permits specification of trade employment in the basic format of equation 3.2 with Q^i measured by deflated sales. Furthermore, use of the sales data allows specification of interarea spillover effects of tourism. Using data from tourism surveys, area-specific series on restaurant and bar sales were disaggregated into purchases made by local residents, purchases made by in-state tourists (Arizonans residing outside a particular substate area, but visiting the region), and purchases made by out-of-state tourists. Explicit representation and estimation of the in-state tourism component of sales allows appropriate representation of the interarea spillovers that operate through Arizonans traveling around their own state.

For tourist-impacted sectors other than restaurants and bars for which explicit sales disaggregation is not feasible, the impact of tourism is specified by using deflated tourist restaurant and bar sales as an index of tourist activity. In general, real sales series are estimated using a standard consumer demand model, real income (augmented where necessary by the index of tourist activity), and relative price of the pertinent sales category.

Services. Employment in the heavily tourist-impacted sectors of the service industry, hotel/motel and amusements, is estimated similarly to the tourist-impacted trade sectors. In the case of medical services, both Phoenix and Tucson serve as exporting centers. Consequently, a model analogous to nondurable manufacturing is used, but the variable internalization is applicable only to the "balance of state" region and the difference between hypothetical and actual employment in that area is distributed to both metropolitan regions, two-thirds to Phoenix and one-third to Tucson. The basic state-level equation for fully internalized employment is a per capita specification using format 3.2 and the third option of Q^i noted at the end of section III.A.2—namely, underlying demand determinants, particularly real per capita income.

Estimation of employment in the large "other services" category requires a specification which permits integration of government expenditures on services with private sector expenditures. Similarly to nondurable manufacturing, national data on personal consumption expenditures in the pertinent service categories are used to estimate an equation for real per capita expenditures as a function of real per capita disposable income and relative prices. Using area-specific income and population data, the nationally estimated equation was used to derive local series on deflated personal expenditures on other services. Deflated government expenditures on services can be directly added to the derived series to obtain a series reflective of real expenditures made by government and individuals. However, specification of "other services" employment as a function of this deflated expenditure series and relative labor costs (similar to the trade sectors) would be incomplete. In particular, it would not contain the impact of service expenditures made by businesses. Data were not available to explicitly estimate service expenditures of private businesses so this interindustry impact is treated similarly to manufacturing employment derived from activity in other sectors, i.e., demand is indicated by employment in these other sectors. Consequently, "other services" employment is a function of deflated government and personal expenditures and private sector employment outside of "other services".

Other Private Sector Employment.   Estimation of employment in the transportation/communication/utilities and finance/insurance/real estate sectors primarily is of the form of equation 3.2, with Q^i denoted by underlying population and real disposable income determinants and price variables including interest rates in the pertinent financial sectors. All of these sectors, outside of transportation and other insurance services, are directly impacted by construction activity, either through construction-derived demand for financial and real estate services or—in the cases of communications and utilities—through construction-derived demands for line expansion and new hookups. These direct interindustry impacts are specified by inclusion in the equation of either construction employment or construction output, e.g., housing starts. In addition, banking and financial services are among the local-serving sectors subject to changing levels of internalization. Consequently, specification of employment in these industries embodies the hypothetical/actual analysis characteristic of nondurable manufacturing and medical services.

The above section and section III.D.6 below, cover specification of nonagricultural wage and salary employment. The aggregate of these categories is the majority of employment in Arizona, approximately 91 percent of total employment. By source of data, there are two other classes of employment in the model, agricultural employment and a residual category—the difference between total employment and the sum of agricultural and nonagricultural wage and salary employment. The residual category, which embodies self-employment, proprietorships, and a correction for multiple job holding in the salaried sector, is modeled as a function of labor force, declining as a proportion of the latter as area size grows. Agricultural employment is specified to trend slowly downward over time.

B. Population

Population estimation is subdivided by area into natural increase and net migration. The former, expressed as a rate relative to population, is on average higher than the national rate in all areas of Arizona, but its long-run trends parallel those in the United States as a whole. Net migration specification combines both direct employment impacts on migration and relative economic attractiveness of the areas as determinants of population flows. In particular, migration is modeled as being responsive in part to direct employment change, with greater weight being given to employment change in higher wage sectors. Using a pooled cross-section time-series estimation on subareas in Arizona, the migration impact of absolute employment change is seen to vary inversely with area size, a phenomenon reflecting the fact that larger labor markets can more readily absorb a given absolute change in employment by varying resident employment than can smaller labor market areas. Thus, the direct employment pull component of the migration equation is of the form:

$$(\alpha_0 + \alpha_1/P^i)(\beta_0 \Delta L_0^i + \beta_1 \Delta L_1^i + \beta_2 \Delta L_2^i) \qquad (3.8)$$

where P^i is population in area i, ΔL_j^i is change in employment in one of three sectors in area i (L_0 = construction, L_1 = mining and manufacturing, and L_2 = all other industries), all coefficients exceed zero and $\beta_0 > \beta_1 > \beta_2$.

The other component of migration determination is lagged response to relative economic attractiveness of the area as measured by relative unemployment rate. The current and temporal interactions among employment, migration, and labor market conditions assures that migration both affects and is affected by employment growth.

C. Income

Personal income determination is subdivided into estimation of seven components: labor compensation (which is further disaggregated into one-digit industrial components), nonfarm proprietors income, farm proprietors income, transfer payments, dividends/interest/rent, personal contributions to social insurance, and residence adjustment. Substate income from the Bureau of Economic Analysis does not directly permit separation by industrial category of compensation of wage and salary employees from earnings of self-employed and proprietors. Earnings of proprietors were netted from industry-specific earnings data using more detailed state information. In particular, it was assumed that

$$P_j^i = (P_s^i/P_s^T)P_j^T \qquad (3.9)$$

$$W_j^i = E_j^i - P_j^i \qquad (3.10)$$

where superscript i denotes industry (T = total) and subscript j denotes area

(s = state), P is proprietors earnings, W is compensation of wage and salary employees, and E is total labor compensation.

Industrial earnings components, the W_j^i above, are generally derived by identity from separately estimated employment and compensation per employee.[1] In the private sector, both leading industry and leading region models of compensation per employee are used. In the former case $(W/L)_j^i$, earnings per employee in industry i in area j, are a function of corresponding earnings in a leading industry in the area, typically manufacturing. In the leading region model, $(W/L)_j^i$ is a function of the analogous variable in another area—a more dominant metropolitan area in the state, the state as a whole, or the nation. This leading region specification in addition includes lagged unemployment rate in the area relative to that in the leading region to allow for differential impacts of labor market tightness on compensation levels. Variants of these two basic models include: (1) addition of legislated impacts on wages (e.g., effect of increases in the minimum wage on earnings per employee in trade sectors); and (2) separate estimation of earnings per full-time employee and the ratio of full-time to total employees in industries characterized by clear long-run trends in the latter ratio. Nonfarm proprietors income is also estimated by identity from earnings per employee and employment (with employment measured by the difference between total employment and the sum of agricultural and nonagricultural wage and salary employment). The earnings-per-employee variable is a function of earnings per wage and salary employee in the sectors in which proprietorships tend to be concentrated—namely, services and trade.

Changes in transfer payments per capita primarily reflect changes in federally legislated benefit levels of transfer programs and consequently, U.S. transfer payments per capita is a major determinant of local per capita receipts. However, since welfare-type payments are responsive to economic conditions, the specification includes area unemployment rate relative to national as a determinant of local deviations from national average resulting from different economic conditions. Personal contributions to social insurance are modeled as a function of total labor earnings and the legislated income base and contribution rate for personal social security payments. Farm income and residence adjustment are both small components of income in all Arizona areas. The former is determined by agricultural prices and activity and the latter varies with the total earnings of employees.

Two aspects of income determination, estimation of the component dividends/interest/rent and the transition from total to disposable income, are both linked to the government revenue/expenditure process. Consequently, they are covered in section III.D.7 below.

D. State/Local Government Revenues and Expenditures

1. Overview. The public budgetary process provides the framework for state and local government revenue and expenditure modeling. National models necessarily focus on federal spending, federal government receipts, and the associated economic impacts of federal deficits. State and local governments, in contrast, are typically required by constitution or charter to maintain a balanced budget. Consequently, the focus for regional modeling is on establishing a strong and direct link between revenues and expenditures. The model permits a choice of two methods by which revenues constrain expenditures: (i) a strict identity linking revenues and expenditures for each level of government in a given time period and (ii) a perhaps more realistic limited information framework in which expenditures in year t is a function of revenues in year t and $t - 1$.

While the budgetary constraint is the dominant structural feature linking public revenues and expenditures, it is important to recognize that the model embodies the entire revenue/expenditure process within a simultaneously determined public–private interaction. Government revenue/expenditure models are often treated as add-ons to a basic economic model of population, income, and employment. That is, data from the latter are used to derive revenue estimates, but there is then no feedback to the private sector. An essential feature of the present model is the complete integration of the public budgetary process with private employment and income generation, all components being simultaneously determined. Not only does private sector economic growth impact regional government revenues collected, the government fiscal process also affects private sector development. As detailed in the sections below, revenue generation and public expenditure impact the private sector via four major channels:

a. Sales and excise tax rates modify relative prices of particular goods and services, and these relative price changes in turn affect individual consumption decisions, level of sales, and hence employment in specific categories. Recall that deflated sales directly enter employment determination in many sectors in section III.A.

b. State/local government taxes have two direct effects on income. Property taxes enter determination of personal income as a reduction in gross rent received by individuals, where gross rent includes both monetary rents and imputed rents received by owner-occupants. Furthermore, other taxes and payments to government determine the translation of personal income into disposable income, the latter being a critical determinant of employment in many local serving sectors.

c. Revenues collected are primary inputs to the determination of the
    number of government employees and the wages these employees are
    paid. As with any industry generating personal income in a community,
    there are private sector impacts from the spending of this income in
    the region.
d. A significant volume of government expenditures is directly channeled
    through the private sector via government purchases of locally pro-
    duced goods and services. Variations in these public expenditures have
    employment impacts analogous to similar expenditure variations de-
    rived from private individual and private business spending. In partic-
    ular, government expenditures on services and construction directly
    determine employment in these sectors as outlined in section III.A.[2]

2. Aggregation and State/Local Linkages.   Specification of the revenue-
expenditure link requires that *all* revenues and expenditures be accounted
for in the model. However, this is an aggregate link and by itself does not
determine the level of detail at which revenues and expenditures should be
modeled. Major revenue classification treated separately in the model are
shown in table 3-3 and were derived from four considerations:

a. *Representation of public and private sector linkages*:   Explicit modeling
    of the various routes through which public policy impacts the private
    sector prohibits a number of aggregations. As an example, lumping
    together corporate and personal income taxes would preclude deriva-
    tion of disposable income.
b. *Legal basis of determination*:   The underlying bases of the revenue
    sources differ significantly, covering a variety of local economic aggre-
    gates (sales, income, wealth). Even more diverse are the bases for
    revenues generated from own sources and revenues derived from feder-
    al aid, the "base" for the latter essentially being federally legislated
    grants to states. These broadly different legal bases of determination
    result in a number of the major disaggregations shown in table 3-3,
    federal aid, income taxes, sales taxes, and property taxes.
c. *State/local revenue linkages*:   A major source of funds to local govern-
    ments are state-shared taxes, taxes pooled at the state level and then
    distributed by sharing formulas to local government entities. However,
    not all state revenues are shared and sharing formulas differ across
    classes of shared revenues. Consequently, in order to determine local
    revenues and expenditures, it is necessary to isolate the three major
    classes of shared revenues—sales taxes, highway revenues (both fuel
    and nonfuel), and income taxes. This necessity precludes, for example,

Table 3-3.   State and Local Government Revenues Estimated in the Model (by source)

Source	State[a]	Local[a]
Intergovernmental revenue	509.4[b]	1,511.1[b]
From federal government	509.4	247.1
From state government	—[c]	1,278.7[b]
Shared transaction privilege tax	—	221.4
Shared income tax	—	65.1
Shared highway revenues	—	93.0
Fuel	—	55.3
Nonfuel	—	37.7
State grants-in-aid	—	899.2[d]
Revenues from own sources	2,364.4	1,874.3
Specific taxes	1,683.5	786.5
Real property taxes	84.3	786.5
Fuel taxes	125.5	—
Gasoline	108.1	—
Usefuel	17.4	—
Nonfuel highway	117.9	—
Income tax	553.8	—
Corporate	114.8	—
Individual	439.0	—
Sales	789.2[e]	185.5[c]
Mining	43.5	—
Utilities	90.7	—
Communications	21.4	—
Restaurants and bars	58.5	—
Retail	391.7	—
Contracting	86.6	—
Rentals	54.8	—
Other Sales	42.0	—
Use tax	12.8	—
Other taxes, charges, and miscellaneous	680.9	902.3
Total revenue	2,873.8[b]	3,370.8[b]

[a] Values are for fiscal year 1981–1982, in $ million.

[b] Net of 14.6 intergovernmental transfers from local to state government.

[c] Dash (—) indicates nonexistent categories.

[d] Almost 90 percent is state aid-to-education.

[e] State taxable sales categories are estimated at the substate level and summed to derive the state aggregate.

[f] Locally levied sales taxes are estimated off an aggregated base.

Source: Compiled by the authors from *Governmental Finances in 1981–82* (GF82No. 5), U.S. Department of Commerce; *1981–1982 Annual Report*, Arizona Department of Revenue; *State of Arizona Tax Handbook* 1983, Arizona's Joint Legislative Budget Committee Staff; unpublished revenue data, Arizona's Department of Transportation; *Annual Financial Report 1981–82*, State of Arizona; *Arizona Property Tax Rates and Assessed Valuations*, Arizona Tax Research Association.

lumping of nonfuel highway revenues into a broader residual category. A completely different type of state-to-local revenue link is the separately treated state grants-in-aid to local areas which are largely state aid to school districts.

d. *Magnitude of revenue class*:   Trade-offs between estimation problems of small, narrowly defined series and estimation problems of aggregated heterogeneous series exist for revenue determination analogously to employment determination. Disaggregation within the major classes of sales taxes and highway revenues primarily reflects a balancing of these considerations. For example, periodic tax law changes create, eliminate, and change the relative magnitudes of subcomponents of the fee-type nonfuel highway revenues rendering the aggregate of these much more explicable than any particular subcomponent. In contrast, consistent data on major categories of sales taxes permit disaggregation and differentiation of economic factors impacting the seven major classifications that account for approximately 95 percent of total sales tax collections. In addition, these sectoral-specific deflated sales data are used in employment determination as discussed in section III.A.

Compilation of consistent data on expenditure disaggregation is far more complex than revenue disaggregation. Consequently, the sole criterion was minimum sufficient expenditure disaggregation to permit the appropriate feedback from the government sector to the private. State and local government expenditures are subdivided into wages and salaries of government employees (over 40 percent of total expenditures), construction (approximately 20 percent), purchases of services other than compensation of government employees (approximately 20 percent), and a residual comprising such items as purchases of capital goods and nondurable supplies.

Two aggregation issues arise in specification of the public sector which are not factors in the private sector analysis. Although there is just one state government, there are numerous types of local government entities—city, county, school district, special district. For revenue and expenditure analysis, these local governmental units are aggregated into a single local government sector. Problems of constructing consistent and comparable revenue and expenditure data series were formidable even with this aggregation. Furthermore, attempts to disaggregate by local government unit would contribute little to the overall public/private sector analysis, which is focused on the county, or broader, geographical level. None of the local government jurisdictions cross county lines.

For employment, population, income, unemployment rate, etc., variables are consistently estimated at the substate level and aggregated appropriately to derive statewide measures. This is neither feasible nor logical for all components in the public revenue/expenditure process. With regard to taxes there are three major categories to be considered: (i) income taxes (both personal and corporate) and nonfuel highway taxes; (ii) sales taxes and fuel taxes; and (iii) property taxes. Items in (i) are only levied and administered on a statewide basis so they must be estimated at that level of aggregation. There are no substate data, for example, to determine areas the income tax is being collected from. Items in (ii) are collected at a local level, pooled into an aggregate state fund, and partially redistributed back to local governments based on sharing formulas which include, but are not restricted to, share of total tax collected in the area. These taxes not only can be estimated at the local level and summed to determine statewide collections, they in fact must be in order to endogenously determine the sharing formulas. Note that some items from (i) are also partially shared back to local governments (personal income tax and nonfuel highway revenue). However, in these cases, the sharing formulas do not include area-specific collections. The property tax, item (iii), is separately levied at state and local levels, with no aggregation of local collections or sharing of state collections. However, the same net assessed valuation tax base is used in determination of both state and local levies. Consequently, for this tax, the base is estimated at the local level, local levies calculated by individual areas, and the state levy derived from the aggregated substate bases. State to local transfers that are not shared revenues are treated analogously to personal income and nonfuel highway taxes, i.e., a state pool to be shared is first determined and then its goegraphical distribution is estimated.

Treatment of local expenditures by local governments is straightforward, but state expenditures are logically constrained on an aggregate basis at a statewide level. After determining this overall constraint from state revenue estimates, the geographical distribution of state expenditures is determined by the regional distribution of both on-going commitments (e.g., the relative sizes of state universities in the different areas) and population growth. The total of state and local government expenditure within each area is then finally disaggregated by type—wages and salaries of government employees, construction, etc. Note that type of expenditure by type of government (state vs. local) is not estimated—e.g., construction expenditures of local governments in a particular area. The distinction is not necessary for the public/private sector impact analysis because the impact of a particular expenditure is largely independent of whether the state government makes the expenditure or a local government does. There are also conceptual problems with attempting to make the distribution because of cooperative state-local projects. Furthermore, available data for Arizona do not permit separation of state and local government employee compensation, and as noted above, this is the single largest expenditure category.

3. Tax Specifications. When estimating revenues, emphasis is placed on modeling tax bases and expressing collections as the base times the appropriate rate or fee. This permits bases to respond to changes in economic and demographic conditions and allows changes in tax rates to have explicit direct first-round impacts on revenues. Tax price effects are specified by incorporating tax rates or fee levels into appropriate price variables. Tax rates, fee levels, and other policy variables are entered exogenously to provide a framework for policy stimulations.

Transaction Privilege (Sales or Gross Business Income) Taxes. Of the eight taxable business income categories estimated in the model, all but mining are based on sales to consumers of commodities or services. Assuming utility maximization and well-behaved utility functions, sales-related tax bases in each substate area are specified as

$$RB_i/P = f_1(RYOP/P, p_i/p) \tag{3.11}$$

or, in its sometimes modified form,

$$RB_i = f_2(P, RYP, p_i/p) \tag{3.12}$$

where RB_i is the real or deflated consumption of the goods and services in category i; P is population; $RYPO/P$ is real per capita disposable income; and p_i/p is the relative price of goods or services in i, including the impact of tax rates on relative prices.

Taxable business income in mining is specified as a function of the market value of production (production times the nominal price of copper) and an indicator of copper demand to allow for inventory adjustments.

Fuel Taxes. Gasoline consumption is estimated using the same general specification as transaction privilege taxes, i.e., as a function of the relative price of gasoline (including taxes) and real income. The basic equation is expanded to include the tourism index since the proportion of gasoline sales to nonresidents (Arizona tourists and travelers en route) is high for Arizona.

Use fuel (UF) is a factor of production in the trucking industry and is modeled as a derived demand for inputs:

$$UF = f_3(O_T, p_F/p_I) \tag{3.13}$$

where O_T is output in the trucking industry and p_F/p_I is the price of fuel (including taxes) relative to other inputs. Unavailable output measures are replaced by local and/or U.S. (for enroute trucks) determinants of shipping demand, e.g., local government or real income, deflated retail sales, or real U.S. consumption of goods. Determinants of shipping demand are also used to model other receipts from freight carriers.

Net Assessed Valuation. Net assessed valuation (NAV), the base for the property tax, at a time t can be written as the identity

$$NAV_t = (1 + \alpha)(1 - s)NAV_{t-1} + VNC_{t-1,t} \qquad (3.14)$$

where s is the proportion of valuation in $t - 1$ lost to demolition between $t - 1$ and t, $(1 + \alpha)$ is the appreciation rate on land and existing structures, and $VNC_{t-1,t}$ is the current value of structures constructed between $t - 1$ and t. The term $(1 + \alpha)$ is specified as the ratio of current to lagged U.S. implicit price deflator for investment in residential structures, $PICR_t/PICR_{t-1}$. Dividing through by $PICR_t$, equation 3.14 is specified in real (or deflated) terms:

$$RNAV_t = (1 + \alpha)(1 - s)RNAV_{t-1} + RVNC_{t-1,t} \qquad (3.15)$$

In estimation, $RVNC_{t-1,t}$ is replaced by measures of indicators of building activity, e.g., housing starts or construction employment.

Income Taxes. The specification for state per capita taxable personal income is based on the following accounting relationship:

$$TYP/P \equiv (GYP/P - NTYP/P - D/P) - E/P \qquad (3.16)$$

where TYP is taxable income in Arizona (constructed data), P is population, GYP is Arizona's gross income (Arizona personal income plus personal contribution to social insurance), $NTYP$ is nontaxable income and D and E are deductions and exemptions, respectively. Personal exemption levels and exemptions for dependents, the aged, and blind remained fixed from 1962 until 1978 when they were tied to the state CPI (CPI^{AZ}). They are assumed to be proportional to population and are represented by the coefficient β_1 in the following linear regression:

$$TYP/P = \beta_1 EI + \beta_2(TXB/P) \qquad (3.17)$$

where EI is an exemption index, represented by ones from 1962 to 1977 and by $CPI_t^{AZ}/CPI_{1977}^{AZ}$) for $t = 1978, 1979, \ldots$. The other three items in expression 3.16 are combined into a single proxy for income available for taxation,

$$TXB = GYP - NTYP - D \qquad (3.18)$$

where $NTYP$ is measured by transfer payments to Arizonans; and deductions, D, is the sum of federal personal income taxes ($FYPT$), state personal income taxes, sales taxes, fuel taxes, and property taxes paid by individuals in Arizona. Total state individual income tax liabilities, L, withholdings, W, and tax payments due in April, TXP, are given by the following set of equations:

$$L = r \cdot TYP \tag{3.19}$$

$$W/L = f_4(FYPT/L) \tag{3.20}$$

$$TXP = L^L - W^L \tag{3.21}$$

where r is the state income tax rate and superscript L denotes a one-year lagged value. Individual taxpayers elect to have either, 0.1, 0.15, or 0.2 times their federal withholdings withheld for the state, consequently $FYPT$ is the primary determinant in equation 3.20. FYPT is specified as follows:

$$FYPT/P = f_5[r_f(FTXB/P), (FTXB/P)/(USFTXB/USP)] \tag{3.22}$$

where r_f is the U.S. effective federal income tax rate, $FTXB$ is Arizona's federal income tax base and the prefix US denotes corresponding U.S. values. $FTXB$ is proxied similarly to TXB in equation 3.18; however, federal personal income taxes and fuel taxes are deductions for the latter but not the former.

Corporate taxable income in Arizona (TYC) is modeled off of U.S. corporate taxable income ($USTYC$) and a measure of Arizona's economic activity. Corporate tax collections equal the corporate income tax rate times taxable income, i.e.,

$$TYC = f_6(USTYC, GBY) \tag{3.23}$$

$$TXC \equiv cr \cdot TYC \tag{3.24}$$

where TYC and TXC are, respectively, Arizona corporate taxable income and corporate income tax collections; GBY is a measure of gross business income (i.e., transaction privilege tax bases, described above); and cr is the corporate income tax rate.

4. State-to-Local Government Transfers. State-to-local government transfers consist of state-shared revenues and state grants-in-aid. The latter is primarily aid to local school districts and is estimated as follows for each substate area j:

$$SAID_j/P_j = f_7\{SAID/P, [YD_j/P_j/(YD/P)]\} \tag{3.25}$$

where $SAID_j$ is state aid to local schools received by area j; variables with subscript j refer to the jth substate area and those without are state values. When necessary, $\Sigma_j SAID_j$ is constrained to equal $SAID$. Total state aid to schools is estimated as a function of state revenues.

Shared revenues are allocated to substate areas by identities that distribute revenues among the substate government units according to legislated formulas. The state's urban revenue sharing program allocates 15 percent of the income tax revenues collected two years previously to incorporated cities and towns according to relative municipal populations. State transaction privilege tax revenues are distributed both to incorporated cities and towns and to county governments. The portion going to cities and towns is distributed according to municipal population; the portion going to counties is distributed with a two-part formula whereby half is allocated according to county net assessed valuation and half is allocated proportionately to sales (i.e., tax base) generated in each county. State-shared highway revenues are distributed to counties according to relative levels of county fuel sales (both gasoline and use-fuel gallons). Incorporated cities and towns receive their share of highway revenues on the basis of a two-tiered formula. In the first tier, funds are allocated to county areas according to fuel sales. These amounts are then divided among the incorporated cities and towns within each county according to municipal population.

5. Federal Transfers to State and Local Government. Specification of federal government transfers to state and local governments consists of three equations:

$$RFSL/P = f_8[(USRFSL/USP), (YD/P)/(USYD/USP)] \qquad (3.26)$$

where $RFSL$ is real federal transfers to state and local governments in Arizona. The share of nominal RFSL going to local governments (FL/FSL) is estimated by

$$FL/FSL = f_9(PM/P, USP^{-1}) \qquad (3.27)$$

where PM is population living in municipalities and USP^{-1} acts as a trend. Real per capita federal transfers to local governments in substate area j is estimated as follows:

$$RFL_j/P_j = f_{10}(USRFSL/USP) \qquad (3.28)$$

Again, $\Sigma_j FL_j = FL$.

6. Expenditures. As covered in section III.D.1, total expenditures are constrained by total revenues and allocated to substate areas as described in section III.D.2. These state and local total government expenditures by area are subdivided into compensation of government employees (disaggregated into employment and earnings per employee), construction expenditures, service expenditures, and other.

State and local government employment in each substate area ($ESLGOV$) is determined by prior and ongoing commitments (hence, a lagged dependent variable), deflated state and local revenues spent in the area ($SLREV/C$), and a measure of labor costs relative to other inputs. On a per capita basis, the equation is

$$ESLGOV/P = g_2(ESLGOV/P^L, SLREV/C/P, WSLGOV/WPI) \qquad (3.29)$$

where $WSLGOV$ is per employee state and local government income in the substate area and WPI is the wholesale price index. $WSLGOV$ is specified relative to a comparable U.S. figure as a slowly adjusting function of recent revenue conditions and the compensation rate in a competitive industry:

$$WSLGOV/USWSLGOV = g_3(SLREV/E/USWSLGOVM2,$$
$$WMAN/USWSLGOV^{L2}) \qquad (3.30)$$

where the Mk suffix denotes a k-period moving average, superscript Lk denotes k-period lag and $WMAN$ is a per employee labor income in manufacturing in Arizona or a substate area. When revenue conditions improve, there is an upward pressure on both government employment levels and per employee compensation in the government sector, with the revenue impact on the latter dampening the effect on the former.

For each substate area, the jth nonemployee-compensation expenditure category ($GEXP_j$) is deflated and specified on a per employee basis as a function of lagged values and the change in deflated revenues per employee:

$$IGEXP_j/C/ESLGOV = g_4(GEXP_j/C/ESLGOV^L, SLREV/C/$$
$$ESLGOVCH) \qquad (3.31)$$

where the I prefix denotes an intermediate value and CH a one-period change in the variable. Although revenue levels or changes in revenues determine each expenditure category, there is no guarantee that these intermediate values of expenditure categories will sum to the total state and local expenditure figures ($GEXP$) that were related directly to total revenues by either an identity or an estimated equation. Consequently, final values of each nonemployee-compensation expenditure category for each substate area are given by

$$GEXP_j = (IGEXP_j/\Sigma_j IGEXP_j) \cdot (GEXP - WSLGOV \cdot ESLGOV) \qquad (3.32)$$

Then, for each substate area,

$$GEXP \equiv WSLGOV \cdot ESLGOV + \Sigma_j GEXP_j \qquad (3.33)$$

7. Revenues and Income Determination. A significant revenue-economic linkage in a state-substate system is that between what individuals receive in personal income and what they have left to spend after all payments to governments have been made (i.e., disposable income). Personal payments to governments are, in order of importance, federal personal income taxes (*FYPT*), state personal income taxes (*W* + *TXP*), property taxes paid by individuals, and several significantly smaller categories. The first two and the aggregate of the smaller categories are incorporated into the framework as deductions from personal income to get disposable income, i.e.,

$$YD \equiv Y - FYPT - (W + TXP) - TNTO$$

where *YD* is disposable income, *Y* is personal income, and *TNTO* is all other tax and nontax payments. Estimation of the income taxes, *FYPT*, *W*, and *TXP*, is described in the previous sections. The small category, *TNTO*, is a function of personal income.

BEA personal income figures treat property taxes as reduction in gross rents received by individuals, where gross rent includes both monetary rents and imputed rents received by owner-occupants. Consequently, in the model, property taxes paid by individuals are added to the dividends, interest, and rent component of personal income for estimation. Property taxes are subsequently resubtracted and the net dividends, interest, and rent fiture is summed with other income components to get total personal income.

IV. Simulation Analyses

A number of simulations were run with the model and illustrate the significance of the various linkages emphasized and detailed in previous sections. The first pair of comparative simulations focuses on variable substate production internalization and its role in overall regional growth. Three sets of simulations, examing the impact of a change in export-base manufacturing employment, permit derivation of (1) the role of population growth in determination of regional multipliers; (2) industrial composition of induced employment change; (3) the relative magnitudes of state and substate multipliers. The final three simulations study the model relationships in terms of changes in state/local tax structure.

A. Substate Internalization and Long-Run Growth

Figure 3-1 plots the long-run growth path for Tucson SMSA nonagricultural

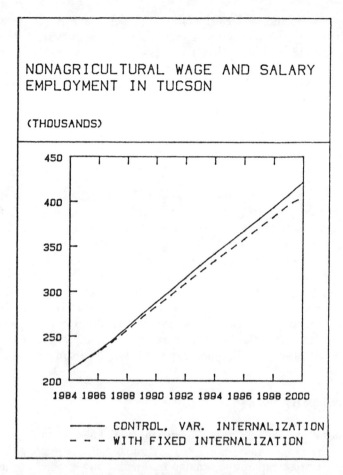

NONAGRICULTURAL WAGE AND SALARY
EMPLOYMENT IN TUCSON

(THOUSANDS)

─────── CONTROL. VAR. INTERNALIZATION
─ ─ ─ WITH FIXED INTERNALIZATION

Figure 3-1. Nonagricultural Wage and Salary Employment in Tucson (thousands)

wage and salary employment under two alternative assumptions with respect to substate internalization of production of goods and services. The
solid line tracks the control solution which embodies increasing Tucson
internalization of nondurable manufacturing and banking services as outlined in section III.A.3. In the alternative growth path solution, shown by
the dashed line, it is assumed that Tucson's ratio of hypothetical to actual
employment in nondurable manufacturing and banking remains constant at
1984 levels throughout the projection horizon. Clearly the allowance for
changing levels of economic integration impacts overall growth, a little at

first, but cumulating to a difference of almost 16 thousand employees or 3.8 percent of nonagricultural wage and salary employment by the year 2000. Of the additional employees in the control run by 2000, 8.4 thousand are in directly affected sectors of nondurable manufacturing and banking. The remaining employees are spread among other local-serving sectors, further growth having been induced by income multiplier impacts in Tucson associated with internalization of own production. It is impossible to calculate a well-defined multiplier for the increased internalization effect because there is not a fixed, temporally constant change in employment in a given sector between the two simulations. However, the simple ratio of total Tucson employment change in 2000 to nondurable manufacturing and banking employment change in 2000 yields a multiplier-type calculation of approximately 2. In comparison with multipliers reported in the next section, this is a figure between a one-year impact multiplier and a long-run multiplier for Tucson. This intermediary result is reasonable since the internalization effects are building up and cumulating slowly over the period of projection.

It should be noted that the model's embodiment of changing internalization of Tucson production has almost no effect on statewide employment projections; the internalization affects the distribution of employment between Tucson and the higher-order city Phoenix from which Tucson otherwise imports nondurable goods and financial services. The Phoenix nonagricultural wage and salary employment by the year 2000 is 17 thousand jobs higher in the simulation in which Tucson internalization is held constant at 1984 levels. Again, approximately half the employment difference is in the immediately impacted sectors, nondurable manufacturing and banking, and the remainder reflects multiplier impacts in the Phoenix area economy.

B. Population Growth and Employment Multipliers

The solid line in figure 3-2 plots the time path of the nonagricultural wage and salary employment multiplier in Tucson resulting from a 1000-employee increase in defense/scientific instruments manufacturing in that SMSA. The employment increase is initiated in 1985 and maintained through the year 2000. The impact multiplier is 1.57 in 1985, but grows to 3.24 by the year 2000. Similar to a national multiplier analysis, a part of the multiplier growth reflects lagged adjustment of private expenditure to income growth and lagged adjustment of employment to changed output levels. Further, there are state and local public sector impacts as private sector income and expenditure growth generates more public revenues and public expenditures are adjusted to the higher revenue levels. Of particular importance, and in

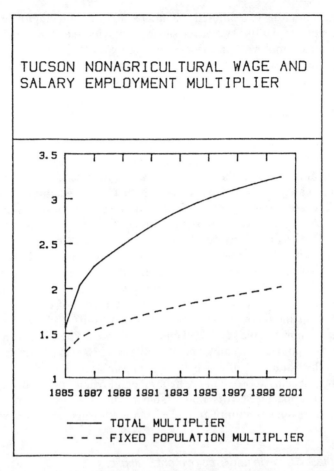

Figure 3-2. Tucson Nonagricultural Wage and Salary Employment Multiplier

contrast to most nationally aggregated impact analyses, the new manufacturing employment and consequent improved economic climate of Tucson
stimulates migration to the SMSA and the demographic change initiates a
cycle of further growth.

The role of population growth in regional multiplier determination can be
highlighted by comparing this total multiplier path with that generated by a
multiplier run in which population is held constant at the levels implied by
the solution of the model without the additional 1000 manufacturing employees (the control solution). This "fixed-population" multiplier path is

tracked by the dashed line in figure 3-2. Note that in determination of the fixed-population multiplier path, Tucson population is not held constant over time. Population levels are held at control values (which increase over time) and not allowed to deviate because of the marginal increase of the 1000 manufacturing employees.

In the fixed-population case, the multiplier in 1985 is 1.3 and rises to 2.0 by the year 2000. While the total multiplier in 1985 is only 20 percent above the fixed-population multiplier, population growth causes it to increase to over 60 percent above the fixed-population multiplier by the year 2000. The demographic effects of the manufacturing increase tend to be concentrated in the early years of the simulation so that the ratio of the total multiplier to the fixed-population multiplier rises rapidly from 1.2 to 1.5 over the period 1985–1988, gradually increases to 1.6 by 1993, and remains approximately constant at the latter level out to the year 2000.

This pattern of change in the ratio of the multipliers reflects the pattern of comparative net in-migration levels simulated in the two multiplier analyses. For the first three-year period, 1985 through 1988, net in-migration in the total-multiplier solution is 3.7 percent above control solution migration (which by construction is identical to migration in the fixed-population multiplier simulation). For 1988–1990, it has dropped off to only 0.8 percent above control levels, and for 1991–1993, migration has almost returned to control levels, being less than half a percent higher in the total-multiplier simulation. In the year 1998, the total-multiplier run simulates the same level of migration as the control run.

There is in fact some overshooting of population growth by the mid-1990s in the total-multiplier simulation. There is overshooting in the sense that comparative labor force and employment increases result in a slightly higher unemployment rate in 1997 and 1998 in the total-multiplier run compared with the control run. As a consequence, net inmigration to Tucson in 1999 and 2000 in the total-multiplier simulation is marginally below control levels.

By the year 2000, total population growth in Tucson associated with the 1000 employee manufacturing increase is 3038 persons. Assuming the same ratio of wage and salary employment to population in the additional group compared with the control level population, the new persons account for absorption of approximately 40 percent of the total wage and salary employment increase of 3242 jobs. The remaining 60 percent of the new jobs generated by the marginal manufacturing employment change are implicitly held by preimpact population. As noted above, the unemployment rate is slightly higher in the total-multiplier run compared with control by the end of the projection horizon. This result is consistent with the increased ratio of wage and salary employment to population because (1) labor force partic-ipation rates are higher in the total-multiplier run and (2) some of the new wage and salary jobs (approximately 2.8 percent) are filled by shifts from the nonsalaried to the salaried sector.

This section, as well as the previous one and the following one, use simulations on the Tucson area as examples. Comparative results hold for other regions, although to differing degrees. Some of the differences among substate area multipliers are discussed in section IV.D below.

C. Industrial Composition of Employment Multipliers

Table 3-4 summarizes by industry the induced employment impacts over time in Tucson of a 1000-employee increase in defense/scientific instruments manufacturing—in that SMSA—which is again initiated in 1985 and main-tained through the year 2000. With the exception of the copper mining industry, employment in all major industrial categories is higher as a result of the manufacturing increase. Note, however, that the industrial composi-tion of employment increase shifts markedly over time. As discussed in the previous section, population growth induced by the employment spurt tends to be concentrated in the early years of the simulation. The residential investment stimulus of this growth causes construction and construction-impacted employment (especially in durable manufacturing, transportation/communication/utilities and finance/insurance/real estate) to figure much more significantly in the industrial employment change in the earlier years of the simulation compared with the latter years. For example, in 1986, con-struction employment accounts for 16.2 percent of induced employment change, but by the year 2000, it is only 4.3 percent of industrial change. Similarly, declines in induced employment share characterize the construc-tion-impacted employment in durable manufacturing, transportation/com-munication/utilities and finance/insurance/real estate.

In table 3-4, shares vary, but absolute employment impact still is positive in all major industrial categories. However, it should be noted that when more specific industrial categories are examined, this is not true. The initial manufacturing employment spurt tightens labor market conditions in Tuc-son, resulting in increased manufacturing wages in this SMSA relative to elsewhere and relative to the prices of nonlabor inputs to the manufacturing process. While this wage increase is not sufficient to offset the demand stimulus to employment growth in local-serving sectors, it does reduce em-ployment in Tucson in the durable manufacturing industries that produce for national markets, particularly the machinery sector. This absolute de-

Table 3-4. Industrial Distribution of Induced Employment Change from a 1000-Employee Increase in Defense/Scientific Instruments Manufacturing in Tuscon

				Number of Employees (Percent of Total Induced Change)[a]			
Industry	Year: 1985	1986	1987	1988	1990	1995	2000
Mining	0 (0.0)	0 (0.0)	0 (0.0)	0 (0.0)	0 (0.0)	0 (0.0)	0 (0.0)
Construction	75 (13.1)	168 (16.2)	162 (13.0)	132 (9.6)	109 (6.9)	103 (5.1)	97 (4.3)
Manufacturing	83 (14.5)	122 (11.6)	135 (10.8)	131 (9.6)	125 (7.9)	128 (6.4)	131 (5.9)
Durable goods	67 (11.7)	85 (8.1)	84 (6.7)	71 (5.2)	57 (3.6)	56 (2.8)	63 (2.8)
Nondurable goods	16 (2.8)	37 (3.5)	51 (4.1)	60 (4.4)	68 (4.3)	72 (3.6)	68 (3.1)
Transportation, communications, utilities	58 (10.1)	72 (6.9)	79 (6.3)	84 (6.1)	89 (5.6)	98 (4.9)	101 (4.5)
Trade	105 (18.4)	187 (18.0)	252 (20.2)	306 (22.4)	396 (24.9)	526 (26.2)	588 (26.3)
Finance, insurance, real estate	38 (6.6)	118 (11.4)	131 (10.5)	135 (9.9)	138 (8.7)	145 (7.2)	152 (6.8)
Services	131 (22.9)	227 (21.9)	306 (24.6)	378 (27.6)	497 (31.3)	718 (35.8)	857 (38.3)
Government	82 (14.3)	144 (13.9)	180 (14.5)	203 (14.8)	235 (14.8)	286 (14.3)	313 (14.0)
Total nonagricultural	572 (100.0)	1,037 (100.0)	1,246 (100.0)	1,369 (100.0)	1,590 (100.0)	2,002 (100.0)	2,242 (100.0)

[a] Does not include direct 1000 increase in defense/scientific instruments manufacturing.

cline contributes to the drop in durable manufacturing's share of induced employment from 11.7 percent in 1985 to under 3 percent in 1995.

In contrast, the share of induced employment accounted for by trade and services rises steadily in the simulation period. In 1985, these two sectors account for 41.3 percent of induced change; and by the year 2000, almost two thirds of induced change is in these local-serving industries. Lagged adjustment to higher income and population levels and lesser sensitivity to the peaking construction impacts results in this steady share growth. Furthermore, compared with other industries, retail trade is characterized by a more rapid decline over time in the ratio of full-time to total employees. Since employment data reported in table 3-4 are head counts, trade's share of induced employment tends to rise more than it would if it were possible to calculate share of "full-time equivalents" growth.

Unlike either trade/services—with temporally increasing shares of induced employment—or construction-related industries—with decreasing shares—the government sector's share of induced employment is almost constant over the 15-year horizon in table 3-4. In general, the elasticity of state and local public revenue with respect to personal income growth in Arizona is less than one, reflecting both revenue-base erosion from emphasis of the tax structure on the retail sector as opposed to the more rapidly growing service sector, and independence of several tax sources (e.g., mining, interstate trucking, out-of-state tourists) from local income-population growth. Consequently, in the multiplier simulation, government expenditure growth in Tucson does not expand as rapidly as personal income; concomitantly, government employment expansion is less than that of trade and services. However, induced employment growth in the government sector is smoother and more consistent than that of the construction-impacted industries. Even the peaking of construction is smoothed in its effect on the government sector—e.g., in one period, (a) increased revenues are generated as a result of higher construction incomes; (b) these are replaced later by increases in property tax revenues as construction projects are completed; and (c) the expenditure adjustments to these revenue changes are not immediate, but phased in. Thus, growth of induced employment in the government sector is steadier than in construction-related industries and less rapid than in trade and services—which have the net effect of an approximately constant share of induced employment in the government sector.

D. Comparative State and Substate Employment Multipliers

Table 3-5 reports the employment multipliers of a 1000-employee increase

Table 3.5. Comparative State and Substate Employment Multipliers of a 1000-Employee Increase in Defense Manufacturing

	Phoenix[a]		Tucson[a]		Nonurban[a]	
	Multiplier in		Multiplier in		Multiplier in	
Year	Phoenix	State	Tucson	State	Nonurban	State
	(1)	(2)	(3)	(4)	(5)	(6)
1985	1.63	1.69	1.57	1.67	1.34	1.43
1987	2.24	2.35	2.25	2.33	1.92	1.99
1990	2.54	2.60	2.59	2.54	2.34	2.27
1995	3.02	3.09	3.00	3.02	2.83	2.80
2000	3.39	3.49	3.24	3.35	3.12	3.17

[a] Area of manufacturing employment change.

in defense/scientific instruments manufacturing in each of the three substate areas. The multipliers were calculated with separate simulations; employment was *not* simultaneously increased in all three areas. For each multiplier run, employment in defense/scientific instruments manufacturing was raised 1000 over control levels, starting in 1985 and maintained through 2000. Own-area and statewide multipliers were calculated for each simulation.

Although multiplier levels do not differ drastically, several interesting points emerge from the comparative empirical analysis. In all cases, both the own-area and statewide multipliers increase over time, but the *relative* increase between 1985 and 2000 in own-area multipliers is clearly greatest for the nonurban balance of state. This reflects the much stronger population effects that occur over time in the balance of state for a given absolute manufacturing employment change. Compared, for example, with Phoenix, the smaller labor markets in the balance of state do not as readily absorb the 1000-employee manufacturing increase from initial resident labor force. Hence, population expands more in the nonurban area and the population growth increases the own-area multiplier. By the year 2000, the substate-area population growth associated with the manufacturing employment increase in Tucson is 50 percent higher than in Phoenix, and in the balance of state, it is 100 percent higher than in Phoenix.

Own-area impact multipliers (those occurring in 1985) are ranked from greatest to least as Phoenix, Tucson, balance of state. The statewide impact multiplier is approximately the same for Phoenix and Tucson, but definitely less for the balance of state. The relative own-area Phoenix and Tucson impact results reflect the greater economic integration of the former area compared with the latter. However, the statewide multipliers are similar for the two areas. The goods and services Phoenix is more self-sufficient in are the same goods and services Tucson imports from Phoenix. Consequently, for production in the state as a whole, it does not matter whether consumption occurs in Phoenix or Tucson. The balance of state also imports from Phoenix; but despite this, the statewide multiplier is less when the 1000-employee increase is in the nonurban region. The lower statewide multipliers in the balance-of-state simulations reflect the fact that the initial income impact in the balance-of-state simulation is less than in those for the metropolitan areas—manufacturing wages are lower in the nonurban counties compared with Phoenix and Tucson.

Note from columns (1) and (2) in table 3-5 that the own-area multiplier in Phoenix is consistently slightly less than the associated statewide multiplier, a differential caused by spillovers from Phoenix to the rest of the state via in-state tourism. One of the most interesting results in table 3-5 is that this same relationship between own-area multiplier and associated statewide multiplier is not always true for the Tucson and balance-of-state simulations. In particular, in the period about 1990–1995, the own-area multipliers for these two regions are almost identical to or *exceed* the statewide multiplier. The own-area multiplier can be greater than the statewide multiplier because of employment redistribution within the state. Such redistribution, particularly in the government sector, accounts for the results in the Tucson and nonurban areas. For example, in 1990, in the nonurban-multiplier simulation, the statewide private-sector multiplier exceeds the own-area private-sector multiplier, but 30 percent of the increase in nonurban government employment is at the expense of government employment elsewhere, particularly the Phoenix area. The net result is a higher total substate-area multiplier than statewide multiplier. Some government employment redistribution is also evident in the Phoenix simulations, but it is not of sufficient magnitude to offset the private sector spillovers and cause the total-employment multiplier of the Phoenix area to exceed the associated statewide multiplier. Much stronger government redistribution effects characterize the Tucson and nonurban situations because (1) area population growth induced by manufacturing increase is greater for the non-Phoenix areas; and (2) the relative effect of the absolute 1000-employee increase is much larger for the small substate regions outside Phoenix. Recall from section III.D.2 that population affects the share of state expenditure so that areas characterized by larger demographic impacts of multipliers tend to receive a greater proportion of state expenditure. Item (2) results in a simple algebraic effect on revenue sharing formulas. Suppose there are two areas, numerically measured by A_1 and A_2 with $A_1 > A_2$, and the two area shares are $A_1/(A_1 + A_2)$ and $A_2/(A_1 + A_2)$. Suppose further that the same absolute increase, ΔA, occurs in the total pool and in a given area. It is obvious that if ΔA occurs in area one, then the difference in shares widens; and if it occurs in area two, then the difference diminishes. However, it is also straightforward to show that the extent to which the share difference diminishes in the second case exceeds the extent to which it widens in the first case. That is, the addition of the same absolute impact has a larger redistributive impact if the addition is made to the smaller area. Although for all areas the 1000-employee manufacturing increase raises aggregate state and local government revenues, expenditure, and employment, it also causes reallocation of the pool, with the net result that some local-area multipliers exceed the statewide multiplier.

However, the government redistributive effect wears off as the demographic impacts of employment change diminish. The migration impacts are strongest in the earliest years of the simulations, tending to cumulate population growth for a while, and then leveling off. As the demographic impacts on government redistribution stabilize, the positive private-sector impacts to the rest of the state via imported goods and services and in-state tourism gain relative to the public sector redistribution. By the year 2000, the statewide multipliers exceed the own-area multipliers consistently for all regions.

E. State and Local Revenue–Expenditure Linkage: Increased Federal Aid to Arizona

Table 3-6 summarizes the employment impact of a sustained $100-million increase (in 1985 constant dollars) in federal aid to Arizona. The simulation assumes nominal increases in federal aid of $100 million in fiscal year 1984–1985 (FY85), $107 million in FY86, $113 million in FY87, increasing to $137 million in FY90, $189 million in FY95, and $263 million in FY2000. In addition, assumptions of no change in federal aid to other states or in other U.S. variables as a result of higher transfers to Arizona are made.

The comparatively small first-year total-employment impacts reflects lags in Arizona's state and local government revenue-expenditure relationships that are incorporated into the model. The impact more than doubles between the first and second year as government expenditures catch up to revenues, with further increase diminishing over time. The total-employment impact increases faster than government employment impact because of dynamically increasing multiplier impacts on the private sector. Government share of the total-employment impact decreases from 61.5

Table 3-6. Industrial Distribution of Employment Changes Due to a $100-Million Increase (in 1985 constant dollars) in Federal Aid to Arizona (percent of total employment impact shown in parentheses)

Industry	1985	1986	1987	1990	1995	2000
Mining	0 (0.0)	0 (0.0)	0 (0.0)	0 (0.0)	0 (0.0)	0 (0.0)
Construction	203 (11.1)	514 (12.9)	610 (11.5)	515 (7.4)	514 (6.1)	516 (5.5)
Manufacturing	65 (3.6)	162 (4.1)	214 (4.0)	265 (3.9)	327 (3.9)	352 (3.7)
Transportation, communication, utilities	20 (1.1)	56 (1.4)	85 (1.6)	134 (1.9)	179 (2.1)	202 (2.1)
Trade	148 (8.1)	375 (9.4)	570 (10.7)	944 (13.6)	1332 (15.7)	1566 (16.6)
Finance, insurance, real estate	32 (1.8)	139 (3.5)	224 (4.2)	265 (3.8)	338 (4.0)	383 (4.1)
Services	236 (12.9)	613 (15.3)	947 (17.8)	1615 (23.3)	2293 (27.1)	2279 (28.9)
Government	1129 (61.5)	2142 (53.5)	2664 (50.1)	3202 (46.1)	3491 (41.1)	3689 (39.1)
Total nonagricultural	1833 (100.0)	4001 (100.0)	5314 (100.0)	6940 (100.0)	8474 (100.0)	9437 (100.0)

percent in 1985 to 39.1 percent by 2000. Services and construction receive 12.9 percent and 11.1 percent, respectively, of the first-year impact as a direct result of higher government expenditure. Services' share increases over time throughout the simulation period via multiplier impacts. The increasing and then declining pattern of construction employment and construction-related employment impacts (especially in finance and real estate) reflects the pattern of induced population growth discussed in section IV.B.

An interesting result is the positive induced impact on the government sector. Total state and local revenues increase by more than the exogenous increase in federal aid. Dividing the increase in total state and local revenues by the exogenous increase in federal aid over time results in a revenue "multiplier" of 1.04 in FY85, 1.09 in FY86, 1.14 in FY90, 1.20 in FY95, and 1.24 in FY2000.

F. Redistributive Aspects of State-to-Local Government Transfers in the Arizona Economy

Table 3-7 summarizes the impacts of changing the state-to-local income tax sharing formula on the two major metropolitan areas and the nonurban segment of the state economy. Arizona's existing income tax revenue sharing formula distributes 15 percent of the state income tax revenues collected two years previously to incorporated cities and towns according to relative populations in those municipalities, i.e.,

$$YT_t^i = 0.15 YT_{t-2}(PM_t^i / \sum_{j=1}^{n} PM_t^j)$$

where YT_j^i is the income tax revenues distributed to incorporated municipality i in time t, YT_{t-2} is total income tax collections two years previously, PM_t^i is the population of municipality i at time t, and n is the total number of municipalities in Arizona. Income tax revenues shared to substate area k, YT_t^k, is the sum of shared revenues to municipalities within that substate area, i.e.,

$$YT_t^k = \sum_{i \in \Omega_k} YT_t^i$$

where Ω_k is the set of municipalities in k. Per capita income taxes paid in the metropolitan areas is significantly higher than that paid by persons living in the balance of the state so, on the one hand, the formula tends to redistribute tax monies from metropolitan areas to the balance of state. However, state

Table 3-7.   Impacts of Alternative Income Tax Sharing Formula

Year	Phoenix	Tucson	Nonurban	Total
	Shared Income Taxes (million dollars)			
1985	−15.234	1.625	13.609	0.000
1986	−13.758	1.423	12.335	0.000
1987	−15.974	1.705	14.271	0.002
1990	−21.579	2.562	19.026	0.009
1995	−38.321	5.883	32.464	0.026
2000	−63.402	11.494	51.952	0.044
	Total Wage and Salary Employment			
1985	−200	43	367	138
1986	−475	67	471	64
1987	−639	79	592	33
1990	−912	111	851	50
1995	−1330	197	1220	85
2000	−1735	309	1536	110
	Government Employment			
1985	−125	26	197	99
1986	−272	34	272	34
1987	−338	41	333	33
1990	−450	54	444	49
1995	−603	95	589	80
2000	−752	143	710	101

income tax revenues are shared only to incorporated cities and towns so there is a stronger opposing redistribution away from the balance of state to metropolitan areas because of significant proportions of persons living in incorporated cities and towns in the latter areas. The net effect is to redistribute revenues away from the balance of state to metropolitan counties with the balance of state receiving about 15.5 percent of shared revenues while generating 19.4 percent of state income.

The redistributive aspects of this state-to-local government transfer is examined by replacing the existing sharing formula with one that channels revenues toward the nonurban balance of state. The alternative revenue sharing formula (effective in FY85) distributes income tax revenues to local governments across substate areas on a per capita basis with a formula that is inversely variant with per capita income. Letting substate area j be the area with the highest per capita income, the alternative formula may be expressed in two equations:

$$YT_t^j = (0.15YT_{t-2}(P^j)/\left[1 + \sum_{k=1}^{m} P^k(YP^j/P^j)/(YP^k/P^k)\right]$$

$$\underset{k \neq j}{Y} T_t^j = YT_t^j(P^k/P^j)(YP^j/P^j)/(YP^k/P^k)$$

where P^j and P^k are population in substate areas j and k, respectively, YP^j and YP^k are respective substate area personal income levels, and m is the number of substate areas ($1 \le j \le m$, $k - 1,2, \ldots, m$, and $k \neq j$).

The Phoenix SMSA has the highest per capita income of the three substate areas. Consequently, under the alternative formula, balance of state and Tucson SMSA local governments would receive for each person residing in that area an amount higher than per person amounts received by local governments in Phoenix: balance of state local governments receive almost 30 percent of shared income tax revenues while generating only 19 percent of state income; the Phoenix area's share falls from 67 to 50 percent while retaining 56 percent of state population and 61 percent of state income; Tucson's share increases from 18 percent to just under 20 percent, an amount roughly proportional to Tucson's share of state income.

The total amount of income tax revenues shared to local governments in FY85 is $94.6 million, consequently, balance of state receipts increase from $14.6 to $28.2 million, Tucson's receipts increase from $17 to $18.6 million, and Phoenix's receipts decrease from $63.0 to $47.8 million. The redistribution of funds increases total state local government expenditures in the first year of the simulation because the balance of state's first-year propensity to spend out of a revenue increase is higher than the Phoenix first-year propensity to cut expenditures out of a revenue decrease. Consequently, total state and local government expenditures increase by $6.8 million in the first year; statewide government employment increases by 99 workers; and total wage and salary employment is higher by 138.

The first-year impact diminishes significantly in the second year as the Phoenix spending and employment levels continue to fall, coming into line with the permanent decrease in revenues. Total state and local government spending falls to almost match control-run values. However, state and local government employment is still up statewide by 34 because of adjustment lags in government employment and a sustained higher level of income derived from the first-year impact. Total employment impact is 64 in the second year.

The relative employment multipliers for Phoenix and balance of state affect the total employment impact over time. Balance of state's short-run multiplier is low relative to Phoenix's because of the former's smaller size and fewer interindustry linkages. However, internalization and induced population growth (discussed in subsections A and B above) cause the balance of state's multiplier to grow faster than Phoenix's. Consequently, the total-employment impact continues to fall in the third year but then gradually expands to 110 by the year 2000. The state and local government impact parallels this pattern, falling to 33 in 1987 and gradually increasing to 101. In the year 2000, the increase in state government employment is only 9 less than the increase in total wage and salary employment but there have been other, offsetting, changes in the private sectors. The comparatively lower balance-of-state multiplier reduces state per capita income slightly, diminishing the income-related sectors (services, trade, financial, etc.) However, the population shift to the balance of state (and, to a limited extent, to Tucson) impacts positively on construction and construction-related trade, manufacturing, and utilities sectors. There has also been a significant redistribution of employment among substate areas, with the balance of state gaining 1536 employees, Tucson gaining 309, and Phoenix losing 1735 by year 2000.

G. Private-to-Public Sector Transfers

Figure 3-3 shows the employment impact of doubling the state personal income tax rate. Total personal income tax collections represent less than 1.5 percent of total personal income. Consequently, increasing the rate by a marginal amount for simulation could, because of computer rounding, prohibit analysis of sometimes small indirect impacts. Therefore, the tax rate is doubled for demonstrative purposes even though it is recognized that such doubling is neither politically feasible nor practical. Two opposing impacts of the tax increase are examined, the decrease in disposable income and its effect on the private sector, and the increase in government revenues and its resulting impact on state employment and income through expenditures.

The dashed line in figure 3-3 records the negative impact on the private-sector economy through tax rate-induced reductions in disposable income. The resulting decrease in employment is 2,350 workers in 1985, 4,573 in 1986, 5,924 in 1987, growing to 9,208 in 1990, 13,823 in 1995, and 17,869 in 2000. The solid line represents the total-employment impact of the tax increase including both the private sector impact and the government expenditure impact. The total gap between the solid and dashed line is the

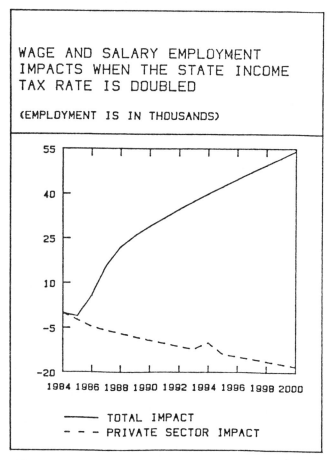

WAGE AND SALARY EMPLOYMENT
IMPACTS WHEN THE STATE INCOME
TAX RATE IS DOUBLED

(EMPLOYMENT IS IN THOUSANDS)

——— TOTAL IMPACT
- - - PRIVATE SECTOR IMPACT

Figure 3-3. Wage and Salary Employment Impacts when the State Income Tax Rate is Doubled (thousands)

government expenditure impact.

Because of lags in the government revenue-expenditure increase and expenditure-employment processes, the income tax rate has a net negative impact in the first year, with total wage and salary employment falling by 960 employees. However, by 1986, government expenditures begin to catch up to "desired" levels and the positive public sector impact exceeds the negative private sector impact by 5,666 employees. This impact grows to 15,427 employees in 1987, 28,930 by 1990, 42,930 by 1995, and 54,207 by 2000. In 1986, the increase in government employment exceeds the total increase in

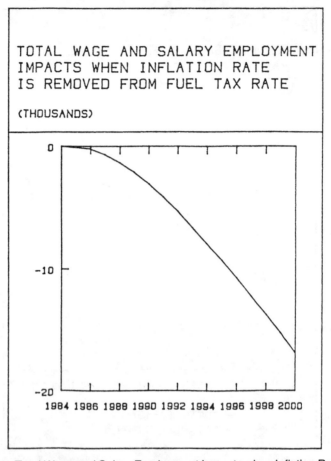

Figure 3-4. Total Wage and Salary Employment Impacts when Inflation Rate is Removed from Fuel Tax Rate (thousands)

employment by almost 490 workers. However, higher overall employment levels induce private-sector multiplier effects so that the total-employment impact exceeds the government-employment impact by 33 percent in 1985. The government employment share falls over time from 75 percent of the total impact in 1987 to 65 percent in 1990, 58 percent by 1995, and 56 percent in 2000.

A similar effect is shown in figure 3-4, which shows the impact of removing the inflation factor from the Arizona state fuel tax rate on gasoline and use fuel (primarily diesel) that is assumed in the control run. In simulation, the fuel tax rate remains at its 1985 level of 13¢ per gallon through the year 2000. The gradually diminishing tax rate used in simulation, relative to that used in the control run, increases fuel consumption thereby increasing fuel-related employment levels. At the same time, however, removal of the inflation factor gradually diminishes government revenues, expenditures, government employment, and employment in other expenditure-impacted private sectors. The combined private and public sector impact is indicated by the solid line. Again, the public sector impact exceeds the private-sector impact resulting, in this case, in employment levels that are lower when the inflation factor is removed than in the control run. This net negative impact increases over time, from 223 employees in 1986, to 698 in 1987, 3,100 in 1990, 9,360 in 1995, and 16,800 in 2000, as the difference between the fixed tax rate and the inflation-related tax rate increases over time.

Several factors contribute to the relatively large differences between the government-expenditure impact and the private sector impact in these simulations. First, significantly larger leakages from the region occur with private sector spending than occur with government spending. Consequently, a private to public sector transfer increases the portion of spending that remains in the state as income. For example, over 40 percent of government expenditures is spent directly on wages and salaries in the state while only about 20 percent of retail sales is retained in the state as income in the trade sector. Private sector leakage is especially high for fuel expenditures because essentially no fuel is produced in Arizona. Second, government sector wage levels are greater than in the tax-impacted private sectors, i.e., primarily trade in the fuel tax simulation and trade and services in the income tax simulation. Per employee labor income in trade and services is 40 and 19 percent lower than per employee government income, respectively. Third, the share of government expenditures on construction is high relative to the private sector share of expenditures on construction. This difference in expenditure mix, combined with interactions between construction employment and induced population growth, tends to make the government-expenditure-induced multiplier higher than the private-sector multiplier. Finally, simulation-specific factors diminish the private sector impact, including the relatively small price elasticity of fuel sales and the deductibility of state taxes from state and/or federal taxable income. The deductability of state personal income taxes from federal taxable income significantly reduces the private sector impact through implicit transfers between the federal and state governments. In addition, the deductibility of state fuel taxes paid by individuals from state taxable income results in slightly offsetting fuel-to-income-tax revenue tradeoffs.

V. Concluding Remarks

Design of multiarea regional econometric models for long-run impact analysis requires a structural framework emphasizing linkages typically not focused on in national econometric models. Identification of these critical linkages is not new in regional analysis; however, they are not generally systematically represented and evaluated in state and metropolitan econometric models. Such a unified, systematic representation was the goal in development of the Arizona state-substate compatible impact model. Particular attention was given to demographic-economic interactions via the migration process, intra-area economic integration, interarea economic relationships, and simultaneous interdependency of the state/local government revenue/expenditure process and private sector economic development.

Population growth has a far more critical role in the multiplier process of subnational areas than in the nation as a whole. As interarea migration occurs in response to changing relative economic conditions, economic expansion is accelerated in some regions and diminished in others. Simulation analyses in the present study confirm the substantial quantitative impact of this phenomenon. For example, the employment multiplier of an exogenous increase in manufacturing employment, after 15 years of adjustment were allowed, was found to be 3.2 in the Tucson SMSA. This number in part reflects the impact of population growth in response to the exogenous change. Without this demographic growth, the multiplier after 15 years would be only 2.0.

Part of local area economic integration parallels standard input-output analysis; output of one local industrial sector is the input to another industry or demand for particular goods or services are directly derived from activity in a particular local industry. Over a longer time period, economic integration also affects the hierarchical relationships among substate centers. As smaller areas grow, they reach critical market masses for internalization of provision of particular services and production of locally consumed commodities. This process can accelerate a particular area's growth, but often at the expense of a higher-order city that had previously provided the goods and/or services. However, not all inter-substate area growth repercussions are of this form. Clearly before critical mass is achieved, growth in one area generates added demands for outputs of another region. Furthermore, long-run systematically positive interarea economic stimuli are observed in industries such as tourism; the substantial volume of instate tourism observed in large, geographically and/or recreationally mixed states spreads growth from one region to the service and trade sectors of another. Structural embodiment of these various intra-area, interarea relationships was emphasized in the present model structure. Their quantitative impact was investigated in terms of simulated long-run growth paths with and without increased internalization, examination of differences in regional multipliers, and analysis of the difference between state and substate area multipliers resulting from a given exogenous change.

While a state and local government clearly has a considerably different economic role from a national government, area development is not unaffected by the fiscal policy of regional government. Government revenue-raising policies affect local disposable income and relative prices. State/local government expenditures directly impact demands made on local private construction and service sectors. The expenditure pattern of governments differs from that of individuals, resulting in multiplier effects when a fixed amount of expenditure is transferred between the public and private sectors. Finally, in many states, the public revenue/expenditure process is an additional channel through which substate areas indirectly interact with each other. Variations in state tax-sharing formulas and grants-in-aid affect relative regional growth rates. In addition to outlining the structural integration of the public and private sectors within the model, specific simulations in the present study have quantified and analyzed absolute and redistributive impacts of local fiscal policy.

A similar model developed for another state and its component areas would undoubtedly yield different numerical simulation results. Consequently, it is not the particular numbers in tables and graphs that should be emphasized. The broader significance of the research derives from the demonstration of the feasibility and importance of simultaneously integrating diverse components of regional analysis into a state-substate multiarea econometric modeling system.

Notes

[1] Military income is treated exogenously and real labor earnings in agriculture, forestry, and fishes are a function of real service earnings and agricultural employment.

[2] State and local government expenditures outside of employee compensation, privately produced construction, and services do not feed back to the private sector. It is not clear that this small residual, about 11 percent of total state and local government expenditures, directly affects the state private sector. For example, the large capital goods purchases in this residual—such as heavy equipment or fleets of cars—are often contracted for directly and purchased from out-of-state supplies.

References

Ballard, K. P., Glickman, N. J., and Wendling, R. M. 1980. Using a multiregional econometric model to measure the spatial impacts of federal policies. In N. J. Glickman (Ed.), *The Urban Impacts of Federal Policies*. Baltimore, MD: Johns Hopkins University Press. Pp. 192–216.

Chang, S. 1979. An econometric forecasting model based on regional economic information system data: The case of Mobile, Alabama. *Journal of Regional Science* 19:437–447.

Duobinis, S. F. 1981. An econometric model of the Chicago Standard Metropolitan Statistical Area. *Journal of Regional Science* 21:293–319.

Friedlaender, A. F., Treyz, G. I., and Tresch, R. 1975. *A Quarterly Econometric Model of Massachusetts and Its Fiscal Structure*. Study funded by the Massachusetts Senate Ways and Means Committee and the Executive Office of Administration and Finance, June 30, 1975, Mimeo.

Glickman, N. J. 1971. An econometric forecasting model for the Philadelphia region. *Journal of Regional Science* 11:15–32.

Glickman, N. J. 1977. *Econometric Analysis of Regional Systems*. New York: Academic Press.

Hall, O. P., and Licari, J. A. 1974. Building small region econometric models: Extension of Glickman's structure to Los Angeles. *Journal of Regional Science* 14:337–353.

Kendrick, J. W., and Jaycox, C. M. 1965. The concept and estimation of gross state product. *Southern Economic Journal* 32:153–168.

Latham, W. R., Lewis, K. A., and Landon, J. H. 1979. Regional econometric models: Specification and simulation of a quarterly alternative for small regions. *Journal of Regional Science* 19:1–14.

L'Esperance, W. L., Nestel, L. G., and Fromm, D. 1969. Gross state product and an econometric model of a state. *Journal of the American Statistical Association* 64:787–807.

Moody, H. T., and Puffer, F. W. 1969. A gross regional product approach to regional model-building. *Western Economic Journal* 7:391–402.

Ratajczak, D. 1974. Data limitations and alternative methodology in estimating regional econometric models. *The Review of Regional Studies* 4:51–64.

Rubin, B. M., and Erickson, R. A. 1980. Specification and performance improvements in regional econometric models: A model for the Milwaukee metropolitan area. *Journal of Regional Science* 20:11–36.

Treyz, G. I., Friedlaender, A. F., and Stevens, B. H. 1980. The employment sector of a regional policy simulation model. *Review of Economics and Statistics* 62:63–73.

4 LINKING REGIONAL ECONOMIC MODELS FOR POLICY ANALYSIS

John R. Kort,
Joseph V. Cartwright,
and Richard M. Beemiller

The authors are Regional Economists with the Bureau of Economic Analysis, U.S. Department of Commerce. The help of many colleagues at the Bureau of Economic Analysis and elsewhere is acknowledged. Views expressed are solely the authors' and not necessarily those of the U.S. Department of Commerce.

I. Introduction

Since the early 1960s, regional scientists have developed a variety of regional economic models for policy analysis. Early efforts focused on the development of economic-base models that provided aggregate Keynesian-type multipliers. The development of regional input-output models followed, mainly in response to the aggregate nature of the multipliers implicit in economic-base models. The input-output model provided a consistent regional accounting framework in which a regional economic structure could be described in great detail. Policy analyses could be extended to disaggregated industry classifications. However, the time paths of economic impacts of policy changes were not captured in these models.

Building on the success of national macroeconometric modelers, regional econometric models were developed in the late 1960s and early 1970s. These early econometric models were typically built as "satellites" to some existing national macroeconometric model, where economic activity in the region was modeled mainly as a function of exogenously determined levels of national economic activity. Thus, changes in economic activity in the region could not have an effect on national economic activity. Moreover, Since these early regional econometric models were typically built for a single region, economic activity in a given region could not affect, or be affected by, changes in other regions.

Recently, the efforts in regional econometric modeling have focused on the development of multiregional systems, in which it is recognized that regions do not grow independently of one another, that significant leakages and stimuli flow from one region into another. The 1980s have seen the development of a number of multiregional econometric models for the United States, as well as for many European and Asian countries.[1] While significantly advancing the state of the art in regional modeling, many of these econometric models have shortcomings. First, they do not aggregate consistently to national totals. Often these multiregional models retain the character of the earlier single-region models, where the direction of causation is from the nation to the region and not vice versa. Second, many of these models have been built as a multiregional system, but do not adequately take into account interregional interaction. Interregional interaction has often been based on aggregate data that do not capture the full extent of trade among industries and regions. Third, the industrial detail is often very aggregated usually at the one-digit Standard Industrial Classification (SIC) level or, at most, the two-digit SIC level. Finally, mainly because of a lack of regional data, these systems do not present a complete regional accounting framework with all final demand and interindustry relationships specified. Therefore, policy questions relating to the interindustry effects of a given change in final demand cannot be answered with these econometric systems, whereas such questions are exactly what the input-output model is designed for.

Based on the work of Garnick (1970), Garnick et al. (1971), Drake (1976), and Ballard et al. (1980), the regional economics program in the Bureau of Economic Analysis (BEA) has continued to develop both multiregional econometric models and regional input-output models. Recent research has focused on enhancing a multiregional econometric model, NRIES II (National-Regional Impact Evaluation System), and a regional input-output model, RIMS II (Regional Input-Output Modeling System), for use in policy analysis. The purpose of this chapter is to describe the characteristics, advantages, and limitations of these two modeling systems and to describe the procedure developed to link the systems for policy analysis. The following section describes the econometric model, NRIES II, and the third section describes the input-output model, RIMS II. The fourth section describes the motivation and procedure for linking the two models for policy analysis and provides an application of the procedure. The final section presents a summary and conclusions.

II. NRIES II Description

NRIES II is an annual econometric projection and impact model used to estimate the spatial distribution of impacts of alternative policies and to provide short- to medium-term projections of state economic activity.[2] NRIES II consists of 51 individual state econometric models, a national model, and a set of indexes that measures trade flows among states.[3] NRIES II is structured so that (1) coefficients of equations pertaining to variables that differ little among states, such as federal fiscal and monetary variables, are estimated within the national model; and (2) coefficients of equations pertaining to variables that differ substantially among states, such as industry product, employment, and income, are estimated within the individual state models. Variables projected within the national model are called "top-down," while those projected within the state models are called "bottom-up." When bottom-up variables are aggregated to national totals, they are called "sum-of-states," and those sums are the national projections of bottom-up variables. An advantage of this hybrid (top-down, bottom-up) modeling approach is that changes in individual state economies can both affect, and be affected by, changes in the national economy.

The hybrid approach to multiregional modeling employed by NRIES II is shown in figure 4-1. The 51 individual state econometric models form the core of the system. Within each state model there are 320 equations, of which 95 are behavioral. Behavioral variables include output, employment, wage rates, nonwage sources of income, population, state and local government revenues and expenditures, investment, labor force, unemployment, and retail sales. Equations are estimated over the period 1958–1982 using ordinary least squares (OLS), with Cochrane-Orcutt corrections where serial correlation is evident. Each of the variables estimated in the state models is summed to derive national totals. This is shown by the shaded outline of the United States outside the core 51 state models in figure 4-1. This feature is referred to as the bottom-up element of NRIES II.

The top-down element of NRIES II, the national model, is shown on the right side of figure 4-1. In this component of the system, variables are esti-

Figure 4-1. NRIES II Configuration

mated at the national level and are used as explanatory variables in individual state models. For example, interest rates estimated in the national
model are used as explanatory variables in investment equations in the state
models. Conversely, variables estimated in individual state models, when
summed to national totals, are used as explanatory variables in the national
model. For example, sum-of-states income is a right-hand-side variable in
the personal consumption expenditures equations in the national model.
This interaction between variables in the state models and variables in the
national model is one of the unique features of NRIES II. As indicated
earlier, state-to-nation feedback does not exist in satellite single-region
models. Similarly, top-down multiregional models are configured such
that state (regional) economic activity cannot have an effect on national
economic activity. In NRIES II, state and national economic activity are
simultaneously and interactively determined.

Variables in the national model include final demand components, federal government receipts and expenditures, money supply, interest rates,
consumer and producer prices, implicit price deflators for gross product

originating, consumer confidence indexes, tax rates, birth and death rates, and various social security variables. There are a total of 190 variables in the national model, of which 40 are behavioral, and about 40 are exogenous policy variables. Like endogenous variables in the state models, national behavioral variables are estimated over the 1958–1982 period using OLS.

The final component of the NRIES II system is the interstate interaction, measured by two-digit SIC manufacturing state-to-state commodity flow indexes derived from the Census of Transportation, Commodity Transportation Survey (CTS). NRIES II, like most regional econometric models, adopts the economic-base theory approach to output specification whereby states' economies are divided into production for export out of the state (basic activity), and production for local consumption (nonbasic activity). In NRIES II, basic activity is defined as that occurring in the manufacturing sector. Manufacturing output equations are therefore specified, in part, as a function of an external demand variable, defined as interstate interaction indexes derived from state export-import data from the CTS. Thus, in addition to the state-to-nation and nation-to-states feedbacks in NRIES II, there is also state-to-state feedback through a set of interaction indexes. This, too, is a unique feature of the model.

II.1. State Models

The internal structure of a typical state model is shown in figure 4-2. Output, generally considered the most comprehensive measure of economic activity, is estimated in constant (1972) dollars and derived from the Kendrick-Jaycox technique.[4]. The output equations are estimated for 30 industries: one-digit SIC level for nonmanufacturing industries, and two-digit level for manufacturing industries. Since NRIES II adopts the economic-base theory approach to output specification, output in the nonmanufacturing industries is mainly a function of local demand variables like state disposable income or population, in addition to several national model variables. The exception is the construction sector, where construction output is a function of state investment in residential and nonresidential structures. Output in the manufacturing industires is mainly a function of the two-digit interstate interaction indexes derived from the CTS, as well as state relative costs and national model variables.

Employment is specified based on a linear factor-demand relationship that assumes all firms are short-run profit maximizers. Therefore, employment, estimated at the one-digit SIC level for all industries, is mainly a function of corresponding industry output. In addition, relative wage rates

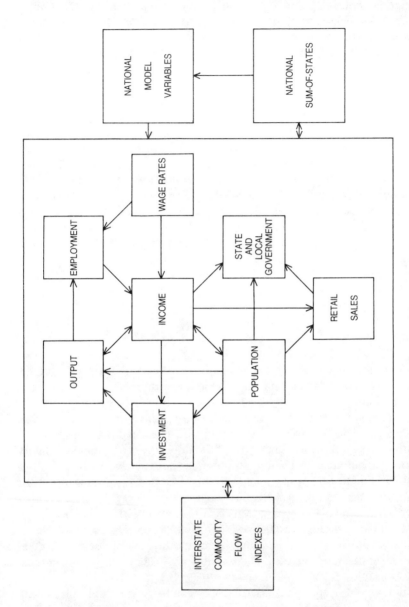

Figure 4-2. Internal Structure of a Typical NRIES II State Model

(state as a percent of the nation) and national model variables determine employment. Wage rates, also estimated at the one-digit SIC level, are functions of consumer prices from the national model, and of state or relative unemployment-rate variables, the latter reflecting a regional Phillip's-curve specification. In combination with employment, wage rates determine the largest components of total income, wage and salary disbursements at the one-digit SIC level. Nonwage income components—transfer payments; dividends, interest, rent; personal contributions for social insurance; and residence adjustment—are specified as functions of state and national model variables.

The investment components estimated for each state model are: residential structures, nonresidential structures, manufacturing equipment, and nonmanufacturing equipment. For residential structures, an investment series was estimated using the techniques devised by Conway and Howard in their work on a model of regional housing construction for the state of Washington.[5] For manufacturing structures and equipment, state data directly available from the *Annual Survey of Manufacturers* are used. For nonmanufacturing structures and equipment, national data are allocated to states. Per capita investment in residential structures is specified as a function of three lagged variables: relative housing costs, defined as the ratio of the Boeckh construction cost index to the consumer price index for rent; credit availability, defined as the difference between the long-term and short-term interest rates; and per capita disposable income. Investment in nonresidential structures and equipment is specified as a function of interest rates and state total output, with a distributed lag (inverted V) formulation.

Population is specified for five age cohorts: under 5, 5–17, 18–44, 45–64, and 65 and older; plus births, deaths, and net migration. The specification is based upon the growth-composition-analysis formulation (see Isard, 1960), where current-period population is equal to past-period population plus births, minus deaths, adjusted by net migration. Each of the five cohort variables is specified using variations of this standard formulation. Births and deaths are specified as functions of state economic variables and national birth and death rates, respectively.

State and local government revenues are divided into own-source revenues and intergovernmental transfers. Within the own-source category, tax revenues are specified as a function of state disposable income, to capture the state income tax portion of the revenues; state total output, to capture corporate-related state taxes; and state retail sales, to capture sales taxes and taxes levied on commercial inventories. Charges and miscellaneous revenues are specified as functions of state income and population variables, since these revenues are typically derived from user charges for

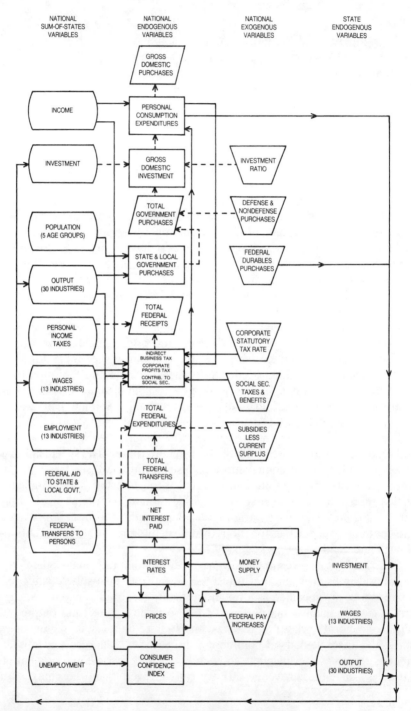

Figure 4-3. The Structure of the NRIES II National Model

services provided to citizens. Intergovernmental transfers are specified as a function of a "need index," calculated in a manner similar to federal revenue sharing formulas. State and local government expenditures are specified as a function of revenues, to account for the available pool of funds, and of the state unemployment rate, to account for budgetary actions associated with business cycle fluctuations.

Retail sales equations are estimated for five groups: food stores, eating and drinking establishment, automotive dealers, gasoline stations, and other retail sales. Each of the retail sales groups is specified as a function of state income and/or population variables, in addition to national consumer price indexes.

II.2. National Model

The structure of the NRIES II national model is shown in figure 4-3. The first column depicts the variables that are obtained by summing (or averaging) the values of the state variables. The second and third columns show the national endogenous and exogenous variables, respectively, which form the top-down component of NRIES II. The fourth column shows the state variables that have national variables as determinants. It is included to better illustrate the two-way feedback between the nation and states.

The national endogenous variables (second column) can be classified into the following four categories: final demand, federal governmental receipts and expenditures, interest rates, and price indexes and consumer confidence index. Within the final demand sector, gross domestic purchases are the sum of personal consumption expenditures, gross domestic investment, and total government purchases. Personal consumption expenditures for durable goods and nondurable goods and services are estimated as a function of state-summed disposable income and nationally determined output prices. The NRIES II measure of gross domestic investment and the national income and product accounts (NIPA) measure are made equal by adjusting the state-summed investment variable within the national model.[6] The sole purpose of this adjustment is to reconcile the NRIES II final demand account for the nation with that from the NIPA. The adjustment is not allocated back to the states.

Total government purchases are the sum of state and local government purchases and federal government purchases. The state and local purchases variable is a function of two population variables, total population and school-age population expressed as a percentage of total population, and of state and local government output. To be consistent with the NIPA, federal purchases are expressed in an identity as the sum of defense and nondefense expenditures.

Total federal receipts are the sum of state-summed personal income taxes, indirect business taxes, corporate profits taxes, and social security contributions. Federal indirect business taxes, being primarily excise taxes, are a function of personal consumption expenditures. Corporate profits taxes are a function of output, of the exogenously assumed statutory tax rate, and of labor's share of income expressed as the ratio of wages and salaries to output. The remaining component of total federal receipts, contributions to social security, is a function of income, employment, and exogenously assumed coverage and benefit rates.

Total federal expenditures, excluding purchases of goods and services, are the sum of federal aid to state and local governments, subsidies less current surplus, net interest paid, and total federal transfer payments. Of these, only transfers and net interest paid are estimated in behavioral equations of the national model. The total federal transfers variable is a function of state-summed transfers to persons while net interest paid is a function of the short-term interest rate.

Both the long-term and short-term interest rates are endogenous variables. The short-term rate, defined as the yield on six-month commercial paper, is determined by prices and the exogenously assumed money supply. The long-term rate, defined as Moody's commercial bond yield, is a function of the consumer confidence index and the short-term interest rate. The consumer confidence index enters as a proxy measure of the risk premium required on instruments of longer maturity.

A number of price indexes are estimated as well as the consumer confidence index. There is a price index for each of the industrial categories in NRIES II and for each of the final demand sectors. In addition, indexes are estimated for consumer and producer prices. In general, both the output price and consumer price equations emphasize raw material and wage cost variables.

As indicated above, inclusion of the fourth column in figure 4-3 illustrates the two-way feedback between the nation and the states. Column 4 shows the state model variables that have national variables in their specification. For example, personal consumption of durable goods enters into the state durable goods output equations, consumer prices enter into the state wage-rate equations, and interest rates enter into the state investment equations. Output, investment, and wages are then summed to U.S. totals and enter into the specification of national endogenous variables, as shown in columns 1 and 2.

II.3. Interstate Interaction Indexes

The final component of the NRIES II system is the interstate interaction indexes. Derived from the CTS, these indexes are calculated for each of the 20 two-digit manufacturing industries and are used as explanatory variables in corresponding two-digit manufacturing output equations. Data in the CTS provide information on commodity shipments by type, weight, value, mode of transportation, and by origin and destintion state for up to five-digit transportation commodity code classifications. Although the CTS is the most comprehensive and statistically reliable source of information on inter-state commodity shipments, it is only compiled for economic census years— 1963, 1967, 1972, and 1977—and only in 1977 is the information considered comprehensive. Since NRIES II is a time-series econometric model requir-ing annual data, a procedure to augment the 1977 CTS data was developed. First, the following "interaction weight" was constructed from the CTS two-digit interstate trade data:

$$\frac{S_{e_i^r} - S_{m_i^r}}{\displaystyle\sum_{\substack{r=1 \\ r \neq s}}^{51} S_{e_i^r}} \tag{4.1}$$

where,

$S_{e_i^r}$ = state s exports of industry i's product to state r
$S_{m_i^r}$ = state s imports of industry i's product from state r

The numerator is simply net exports of industry i by state s, with respect to state r. The denominator is total gross exports of industry i from state s, excluding shipments to itself ($r \neq s$ in the summation). Given the total amount of shipments out of state s, the interaction weight measures what proportion of this total is demanded by, and shipped to, state r, on a net basis.

Next, a temporal allocation of the new interaction weight was constructed using relative location quotients (LQ's).[7] The pairwise ratio of output-based LQ's was calculated for each pair of states for each year, 1958–1982, and then put on a 1977 index basis as in expression 4.2:

$$\frac{S_{LQ_{it}}/r_{LQ_{it}}}{S_{LQ_{i,77}}/r_{LQ_{i,77}}} \tag{4.2}$$

The numerator of the relative LQ in equation (4.2) can be interpreted as state s's export position in industry i, relative to state r's export position. If the ratio is greater than 1 (although both states' LQ's may be less than 1), then state s is said to be relatively more self-sufficient in producing industry i's output than is state r. If the ratio is less than 1, then state r is relatively more self-sufficient. The numerator, the current-period LQ ratio, is divided by the corresponding ratio for 1977 since the export-import positions of states (the interaction weights) are based on the 1977 CTS.

To complete the interaction index, a measure of demand from all states r, $r \neq s$ (output or income), was multiplied by the interaction weight times the temporal allocation:

$$s_{\mathrm{II}_{it}} = \sum_{\substack{r=1 \\ r \neq s}}^{51} \left(\frac{s_{e_i^r} - s_{m_i^r}}{\displaystyle\sum_{\substack{r=1 \\ r \neq s}}^{51} s_{e_i^r}} \right)^{77} \left(\frac{s_{\mathrm{LQ}_{it}}/r_{\mathrm{LQ}_{it}}}{s_{\mathrm{LQ}_{i,77}}/r_{\mathrm{LQ}_{i,77}}} \right) r_{Q_t} \qquad (4.3)$$

For 1977, the interaction index simply equals the interaction weight times output (or income), since the middle term, the temporal allocation, is equal to one. For every other year, the interaction weight is inflated (deflated) by factors of, say, 1.02 or 0.98, and so on, depending upon the extent to which the relative LQ position of s-to-r changed in year t vis-á-vis 1977. If s specializes relatively more in industry i (vis-á-vis r) than it did in 1977, then s's interaction weight is inflated (multipled by a factor greater than 1) above the 1977 value. If s specializes relatively less in industry i (vis-a-vis r) than it did in 1977, then s's interaction weight is deflated (multiplied by a factor less than 1) below the 1977 value.[8]

The interaction index, thus formulated, has several major advantages: (1) it is based on actual trade flow data among states for 1977; (2) it allows for trading patterns among states to change through time; and (3) since the temporal allocation—the ratio of the LQ's relative to the 1977 ratio—is based on output variables, and output is predicted in the NRIES II model, the interaction index is itself interactive with respect to the rest of the model. That is, for a projection period, the LQ's are actually predicted within the framework of the model solution procedure.

II.4. Advantages and Limitations of NRIES II

There are several advantages to the approach employed by NRIES II. First, because of its interregional elements, NRIES II can be used to analyze the regional or spatial distribution of policy impacts. For example, this might include the measurement of the effects of economic changes in one region upon all other regions. Second, NRIES II simultaneously determines the level of both national and regional activity. In contrast, many existing regional models distribute given national totals among regions, thereby ignoring the effects that the changes in regional activity could have on the nation as a whole. Third, by integrating regional and national models, the NRIES II structure enables the analyst to assure that the sum of regional activity is consistent with reasonable forecasts of national activity. In contrast, individual state models, when summed, can produce overstatements or understatements of growth when no comprehensive national framework is present. Finally, unlike other existing multiregional models, NRIES II is able to examine the effects of concurrent national and regional policy changes. This type of application might include the analysis of the effects of construction activity that takes place in one state but is funded by a federal tax imposed on all states.

As is the case with any econometric model, NRIES II has certain limitations that affect the ways in which it should be employed. First, since it is an annual model, NRIES II is better employed for the purpose of medium range projections and impact analysis rather than for analyzing short-run cyclical fluctuations. Second, the industrial and spatial detail of NRIES II is relatively aggregate. The impacts of changes in economic policy can be analyzed only at the one-digit SIC level for nonmanufacturing industries, and at the two-digit level for manufacturing industries, and only at the state level. In contrast, an I-O framework may be capable of analyzing impacts at the four-digit SIC and county levels. Third, NRIES II is predominantly a demand-driven model, and, to some extent, ignores supply constraints. These three limitations however, are largely due to the lack of sufficient regional data, rather than to any weakness in the model structure.

II.5. Model Validation

Evaluation of the performance of NRIES II is based upon simulation errors associatd with five variables—gross domestic product, employment, personal income, population, and gross domestic investment. A statistic commonly used to measure errors in regional models is the mean absolute percent error (MAPE), represented in equation 4.4:

$$\text{MAPE} = \frac{1}{n} \sum_{t=1}^{n} \frac{|Y_t - \hat{Y}_t|}{Y_t} \cdot 100 \qquad (4.4)$$

Table 4-1. Dynamic Simulation for 1973 to 1981, Mean Absolute Percent Error for Major Aggregate Variables: U.S., BEA Regions, and States

Regions/States	Gross Domestic Product	Employment	Personal Income	Population	Gross Domestic Investment
United States	1.88	1.58	1.73	0.13	5.08
New England	1.42	1.49	1.18	0.75	4.54
Mideast	1.58	1.71	1.29	0.47	5.41
Great Lakes	2.39	1.88	2.32	0.32	4.93
Plains	1.67	1.46	1.96	0.42	3.32
Southeast	2.34	1.89	2.14	0.82	9.28
Southwest	2.02	1.36	2.01	0.35	4.22
Rocky Mountain	2.57	1.90	2.38	0.44	4.71
Far West	2.93	1.99	2.59	0.83	6.11
Alabama	4.07	3.63	4.28	1.56	6.49
Alaska	4.59	3.20	5.24	1.77	7.57
Arizona	4.66	3.69	3.73	2.03	20.53
Arkansas	2.76	2.19	2.55	0.87	4.11
California	3.07	2.14	2.75	0.91	5.96
Colorado	2.57	2.00	2.23	0.58	6.55
Connecticut	1.66	1.45	1.25	0.64	5.62
Delaware	3.38	4.97	3.71	2.48	11.12
District of Columbia	3.86	3.62	3.68	3.25	5.05
Florida	3.57	3.11	2.66	1.74	30.13
Georgia	2.47	2.02	2.14	0.67	5.32
Hawaii	2.53	2.87	2.45	0.78	3.08
Idaho	2.27	2.12	2.65	0.78	5.95
Illinois	3.12	2.67	3.04	0.31	6.90
Indiana	3.18	2.52	2.89	0.58	3.83
Iowa	1.89	1.88	2.31	0.67	3.81
Kansas	2.97	2.89	2.91	0.77	2.80
Kentucky	3.45	3.08	3.65	1.46	6.62
Louisiana	1.77	0.67	1.42	1.02	6.25

Maine	1.77	1.40	1.66	1.22	9.45
Maryland	1.11	1.18	1.04	2.13	5.77
Massachusetts	1.40	1.70	1.39	1.48	5.95
Michigan	2.42	1.84	2.27	1.12	5.58
Minnesota	2.65	1.80	2.39	0.36	6.12
Mississippi	2.42	1.76	2.71	1.27	5.44
Missouri	1.71	1.15	1.92	0.44	4.94
Montana	3.15	2.00	2.41	1.39	2.27
Nebraska	2.13	1.38	1.85	0.60	2.90
Nevada	4.82	4.78	4.38	2.63	17.29
New Hampshire	2.36	1.88	2.22	0.73	6.16
New Jersey	1.47	1.67	2.17	2.26	5.31
New Mexico	2.02	1.48	2.73	0.47	6.38
New York	1.98	1.93	1.39	0.49	5.51
North Carolina	2.05	2.19	1.65	0.44	6.55
North Dakota	1.90	1.52	2.01	0.65	4.98
Ohio	2.58	1.66	2.19	0.35	5.27
Oklahoma	2.42	1.03	2.32	0.46	5.28
Oregon	3.50	2.01	3.37	0.72	7.32
Pennsylvania	2.22	1.76	2.25	1.48	5.70
Rhode Island	3.46	3.05	2.82	2.22	6.44
South Carolina	2.75	2.22	2.55	2.09	5.25
South Dakota	4.04	0.88	1.32	1.43	4.81
Tennessee	3.93	3.46	4.35	2.03	6.83
Texas	1.99	1.50	2.35	0.33	3.12
Utah	4.44	3.13	4.12	0.57	6.62
Vermont	1.21	0.82	0.89	0.76	4.54
Virginia	1.83	1.43	1.52	0.43	3.99
Washington	3.52	2.55	3.18	0.74	11.69
West Virginia	3.19	2.51	3.69	1.02	3.93
Wisconsin	2.21	1.46	1.92	0.25	3.03
Wyoming	4.75	2.46	4.87	1.81	9.12
State average	2.77	2.20	2.62	1.12	6.69

where,

n = the number of periods in the simulation
Y_t = the actual value of the variable Y in time period t
$\hat{Y}_t$ = the projected value of the variable Y in time period t

Table 4-1 shows MAPE values for a dynamic solution. Generally, the MAPE values associated with output, employment, and income range from 1.0 percent to less than 5.0 percent. Population exhibits the lowest values among the five variables, largely due to the low variability in population trends. On the other hand, investment is one of the most volatile sectors of the economy and, as such, is difficult to project. This is reflected in the higher MAPE values associated with this variable. The higher values can be attributed, in large part, to the 1974–1975 recession, when investment in many states declined sharply. In general, states with the highest values experienced declines that were both more severe and more extended than those of other states. It is likely that factors in addition to the recession contributed to the extended declines in these states. For example, in Florida—the state with the highest MAPE value—the ending of a period of speculative overbuilding, along with the recession, tended to depress investment through 1976. In general, there is very little difference between these results and the MAPE values of selected single-region models. For example, the average value associated with output for the single-region models is 1.8, and it is 1.9 for NRIES II.[9]

III. RIMS II Description

RIMS II is designed to estimate regional I-O coefficients and multipliers for use in estimating the regional impacts of economic policies.[10] Coefficients and multiplers can be estimated for any county or group of counties in the United States and for all of the approximately 500 industries in BEA's benchmark national I-O tables. Currently, RIMS II developmental research (represented by equations 4.13 through 4.18 below) is focused on estimating regional transactions tables, and comparing RIMS II estimates of state-specific imports and exports with survey-based estimates from the CTS. RIMS II is also being adapted to analyze the regional and industrial impacts of defense procurement.

III.1. Deriving Regional Purchase Coefficients and Multipliers

RIMS II is based on the following regional I-O accounting identities:

$$x_i^r = \sum_j x_{ij}^r + fd_i^r + e_i^r \tag{4.5}$$

where,

x_i^r = total output of regional industry i
x_{ij}^r = sales of regional industry i to regional industry j
fd_i^r = sales of regional industry i to regional final demand, which consists of sales to consumption, investment, and government
e_i^r = sales of regional industry i outside of region r—that is, exports of i

$$x_j^r = \sum_i x_{ij}^r + q_j^r + m_j^r \tag{4.6}$$

where,

q_j^r = value added in regional industry j; value added consists of employee compensation, profit-type income, and indirect business taxes
m_j^r = imports by regional industry j

Assuming proportional inputs per dollar of output, equation 4.5 can be expressed by the following production system:[11]

$$x_i^r = \sum_j a_{ij}^r x_j^r + fd_i^r + e_i^r \tag{4.7}$$

where a_{ij}^r is the direct regional purchase coefficient, that is, the proportion of the total output of regional industry j that is accounted for by the purchases of imports from regional industry i.

In matrix notation,

$$X^r = A^r X^r + FD^r + E^r \tag{4.8}$$

or

$$X^r = (I - A^r)^{-1}(FD^r + E^r) \tag{4.9}$$

Assuming the average production system expressed in equation 4.7 is also a marginal production function, changes in total industry-specific output can be estimated as a function of changes in final demand or exports. That is,

$$\Delta X^r = B^r \Delta (FD^r + E^r) \tag{4.10}$$

where $B^r = (I - A^r)^{-1}$—an i, j element of this matrix shows the direct and indirect purchases from regional industry i by regional industry j required to support a marginal change in regional final demand or exports. The matrix B^r is often referred to as a regional-multiplier matrix because it shows both the direct and the indirect impacts on regional output when final demand or exports change. Given the industry-specific output changes estimated by equation 4.10, industry-specific changes in value added (Δq_i^r's) can be estimated based on industry-specific ratios of value added to output. Employee compensation and employment impacts can be estimated similarly.

Estimates of regional interindustry transactions (x_{ij}^r), of regional final demand (fd_i^r), and of regional exports (e_i^r) are not routinely prepared in the United States.[12] For this reason, RIMS II uses a nonsurvey approach to estimate the basic I-O relationships.[13] More specifically, RIMS II uses BEA's benchmark I-O tables, which show the input and output structure of approximately 500 industries at the national level. Input requirements that are not produced in a study region are identified using BEA's four-digit SIC county-level employee compensation estimates. Currently, estimates for 1980 through 1984 can be used. Most often the regional industry-specific employee compensation estimates are used to form location quotients (LQ_i^r's). An LQ_i^r greater (less) than one is taken to mean that r is an exporter (importer) of i.[14] That is,

$$a_{ij}^r = r_i a_{ij}^n \tag{4.11}$$

where

$$r_i = \begin{cases} LQ_i & \text{if} \quad LQ_i < 1.0 \\ 1.0 & \text{if} \quad LQ_i > 1.0 \end{cases}$$

$a_{ij}^n = $ national direct coefficient

Multipliers (b_{ij}^r's) can be estimated by forming the Leontief inverse of A^r.[15] Direct import coefficients can be expressed as the difference between national and regional direct I-O coefficients. That is,

$$m_{ij}^r = a_{ij}^n - a_{ij}^r \tag{4.12}$$

where m_{ij}^r is the proportion of the output of j produced in r that is accounted for by the import of i produced outside r.

III.2. Estimating Regional Transactions Tables

Regional output and interindustry transactions can be estimated by equations 4.13 and 4.14.[16]

$$x_j^r = ec_j^r / a_{ec,j}^n \tag{4.13}$$

where

$a_{ec,j}^n$ = the national ratio of employee compensation to output in industry j

ec_j^r = employee compensation in industry j in region r

$$x_{ij}^r = a_{ij}^r x_j^r \tag{4.14}$$

Having estimated regional import coefficients and industry-specific output, industry-specific imports can be estimated as

$$m_i^r = \sum_j m_{ij}^r x_j^r \tag{4.15}$$

where

m_i^r = region r's total imports of i

$m_{ij}^r x_j^r$ = region r's imports of i as an input to j

Industry-specific value added can be estimated either by equation 4.16 or equation 4.17:

$$q_j^r = x_j^r - \sum_i a_{ij}^r x_j^r - \sum_i m_{ij}^r x_j^r \tag{4.16}$$

$$q_j^r = ec_j^r (q_j^n / ec_j^n) \tag{4.17}$$

Finally, final demand and exports can be estimated as

$$fd_i^r + e_i^r = x_i^r - \sum_j a_{ij}^r x_j^r \tag{4.18}$$

In some cases, the sum of final demand and exports from equation 4.18 has been estimated initially to be negative.[17]

III.3. Advantages and Limitations of RIMS II

There are numerous advantages to RIMS II. First, it is possible to provide estimates of economic impacts without building a complete survey I-O model for each region under study, since RIMS II produces multipliers that are derived from secondary data sources. Second, the RIMS II multipliers are derived from a limited number of secondary data sources, thus eliminating the costs associated with the compilation of data from a wide variety of such sources. Third, because of the disaggregated sectoring plan employed by RIMS II, analysis may be performed at a detailed industrial level, thereby avoiding aggregation errors that often occur when different industries are combined. Fourth, the RIMS II multipliers are based on a consistent set of procedures across areas, thus making comparisons among areas more meaningful than would be the case if the results were obtained from incompatible impact models designed only for individual areas. Fifth, the multipliers can be updated to reflect the most recent regional employee compensation estimates.

The impacts estimated by RIMS II can be crucial for deriving effects not directly estimated by RIMS II itself. For example, the estimation of regional fiscal, labor migration, and environmental effects often depend on the estimation of the regional output and employment impacts of the initial stimulus. Since many of these important effects are often best analyzed on a case-by-case basis, one of the major advantages of using RIMS II is that valuable research resources can be spent on the analysis of these effects, rather than on the construction of an I-O model. Therefore, when using RIMS II, a cost-effective impact study might devote most of its research budget to specifying initial impacts in industry-specific detail, and analyzing the implications for other important aspects of regional economic activity of the RIMS II estimated impacts.

As discussed in greater detail in Cartwright et al. (1981), RIMS II is subject to the same major limitations as other regional and national I-O models. For example, RIMS II multipliers are derived from a linear Leontief production function, which assumes constant returns to scale and no substitution among inputs. Second, the use of the LQ technique to regionalize the national I-O tables is subject to a number of criticisms as discussed in Isard (1960) and Nourse (1968). Third, nonsurvey regional I-O tables, when constructed using LQ's, will be inconsistent with national I-O tables unless residuals (differences between bottom-up summed transactions and the BEA national transactions tables, for example) are distributed by some means. However, individual survey-based regional I-O tables will not likely sum either to a national survey-based I-O table or to the national table as presently constructed by BEA. Finally, RIMS II does not identify the time paths of impacts, and does not take into account the interregional flows of goods and people when analyzing impacts.

III.4. Model Validation

Even though RIMS II estimates are based, in part, on several assumptions about the equality of national and regional production functions (for example, equations 4.11, 4.13, and 4.17), empirical tests of the accuracy of RIMS II multipliers, as reported in Cartwright et al. (1981), indicate that RIMS II yields estimates that are not substantially different from those generated by regional I-O models based on the costly gathering of survey data. For example, a comparison of 224 industry-specific multipliers from survey-based tables for Texas, Washington, and West Virginia indicate that the RIMS II average multipliers overestimate the average multipliers from the survey-based tables by approximately 5 percent; and, for the majority of individual industry-specific multipliers, the difference between RIMS II and survey-based multipliers is less than 10 percent. In addition, RIMS II and survey-based multipliers show statistically similar distributions of affected industries. Earlier studies—for example, Schaffer and Chu (1969) and Morrison and Smith (1974)—found that nonsurvey regional I-O techniques similar to RIMS II consistently overestimated regional coefficients and multipliers when compared with survey-based tables. However, these studies relied on results from aggregate (less than 50-industry) tables. The relative accuracy of RIMS II is due to its use of a disaggregate (approximately 500-industry) sectoring scheme, which better takes into account the regional industrial mix.[19]

Furthermore, as reported in Cartwright and Ambargis (1984), the initial results of on-going research to evaluate the accuracy of RIMS II-estimated transactions tables (equations 4.13 through 4.18) are encouraging. The research to date has established a high degree of correlation between diaggregated LQ's and trade variables developed from the CTS. This suggest that, in place of using the survey-based CTS estimates to adjust national I-O coefficients, disaggregated LQ's may be used, as they are in RIMS II, to estimate regional I-O coefficients.[19] Moreover, in contrast to nonsurvey methodologies that in part directly rely on CTS estimates, RIMS II may be especially useful for years when (or in regions where) no CTS estimates are available. Furthermore, based on extensions of the basic RIMS II methodology, the patterns of imports and exports contained in RIMS II transactions tables are highly correlated with the patterns in the CTS. The high correlations among the RIMS II and CTS estimates provide indications, beyond those reported by Cartwright et al. (1981), of the accuracy of RIMS II coefficients and multipliers.

IV. Linking NRIES II and RIMS II for Impact Analysis

As indicated earlier, one of the limitations of NRIES II, as with most regional econometric models, is the relatively aggregate nature of its industrial detail compared with input-output models. For example, RIMS II has the capability of analyzing 500 industries for any county in the United States, whereas NRIES II has the capability of analyzing only 30 industries for states in the United States. Most disaggregated regional I-O models, including RIMS II, do not provide time paths of impacts of alternative policies, and do not take into account interregional flows of goods and people when analyzing impacts.[20] NRIES II has both of these capabilities.

There are instances where the capabilities of both types of models, econometric and input-output, are required. This is particularly true for impact analysis where, for example, disaggregate industry-specific final demand changes are provided, and the analysis requires both disaggregate and temporal impact results. In most cases, policy analysts think in terms of, and provide information on, final demand changes only, and these changes are typically only for a few key or relevant industries. For example, a policy analyst may be interested in the impacts of a construction project in a particular area, and may have available information only on the value of construction for the project. Yet, changes in construction activity will affect the region's (as well as the nation's) economy in a variety of industries. For example, 50 percent of the total changes in economic activity might occur in construction, while 30 percent might occur in durable goods activity, and another 20 percent in other sectors. Moreover, depending on the extent of the region's self-sufficiency, its size, and its internal interindustry structure, the industry-specific changes in economic activity that result from this construction project might in fact occur in other regions of the country in addition to the local area. To continue the above example, while most, if not all, of the construction activity might take place in the local area, changes in durable goods activity might occur outside the local area, again depending on the local area's industry structure. Thus, the key to an accurate regional economic impact analysis in such cases is the ability to convert the policy analyst's information (on final demand changes) into region-specific, industry-specific output and value-added changes, and then to estimate impacts on other regional variables and impacts in other regions.

One approach to combining both types of models for impact analysis is referred to as the linking approach.[21] The linking approach takes an initial exogenous final demand change, uses it as an input to an input-output model, and derives detailed interindustry output effects. Since output in the I-O convention refers to gross-duplicated output, these output effects are then converted to a value-added basis to be consistent with econometric model conventions. These value-added changes are then used as inputs to an econometric model to produce intertemporal estimates of the total impacts of the initial final demand change.

IV.1. Methodology

To illustrate the procedure, equation 4.10 from section 3.2 may be rewritten as

$$\Delta x_i^r = b_{ij}^r \Delta f d_j^r \tag{4.19}$$

The exogenous final demand change $(\Delta f d_j^r)$ is premultiplied by the elements of the inverse of the direct coefficient matrix (b_{ij}^r) to obtain changes in (I-O definition) output (Δx_i^r). Next, these output changes are converted to value-added changes through the use of value-added to output ratios:

$$q_i^r = (q_i^r / x_i) x_i^r \tag{4.20}$$

These value-added changes (at the I-O disaggregate industry level) are then aggregated to the industry level of the econometric model:

$$q_i^r = \sum q_i^r \tag{4.21}$$

Finally, the value-added changes are used as "add-factors" in the output (valued-added basis) equations in the econometric model to produce an impact solution, that, when compared to a baseline solution, represents the total (direct, indirect, induced, interregional, and intertemporal) effects of the initial exogenous change in final demand.[22]

The NRIES II and RIMS II models have adopted the linking approach of combining input-output and econometric model capabilities. In a linked NRIES II–RIMS II application, the RIMS II model is specified with all final demand and exports exogenous. That is, RIMS II does not account for additional impacts induced by further rounds of household, investment, government, and export spending.[23] Furthermore, as in all RIMS II applications, interregional and intertemporal effects are not specified. RIMS II does provide a detailed set of interindustry effects, and it can translate unique patterns of demand changes into value-added changes. NRIES II completes the framework of impact analysis by providing the induced, interregional, and intertemporal aspects of the impacts to be analyzed.

IV.2. Application

In order to illustrate the results of linking NRIES II and RIMS II for policy analysis, the models were linked to assess the regional economic impacts of a new military base.[24] The specific example adopted is the 1978 proposal (now abandoned) to deploy the MX missile in Nevada and Utah throughout the 1980s. This section examines the estimated impact of the MX construction project in Nevada, Utah, and elsewhere in the United States. The other regional and national economic impacts of the MX program (which include, for example, building the missile and financing the associated DOD expenditures) are not examined.

Information from the Air Force's 1980 Draft Environmental Impact Statement (DEIS) was used to describe the project's direct impacts. Based on the various estimates in the DEIS, RIMS II was used to estimate industry-specific changes in final demand, output, and value added, which in turn became the data inputs to NRIES II. In the course of estimating total impacts, both RIMS II and NRIES II were modified in order to take into account the unique characteristics of the MX project.[25] For example, a defense-adapted version of RIMS II, as described in reports of the Economic Adjustment Committee (1980, 1983), was used in the analysis in order to avoid the simplistic assumption that defense-induced impacts are the same as impacts caused by changes in private-sector activity. Similarly, since a large number of the defense-related in-migrants to Nevada and Utah were assumed to live on the base, an adjustment was made to the NRIES II equations that forecast changes in residential construction output, in part, as a function of population change. This adjustment avoided the contradiction of on-base personnel directly generating a change in the level of off-base residential construction.

The MX-related employment impacts over the 1984–1989 interval are shown in table 4.2. In 1987, employment in Nevada and Utah would increase by 77,000 jobs, relative to the NRIES II baseline projections. The annual total MX-related increase in Nevada and Utah would represent up to 7 percent of the employment in the NRIES II baseline projection for Nevada and Utah. Although this NRIES II–RIMS II analysis did not take fully into account either the regional or national impacts of the entire MX program (which would include, for example, impacts associated with the fabrication of the missile itself), impacts by region and for the nation from the siting of the MX are presented in order to indicate the capabilities of a NRIES II–RIMS II analysis. By Census regions, large positive impacts would take place in the Mountain and Pacific regions, while large negative impacts would occur in the Middle Atlantic and East North Central regions, where NRIES

Table 4-2. MX Employment and Population Construction Impacts: Full Deployment in Nevada and Utah, 1984–1989 (thousands)[a]

Region	Employment						Population					
	1984	1985	1986	1987	1988	1989	1984	1985	1986	1987	1988	1989
United States	18	43	72	73	68	56	0	0	0	0	0	0
Nevada and Utah	18	42	71	77	73	54	20	46	85	108	108	93
Census Regions												
New England	*	*	−1	−1	−1	−1	−1	−2	−4	−5	−6	−5
Middle Atlantic	−1	−2	−5	−8	−11	−12	−4	−9	−18	−24	−27	−27
South Atlantic	*	*	*	*	1	5	−4	−9	−16	−18	−16	−10
East North Central	−1	−2	−5	−8	−9	−9	−4	−10	−19	−25	−29	−29
East South Central	*	*	*	−1	−1	−1	−1	−3	−5	−6	−7	−6
West North Central	*	*	*	−1	−1	*	−1	−3	−6	−8	−9	−9
West South Central	*	*	*	1	2	3	−2	−3	−7	−8	−7	−5
Mountain	18	42	72	79	75	58	19	43	81	104	106	93
Pacific	3	8	13	14	15	14	−1	−3	−6	−6	−5	−3
Addenda:												
Total Nevada-Utah impacts as a percentage of NRIES II baseline	2	4	7	7	6	5	1	2	4	4	4	4
Direct employment impacts from DEIS	7	17	28	29	29	24	—	—	—	—	—	—

[a] Impacts are cumulative and refer to the construction of the MX project in Nevada and Utah—not to the entire MX program. Detail may not add to total due to rounding.

* Less than the absolute value of one thousand.

II estimates significant MX-related outmigration.[26]

The MX-related migration impacts from the siting of the MX over the 1984–1989 interval are also shown in table 4.2. For the nation, the migration impacts are nil, since the MX project is not assumed to initiate foreign in-migration, but is viewed as causing a reallocation of population within the United States. In Nevada and Utah, migration impacts would peak at over 107,000 in 1987 and 1988, and would decline to nearly 93,000 in 1989. By Census region, only the Mountain region (which includes Nevada and Utah) experiences positive migration impacts. However, since even in the Mountain region the total regional impacts are less than those for Nevada and Utah combined, there is migration from the other states in that region to Nevada and Utah. The peak-year MX-related increase in population in Nevada and Utah would represent over 4 percent of the population in the NRIES II baseline projection for Nevada and Utah. As a percentage of the NRIES II baseline projection, MX-related impacts on employment are greater than those on population. This indicates that a share of the total employment impacts would be associated with current residents of Nevada and Utah through increased labor force participation and decreased unemployment. That is, not all newly created jobs will be claimed by inmigrants.

In addition to impacts on employment and population, NRIES II–RIMS II can estimate impacts on a wide range of economic variables in the two states. During the peak construction years, the MX project could increase the labor force participation rate for the working-age population by 2 percentage points, and lower the unemployment rate by 1 percentage point. Measured in impact-year dollars, total personal income in Nevada and Utah would increase by $2.5 billion in the peak years. In 1989, total personal income would be $2.0 billion (or 5 percent) over the baseline value in NRIES II. In that year state and local government expenditures in Nevada and Utah are estimated to be $500 million over those that would occur without the MX project.

V. Summary and Conclusions

The purpose of this discussion has been to describe the structure and performance of two regional models developed at BEA, NRIES II and RIMS II, and to describe the procedure used to link the two models for policy analysis. An application of the linking technique, related to the economic impacts of the MX missile program, was also presented in this chapter.

The multiregional econometric model, NRIES II, was described as adopting the hybrid approach to multiregional modeling, where both top-down and bottom-up elements were present. NRIES II was shown to comprise 51 state econometric models, a national model, and interstate trade indexes. The model compared favorably with single-region models in terms of dynamic simulation error statistics, and was shown to have a number of advantages relative to many other existing regional econometric models.

The regional input-output model, RIMS II, was described as adopting a nonsurvey technique for estimating regional purchase coefficients for approximately 500 industries and more than 3000 counties. It was also shown how RIMS II could be used to construct regional transactions tables. The model compared favorably with more costly survey-based I-O techniques (for example, those constructed for Texas, Washington, and West Virginia), and was shown to have a number of advantages relative to other nonsurvey I-O models in terms of its level of disaggregation and its comparability across regions.

The motivation and procedure for linking the two models for policy analysis was described. The technique produced detailed direct and indirect impacts at a disaggregated level, and total impacts, including intertemporal and interregional effects, at a more aggregate level. The major conclusion of this chapter is that linking NRIES II and RIMS II for policy analysis is not only feasible, but often desirable.

Notes

[1] For a description of the various regional modeling techniques, see Gustely (1978), pp. 2–14. See Adams and Glickman (1980) for a bibliography of multiregional models.

[2] For a detailed description of NRIES II, see Ballard et al., (1980), Kort (1983), and Kort and Cartwright (1981).

[3] For simplicity, the District of Columbia is referred to as a state.

[4] See Kendrick and Jaycox (1965). Output in regional econometric models (derived from the Kendrick-Jaycox technique) is defined as the market value of all final goods and services produced during a given year, before deduction of capital consumption allowances, but after deduction of intermediate products used by business in the year. Thus, in econometric models, output is conceptually equivalent to value added and double counting is avoided as it is in constructing the GNP accounts. In contrast, in input-output models, output is defined as the total production of an industry, including intermediate products. I-O definition output is therefore often referred to as "gross duplicated output." This distinction between output in an I-O model and in an econometric model, illustrated in equations 4.5 and 4.6 in section 3.1, necessitates the conversion of output impacts from the I-O model to value-added terms. Sections III and IV discuss this distinction further. See BEA (1984) for further discussion of I-O and NIPA accounting conventions.

[5] For a discussion of the methodology used to construct the data series and of the Washington housing model, see Conway and Howard (1980). For further tests of the Washington model's general applicability to projecting regional investment behavior, see Kort (1983).

[6] Since the NIPA do not provide regional detail, it is necessary to estimate investment for states using other data sources. Because of differences in coverage and estimation procedures, the data used are not comparable to the NIPA, and the resulting NRIES II state-summed estimates must be adjusted.

[7] A location quotient is defined as the share of total output in a state accounted for by industry i, divided by the corresponding U.S. share. An LQ is typically used as an estimate of a state's self-sufficiency in producing the output of a given industry. If the value of an LQ is less than 1, then the state is assumed to import that industry's product. If the value of the LQ is greater than 1, then the state is assumed to have greater than its share of production of output in that industry and is assumed to export to other states. Thus, the LQ is a proxy measure for the export/import position of a given state. See Israd (1960) for further discussion.

[8] It is important to emphasize that the interaction weight (the first term on the left-hand side of equation 4.3) only applies if it is positive, i.e., if state s is a net exporter of i to state r. If s is a net importer of i from r, then the value would be negative. Applying a negative weight to the demand variable output or income is obviously not appropriate. Therefore, negative interaction weights were given values of zero. Note, however, that this does not mean that information in the CTS file is being lost. If s is a net importer from r (and therefore the weight is given a value of zero), r must be a positive net exporter to s. So the interaction is captured when the index is calculated for state r.

[9] The single-region models used in this comparison are Georgia, Indiana, Mississippi, New York, Ohio, Pennsylvania, and Tennessee.

[10] For a complete description and a detailed evaluation of RIMS II, see Cartwright et al. (1981). A recent bibliography of RIMS II-based impact studies can be found in EAC (1983). For detailed presentations of regional I-O modeling methodologies, see also Richardson (1972) and Schaffer (1976)

[11] Equations 4.7 to 4.10 represent the widely used demand driven I-O model. An alternative I-O model, most often referred to as a supply-constrained model, can be specified from equation 4.6. For additional details, see Giarrantani (1977, 1980) and Cartwright et al. (1982)—the latter develops a RIMS II-based supply-constrained model.

[12] At the state and county levels in the United States, wages and salaries (the major component of employee compensation) and other components of personal income are routinely estimated by BEA. At the state level, some research has been undertaken to specify a full set of multiregional I-O accounts. For details see Polenske (1980), Faucett (1983), and Miller and Blair (1983). For several states (Kansas, Texas, Washington, and West Virginia) survey-based regional I-O tables were estimated in the 1970s.

[13] Other nonsurvey methodologies have been developed to estimate regional I-O coefficients. For details see chapter 2 in Cartwright et al. (1981), Sawyer and Miller (1983), Stevens et al. (1983), and Round (1978, 1979, 1983). In general, as reported in these studies, the methodologies that rely on disaggregated estimates (400 to 500 industries) are far superior to methodologies that rely on more aggregated estimates (less than 50 industries).

[14] RIMS II uses a mixed LQ approach, which is described in Cartwright et al. (1981). To simplify the presentation here, only the employee compensation LQ's are discussed. Regionalizing factors (r_i's) also have been chosen on an ad hoc basis in numerous RIMS II applications. Furthermore, r_i's, initially based on LQ_i^r, as in equation 4.11, have been reestimated as discussed in note 17 below. Finally, within metropolitan areas, r_i's have been estimated by a two-region version of RIMS II. For details see Cartwright (1979, 1980).

[15] In many RIMS II applications, the A^r and B^r matrixes are expanded by the inclusion of a regional household row and column to account for the impacts induced by household spending. For additional discussion of endogenizing households, see chapter 3 in Cartwright et al. (1981)

and note 2.3 below.

[16] Equations 4.13 through 4.18 extended the RIMS II model beyond the estimation of regional I-O coefficients and toward the estimation of regional transactions tables. Evaluation of the accuracy of these techniques is on-going within BEA.

[17] As discussed at the end of chapter 3 in Cartwright et al. (1982), this means that imports have been underestimated. In those cases, imports (r_i's) have been raised (lowered), and the sum of final demand and exports has been constrained to be zero or greater.

[18] In contrast to the RIMS II four-digit SIC estimates, RIMS II multipliers based on two-digit SIC estimates overestimate the average multiplier from survey-based tables by 25 percent.

[19] CTS trade estimates have been used directly in several regional and interregional models—for example, Polenske (1980), Faucett (1983), Miller and Blair (1983), and Stevens et al. (1983). Unlike RIMS II tables, however, regional tables that use CTS estimates directly may be locked into the base year of the survey. Further research on the instability of survey-based trade estimates and the variability of RIMS II estimates over time is warranted.

[20] The exception is the MRIO multiregional input-output model developed by Polenske (1980). However, while MRIO captures interregional interaction in terms of goods, the same is not true for migration.

[21] The other approach is referred to as the embedding approach. This approach has been employed by Almon (1974), Preston (1972 and 1975), Seguy and Ramirez (1975), Bodkin (1976), Bourque et al. (1977), L'Esperance (1971), and Treyz et al. (1980a). For a complete evaluation of the two techniques, see Kort and Cartwright (1981). An early application using the linked approach appears in Glickman (1977).

[22] A baseline solution is defined as a projection of likely trends in economic activity, without changes in current economic policy.

[23] When RIMS II is used alone, households are often made endogenous to account for the impacts induced by household spending. To avoid double counting, when RIMS II is linked with NRIES II, households are made exogenous in RIMS II, and NRIES II estimates the impacts induced by household spending, as well as the interregional and intertemporal impacts. For additional details, see Kort and Cartwright (1981).

[24] A more detailed description of this impact analysis, which relied on somewhat earlier versions of NRIES II and RIMS II, can be found in EAC (1983).

[25] Although this NRIES II–RIMS II analysis captures the major unique characteristics of the MX project, as presented in the DEIS, the estimated total impacts should be viewed as illustrative of the types of results generated by a NRIES II–RIMS II model, rather than as the definitive estimates of MX impacts. For additional details, see EAC (1983).

[26] Regions experiencing negative impacts due to the construction of the MX project in Nevada and Utah experience positive impacts due to other aspects of the MX program, for example, the DOD expenditures associated with the fabrication of the MX missile itself.

References

Adams, F. G., and Glickman, N. J. 1980. *Modeling the Multiregional Economic System*. Lexington, MA: Heath.

Almon, C., Jr., et al. 1974. *1985: Interindustry Forecasts of the American Economy*. Lexington, MA: Heath (Lexington Books).

Ballard, K., Gustely, R., and Wendling, R. 1980. *The National-Regional Impact Evaluation System: Structure, Performance, and Application of a Bottom-up Inter-*

regional Econometric Model. Washington, D.C.: Government Printing Office.

Bodkin, R. 1976. A large-scale input-output econometric model of the Canadian economy (CANDIDE). In Karen Polenske and Jiri Skolka (Eds.), *Advances in Input-Output Analysis.* Cambridge, MA: Ballinger. Pp. 27–44.

Bolton, R. 1980. Multiregional models in policy analysis. In F. G. Adams and N. J. Glickman (Eds.), *Modeling the Multiregional Economy System.* Lexington, MA: Heath (Lexington Books).

Bourque, P., Conway, R., and Howard, C. 1977. *The Washington Projection and Simulation Model.* Seattle, WA: University of Washington.

Bureau of the Census. 1981. *1977 Census of Transportation: Commodity Transportation Survey, TC77–CS.* Washington, D.C.: Government Printing Office.

Bureau of Economic Analysis (BEA) 1984. The input-output structure of the U.S. economy, 1977. *Survey of Current Business* 64:42–84.

Cartwright, J. V. 1979. Estimating the spatial distribution of program impacts within metropolitan areas. Paper presented at the annual meeting of the Southern Regional Science Association, April.

Cartwright, J. V. 1980. The intrametropolitan distribution of program impacts: A multiplier analysis. Paper presented at the annual meeting of The Council of University Institutes of Urban Affairs, March.

Cartwright, J. V., and Ambargis, Z. O. 1984. Location quotients and trade in regional I-O tables. Paper presented at the annual meeting of the Southern Regional Science Association, April.

Cartwright, J. V., Beemiller, R. M., and Gustely, R. D. 1981. *Regional Input-Output Modeling System (RIMS II): Estimation, Evaluation, and Application of a Disaggregated Regional Impact Model.* Washington, D.C.: U.S. Department of Commerce.

Cartwright, J. V., Beemiller, R. M., Trott, E. A., Jr., and Younger, J. M. 1982. *Estimating the Potential Industrial Impacts of a Nuclear Reactor Accident.* NUREG/CR-2591, Washington, D.C.: U.S. Nuclear Regulatory Commission.

Conway, R. S., Jr., and Howard, C. T. 1980. A forecasting model for regional housing construction. *Journal of Regional Science* 20:1–10.

Drake, R. L. 1976. A shortcut to estimates of regional input-output multipliers: Methodology and evaluation. *International Regional Science Review* 1:1–17.

EAC (Economic Adjustment Committee). 1980. *The Regional Economic Impact of Military Base Spending.* Washington, D.C.: U.S. Department of Defense.

EAC (Economic Adjustment Committee). (1983). *Modeling the Regional Economic Impacts of Major New Military Bases.* Washington, D.C.: U.S. Department of Defense.

Faucett, J. G. 1983. *The Multiregional Input-Output Accounts, 1977: Introduction and Summary.* Chevy Chase, MD: Jack Faucett Associates.

Garnick, D. H. 1970. Differencial regional multiplier models. *Journal of Regional Science.* 10(1):35–47.

Garnick, D. H., Trott, C. E., Olson, A., Hertzfeld, H., and Fable, V. 1971. *Toward the Development of a National-Regional Impact Evaluation System and the Upper*

Licking Area Pilot Study. Staff paper in Economics and Statistics No. 18. Washington, D.C.: U.S. Department of Commerce.

Giarrantani, F. 1977. Application of an interindustry supply model to energy issues. *Environment and Planning A* 8:447–454.

Giarratani, F. 1980. The scientific basis for explanation in regional analysis." *Papers, Regional Science Association* 45:185–196.

Glickman, N. J. 1977. *Econometric Analysis of Regional Systems.* New York: Academic Press.

Gustely, R. D. 1978. *Forecasting Regional Economic Activity: The Tennessee Econometric Model (TEM II).* Knoxville, TN: Center for Business and Economic Research, University of Tennessee.

Isard, W. 1960. *Methods of Regional Analysis.* Cambridge, MA: MIT Press.

Kendrick, J. W., and Jaycox, S. M. 1965. The concept and estimation of gross state product. *Southern Economic Journal* 32:153–168.

Kort, J. R. 1983. A multiregional test of the Conway-Howard Regional Housing Construction Model. *Journal of Regional Science* 23(3):413–418.

Kort, J. R., and Cartwright, J. V. 1981. Modeling the multiregional economy: Integrating econometric and input-output models. *Review of Regional Studies* 11(2):1–17.

L'Esperance, W. 1977. Conjoining an input-output with an econometric model of Ohio. *Regional Science Perspectives* 2:54–77.

Miller, R. E., and Blair, P. 1983. Estimating state-level input-output relationships from U.S. multiregional data. *International Regional Science Review* 8:233–254.

Morrison, W. I., and Smith, P. 1974. Nonsurvey input-output techniques at the small area level: An evaluation. *Journal of Regional Science* 14:1–4.

Nourse, H. O. 1968. *Regional Economics.* New York: McGraw-Hill.

Polenske, K. R. 1980. *The U.S. Multiregional Input-Output Accounts and Model.* Lexington, MA: Heath (Lexington Books).

Preston, R. S. 1972. *The Wharton Annual and Industry Forecasting Model,* Philadelphia, PA: Wharton School of Business.

Preston, R. S. 1975. The Wharton long-term model: Input-output within the context of a macro forecasting model. *International Economic Review* 16(1):3–19.

Richardson, H. W. 1972. *Input-Output and Regional Economics.* London: Weidenfeld and Nicholson.

Round, J. I. 1978. An interregional input-output approach to the evaluation of nonsurvey methods. *Journal of Regional Science* 18:179–194.

Round, J. I. 1979. Compensatory feedback effects in interregional input-output models. *Journal of Regional Science* 19:145–155.

Round, J. I. 1983. Nonsurvey techniques: A critical review of the theory and the evidence. *International Regional Science Review* 8:189–212.

Sawyer, C. H., and Miller, R. E. 1983. Experiments in regionalization of a national input-output table. *Environment and Planning A* 15:501–511, 520.

Schaffer, W. A. 1976. *On the Use of Input-Output Models for Regional Planning.* Leiden: Martinus Nijhoff.

Schaffer, W. A., and Chu, K. 1969. Nonsurvey techniques for constructing regional interindustry models. *Papers and Proceedings of the Regional Science Association* 23:83–101.

Seguy, R. M., and Ramirez, J. 1975. The use of input-output analysis in an econometric model of the Mexican economy. *Annals of Economic and Social Measurement* 4(4):531–552.

Stevens, B. H., Treyz, G. I., Ehrlich, D. J., and Bower, J. R. 1983. A new technique for the construction of nonsurvey regional input-output models. *International Regional Science Review* 8:271–286.

Treyz, G., Williams, R., DuGuay, G. E., Stevens, B. H., and Friedlaender, A. 1980a. An overview of the Massachusetts Economic Policy Analysis (MEPA) model. Paper presented at the Harvard/MIT Joint Center for Urban Studies conference on An Assessment of the State of the Art in Regional Modeling.

Treyz, G. 1980b. Design of a multiregional policy analysis model. *Journal of Regional Science* 20:191–206.

5 THE REGIONAL BUSINESS CYCLE: A THEORETICAL EXPOSITION WITH TIME SERIES, CROSS SECTIONAL, AND PREDICTIVE APPLICATIONS

M. Ray Perryman
and
Nancy S. Perryman

I. Introduction

One of the most perplexing aspects of the economic history of the United States and most other advanced countries has been the frequent interruption of the overall pattern of growth and prosperity by periods of contraction and often severe depression. The specific analysis of the nature and causes of these "business cycles" has been one of the dominant themes in the literature of economics for more than a century and, although interest in the area has fluctuated almost as much as the phenomenon itself, remains so today.[1] Moreover, much of the recent activity associated with the construction and simulation of large-scale national econometric models has been fostered by a desire on the part of corporate and government officials to more accurately forecast the nature and timing of major economic disturbances. This emphasis on the detailed exploration of cyclical movements and impacts is presently becoming extremely apparent at the regional level. The construction and application of regional econometric models is, in fact, presently a very high-priority item in most states and in a number of major metropolitan areas.[2]

There is a long history of general recognition that certain industries and,

125

because of their productive mix, certain regions are much more prone to cyclical movements than others. As an obvious example, durable goods manufacturing represents an industrial category that is normally considered to be highly susceptible to fluctuations in economic activity. This correlation results from the fact that purchases of such items may frequently be deferred and, given the uncertainties inherently associated with recessions, it is reasonable to expect declines during such periods. Consequently, a geographic area dominated by durable manufacturing, such as the state of Michigan, is quite likely to be adversely affected by overall business downturns.[3] The differential regional impacts of national economic conditions and the importance of these variations in both governmental and corporate planning strongly suggest the need for a comprehensive measure of both the relative cyclical sensitivity of individual areas on a cross-sectional basis and the temporal evolution of this responsiveness to national economic conditions.

The purpose of this chapter is to illustrate the application of a simple, yet pervasive, measure of the relationship between fluctuations in the national and regional economies and to describe its potential implementation on a broad basis. To demonstrate its viability, this Regional Business Cycle Index, which was previously derived by one of the authors (see Perryman 1981a, 1981b, 1982), is constructed for the economies of Texas, California, and Michigan. This empirical exercise reflects the initial phase of a project designed to accomplish the universal generation of the entire spatial time series for the United States. The chapter achieves its aim still further through the extension of the Index into a forecasting environment. This task is demonstrated for the state of Texas through an application of the Texas Econometric Model, a large-scale empirical system maintained by the authors. In terms of organization, the chapter begins with a brief description of the basic methodology for developing a quarterly Gross State Product series with the requisite degree of industrial disaggregation. This data set, which is presently either available or under construction in many states, is essential to the index construction process.[4] Following this analysis, a discussion of the basis for the cyclical indicator and a synopsis of its formal derivation is given. Utilization of the proposed methodology within the context of the Texas, California, and Michigan economies is then demonstrated, as is the predictive capability of the method in conjunction with the Texas model. Finally, a concluding section summarizes the chapter and its implications for the overall measurement of regional cyclical performance.

II. The Derivation of Gross State Product

Given the fact that quarterly fluctuations in real gross national product (gnp) are employed as the standard measure of the cyclical performance of the U.S. economy, it is initially necessary to construct a comparable measure of regional economic activity, i.e., a quarterly real gross state product (gsp) series. The limitations inherent in the present data base for regional economies, however, preclude the development of a gsp series by the traditional expenditure (consumption, investment, etc.), income (wages, rents, interest, etc.), or usage (consumption, savings, taxes, etc.) approaches. Nevertheless, there is sufficient information to permit the generation of a reasonable series utilizing an "output by industry" procedure.[5] Moreover, this well-known method, which was originally suggested by Kendrick and Jaycox (1965) is particularly suitable to the derivation of the regional cyclical index, which will be described in section III and implemented in section IV. As will be subsequently illustrated, the sectoral detail embodied in this procedure is an essential element of the sensitivity gauge. The construction process evolves from a basic identity of the form

$$GSP \equiv \sum_{i=1}^{n} GPO_i \qquad (5.1)$$

where:

GSP = nominal gross state product
GPO_i = nominal state gross product originating in sector i

Each of the individual sectoral outputs is then deflated by an appropriate price index in order to form the real series, i.e.,

$$gsp \sum_{i=1}^{n} (GPO_i/P_i) = \sum_{i=1}^{n} gpo_i \qquad (5.2)$$

where

gsp = real gross state product
P_i = price index for sector i
gpo_i = real gross product originating in sector i

In actual implementation, the basic relationship given in expression 5.1 may be operationalized as

$$GSP = GPO_{Mi} + GPO_C + GPO_{MaD} + GPO_{MaN} + GPO_W + GPO_R$$
$$+ GPO_F + GPO_{Tr} + GPO_S + GPO_G + GPO_{Ag} \qquad (5.3)$$

where:

GPO_{Mi} = nominal gross product originating in mining
GPO_C = nominal gross product originating in construction
GPO_{MaD} = nominal gross product originating in durable manufacturing
GPO_{MaN} = nominal gross product originating in nondurable manufacturing
GPO_W = nominal gross product originating in wholesale trade
GPO_R = nominal gross product originating in retail trade
GPO_F = nominal gross product originating in finance, insurance, and real estate
GPO_{Tr} = nominal gross product originating in transportation, communication, and public utilities
GPO_S = nominal gross product originating in services
GPO_G = nominal gross product originating in government
GPO_{Ag} = nominal gross product originating in agriculture, agricultural services, forestry, and fisheries.

The Kendrick-Jaycox approach initially makes use of state and national data series on income received (personal income), by industry; and national data on income originating (national income), by industry. The data employed in this basic approach are annual and are available in published or subscription form from the U.S. Department of Commerce. The first stage of the procedure is the calculation of a state income originating series. Such a series may be reasonably approximated by the expression

$$SIO_i = SIR_i \cdot \frac{NIO_i}{NIR_i} \qquad (5.4)$$

where

SIO_i = nominal state income originating in sector i
SIR_i = nominal state income received in sector i
NIO_i = nominal national income originating in sector i
NIR_i = nominal national income received in sector i

State income originating figures must be calculated for each of the eleven sectors identified in relation 5.3. Annual state data for net product originating and gross product originating are then obtained by adding, respectively, indirect business taxes and capital consumption allowances to the income originating series. Specifically, net product originating by industry is obtained as

$$NPO_i = SIO_i + SIO_i \cdot \frac{IBI_i}{NIO_i} \tag{5.5}$$

where

NPO_i = nominal state net product originating in sector i
IBT_i = nominal national indirect business taxes in sector i

The gross product series is then simply

$$GPO_i = NPO_i + SIO_i \cdot \frac{CCA_i}{NIO_i} \tag{5.6}$$

where CCA_i = nominal national capital consumption allowance in sector i. Equations 4.4, 4.5, and 4.6 may be combined to yield a summary formula:

$$GPO_i = SIO_i[1 + (IBT_i/NIO_i) + CCA_i/NIO_i)] \tag{5.7}$$

Once these nominal series are constructed, they are easily converted to real gross product numbers through use of the annual price deflators by sector that are maintained by the Department of Commerce. As described in equation 5.2, the individual sectoral expressions derived in accordance with equation 5.7 are deflated and then summed in order to form the real gross state product series.

The procedure described above is the general approach for computing annual gross state product. Several modifications are also generally employed in an effort to improve the estimates. Initially, there is sufficient state data to permit direct calculation of gross farm product, a major component of GPO_{Ag}. This information is regularly published by the U.S. Department of Agriculture. The basic identity utilized in this computation is

$$GFP = VFP - TIE \tag{5.8}$$

where

GFP = nominal gross farm product
VFP = nominal value of total farm product
TIE = nominal total intermediate production expenses.

This expression may be further decomposed into

$$VFP = CRM + VHC + RVD + \Delta INV - NR \tag{5.9}$$

and

$$TIE = Feed + Lstk + Seed + Fert + ROE + MOE \tag{5.10}$$

where

CRM = nominal cash receipts from marketings
VHC = nominal value of home consumption
RVD = nominal gross rental value of dwellings
ΔINV = nominal net change in farm inventories
NR = nominal net rent to nonfarm landlords
$Feed$ = nominal feed expenses
$Lstk$ = nominal livestock expenses
$Seed$ = nominal seed expenses
$Fert$ = nominal fertilizer expenses
ROE = nominal repairs and operation expenses for farm equipment
NOE = nominal miscellaneous operating expenses

It is also possible to disaggregate the cash receipts total into a large number of individual crop and livestock categories. Moreover, sufficient data on farm prices exist to make it possible to deflate each component separately. Consequently, in this instance it is possible to employ a "double deflation" method which is much more accurate and comprehensive than the standard price adjustment method.

An additional modification of the Kendrick-Jaycox method, originally suggested by Niemi (1972), relates to the manufacturing sector. As is obvious from the description given above, the basic procedure utilizes the implicit assumption that several relationships are proportional between the state and the nation. This postulate is probably reasonable in a number of industries, particularly those that are almost universally labor intensive. Because of the widely varying patterns in the manufacturing base of individual areas, however, this degree of homogeneity may not be realized. As an illustration, Perryman (1980) recently demonstrated that there were highly significant differences between the functional forms of production relationships in several manufacturing subsectors for the United States and Texas. To account for such variations, Niemi maintains that the GPO_{Ma} aggregate should be weighted by the relative ratio of value added to labor payroll between the United States and the state. Formally, this formulation is given by

$$GPO'_{Ma} = GPO_{Ma}\left(\frac{SVA/SLP}{NVA/NLP}\right) \tag{5.11}$$

where

GPO'_{Ma} = weighted calculation of nominal gross product originating in

        manufacturing
SVA = state nominal value added in manufacturing
SLP = state nominal labor payroll in manufacturing
NVA = national nominal value added in manufacturing
NLP = national nominal labor payroll in manufacturing

This weighted number (in both real and nominal terms) may be substituted into the basic gross state product formulas. Given the present analytical framework and data availability, it is possible to generate distinct weighting schemes for both durable and nondurable manufacturing, i.e., GPO'_{MaD} and GPO'_{MaN}.

Finally, the government sector is also somewhat unique. There is no proprietor's income in government and little or no indirect business taxes and capital consumption allowances.[6] The most commonly used approach to the calculation of GPO_G was developed by L'Esperance, Nestel, and Fromm (1969) and is expressed as follows:

$$GPO_G = \left(\frac{NIO_1}{NWS_1} \cdot SWS_1 \right) + \left(\frac{NIO_f}{NWS_f} \cdot SWS_f \right) \qquad (5.12)$$

where

NIO_1 = nominal national income originating in state and local government activity

NWS_1 = nominal national wages and salaries in state and local government activity

SWS_1 = nominal state wages and salaries in state and local government activity

NIO_f = nominal national income originating in federal government activity

NWS_f = nominal national wages and salaries in federal government activity

SWS_f = nominal state wages and salaries in federal government activity

The major advantages of this procedure are (1) its basic consistency with the standard Kendrick-Jaycox method and (2) its inclusion of military output, a major factor in numerous regional economies.

The only remaining task is to describe the generation of the quarterly series. Such a series is necessary in order to measure evolving cyclical sensitivity in that annual numbers are not temporally frequent enough to capture many significant economic fluctuations and may, in actuality, camouflage underlying instability. The basic method for constructing quarterly gross state product was recently suggested by Weber (1979). With respect to the nominal series, it is initially possible to calculate quarterly state income originating using the relationship

$$SIO_{qi} = SIR_{qi} \cdot \left(\frac{NIO_{qi}}{NIR_{qi}}\right) \tag{5.13}$$

where

SIO_{qi} = nominal quarterly state income originating in sector i
SIR_{qi} = nominal quarterly state income received in sector i
NIO_{qi} = nominal quarterly national income originating in sector i
NIR_{qi} = nominal quarterly national income received in sector i

All of the data required for the computation of these numbers are available from the Commerce Department. To convert this series into gross state product, the income originating numbers are multiplied by a ratio of gross national product to national income originating in the relevant sector, i.e.,

$$GPO_{qi} = SIO_{qi} \cdot \left(\frac{GNP_i}{NIO_i}\right) \tag{5.14}$$

where

GPO_{qi} = quarterly nominal state gross product originating in sector i
GNP_i = annual nominal gross state product in sector i
NIO_i = annual nominal gross state product in sector i

The sectoral values may then be summed for each quarter to obtain the aggregate series. Note that, because of the unavailability of sector GNP on a quarterly basis, the multiplicative factor is the same for each quarter. To transform these figures into constant dollars, it is, of course, necessary to utilize sectoral implicit price deflators. These data are only available annually and are generated through a simple linear interpolation process. The basis for the sensitivity index and its derivation are now presented.

III. The Regional Business Cycle Index

Given a gross state product series constructed in the manner described in section II, it becomes possible to derive a simple measure of cyclical sensitivity. To motivate the approach utilized in this process, consider the recent experience of the economy of Texas. Because of its diverse economic base, its geographic locality within the Sun Belt, its resource endowments, and numerous other factors, Texas has long been thought to be largely exempt from the severe cyclical movements in national business activity. Yet there may well be endogenous forces that tend to ameliorate this insulation over time. It is reasonable to expect that, given the locational advantages of Texas, many additional firms are likely to begin operations within the state. In fact, the area has, in recent years, consistently been among the leading states in the country in attracting new firms. To the extent that the new businesses are subject to cyclical variations, however, their presence may erode the noncyclical character of the regional economy. The index described below is designed to measure the degree of cyclical proclivity on a temporal basis.

The proposed indicator of cyclical variation begins from the basic premise that the character of an economy may be viewed as dependent upon the following two critical factors: one, the industrial composition of the region, and two, the cyclical sensitivity of each industry within the region. It may obviously be expected that the greater the concentration of highly volatile industries within the area, the greater its susceptibility to national fluctuations. The construction process is in many ways comparable to traditional economic analyses of the business cycle and is methodologically summarized in i through iv below.

i. The data to be employed (real quarterly gross state product by sector and real quarterly gross national product) should initially be adjusted in order to eliminate seasonal variation and trend factors. Many of the series utilized in developing the gross product estimates are already seasonally adjusted, but a final reevaluation via a standard program with evolving variable weighting patterns (e.g., Census X-11 or the X-11-ARIMA of Statistics Canada) seems well advised. A number of possible techniques for removing the trend component are feasible. For example, simple first differencing of a linear empirical relationship will normally eliminate a consistent temporal pattern in a satisfactory manner. This approach is particularly viable in cases in which an intercept or constant term is retained in the transformed expression (e.g., see Anderson and Jordan, 1968). Another standard detrending procedure is accomplished through the estimation of a regression of the form

$$Y = \alpha + \beta t + \varepsilon \qquad (5.15)$$

where

Y = series to be detrended

t = time index
α, β = parameters to be estimated
ε = a random disturbance term

This empirical expression permits calculation of the "trend" component of the series, i.e.,

$$\hat{Y} = \hat{\alpha} + \hat{\beta}t \qquad (5.16)$$

where

$\hat{Y}$ = trend component of Y
$\hat{\alpha}, \hat{\beta}$ = estimated coefficients

The detrended series to be denoted herein by Y^*, is then given by

$$Y^* = Y - \hat{Y} \qquad (5.17)$$

Somewhat more complex regression specifications are also superior in some cases. As a simple example, an exponential trend component of the form

$$Y = \alpha e^{\beta t} \qquad (5.18)$$

is frequently employed. This equation is, of course, linear with respect to its parameters when given in natural logarithmic form and, thus, is readily estimable. Finally, the purging of temporal elements may be achieved through the estimation of simple time series models, such as those determined via the autoregressive integrated moving average (ARIMA) method suggested by Box and Jenkins (1976). These "purged" data are then employed in the second phase of the computational process.

ii. According to traditional data analysis, any economic series may be divided into seasonal, trend, cyclical, and random components. Once the seasonal and trend components are removed, only the cyclical and random factors remain. A simple strategy for the isolation of the cyclical aspect of each sectoral gross state product series is to specify and estimate an equation of the following form:[7]

$$\Delta gpo^*_{qi} = \alpha + \beta \Delta gnp^*_q + \varepsilon \qquad (5.19)$$

where

Δgpo^*_{qi} = quarterly change in real state gross product originating in sector i, in detrended and seasonally adjusted form
Δgnp^*_q = quarterly change in real gross national product, in detrended and seasonally adjusted form

α, β = parameters to be estimated
ε = random disturbance term

It is obvious, at least from a purely theoretical standpoint, that the intercept term α in i above is equal to zero. Despite the first differenced form, however, it is not desirable to constrain the regressions in order to force the estimated relations through the origins. When regression coefficients are restricted, the coefficient of determination (R^2) does not necessarily vary between zero and one. This statistic, which measures the percentage of the variation in the dependent variable that is explained via the regression, is utilized in the construction of the index and, for this purpose, its range of values must lie between zero and one and it must be a true correlation measure. Moreover, the constant term should, as noted earlier, serve to isolate any remaining trend elements in the first difference expression. The rationale for the utilization of equation 5.5 is simply the fact that quarterly changes in real gross national product represent the standard measure of cyclical sensitivity for the economy of the United States. Hence, the degree of correlation between this variable and sectoral gross state product provides a reasonable relative measure of the cyclical nature of various industries.

iii. Following a calculation of a set of expressions such as equation 5.19, a weighting factor W_i may be defined as follows:

$$W_i = \begin{cases} R_i^2 & \text{if } \hat{\beta}_i \geq 0 \\ -R_i^2 & \text{if } \hat{\beta}_i < 0 \end{cases} \tag{5.20}$$

where

R_i^2 = the coefficient of determination from the estimation of equation 5.19 for sector i

β_i = the parameter estimate of β_i from equation 5.18 for sector i

Note that, if the slope estimate is zero, the coefficient of determination is also zero.

iv. The final Region Business Cycle Index (RBCI) may then be computed as

$$RBCI = \sum_{i=1}^{n} W_i \cdot \frac{qpo_{qi}}{gsp_q} \tag{5.21}$$

where

$RBCI$ = quarterly values of the index
gpo_{qi} = real state gross product originating in sector i in quarter q
gsp_q = real gross state product in quarter q

The ratios of sectoral to total output will vary from quarter to quarter depending upon the output mix of the region.

A brief analysis of this measure and its basic properties is now provided. The index defined can be shown to vary within the open interval $(-1,1)$, with highly negative values representing regions with countercyclical economies, highly positive values representing procyclical areas, and values near zero suggesting economies that are insulated from national fluctuations. By definition, the sum of the ratios of sectoral to total gross product is unity, i.e.,

$$\sum_{i=1}^{n} \frac{gpo_{qi}}{gsp_q} = 1 \tag{5.22}$$

This relationship is essentially a restatement of the earlier expression to the effect that total product is merely the sum of the output from each sector.

The RBCI measure may be reasonably illustrated through consideration of the two polar cases with respect to regional business fluctuations. As one extreme example, assume there is a regional economy dominated by a single industry. Assume further that this industry is countercyclical ($\hat{\beta} < 0$) and that the relationship is near perfect, i.e., R_i^2 approaches one. In this case, RBCI is simply the product of the share of this industry within the total regional economy (i.e., one) and a weighting factor which is near negative one. Hence, the index approaches its lower bound in this contrived situation. Conversely, an area dominated by a strongly procyclical sector would approach the upper bound. As a practical matter, it is unlikely that many sectors will exhibit truly countercyclical patterns at the level of aggregation embodied in the gross state product accounts. Moreover, the use of a state as the geographic unit will generally result in an economic base sufficiently diverse to insure the absence of aggregate countercyclical behavior. Consequently, in the actual implementation of the indicator, it is highly probable that the range of variation will be confined to the $(0,1)$ interval in virtually all cases. On a more realistic basis, the range of values may be narrowed still further. In order to initially test the index, a mock economy was created which exhibited the maximum degree of diversity that is pragmatically feasible within advanced societies. Similarly, a second economy was specified which exhibited the highest conceivable concentration of cyclically influenced industries within the contemporary structure of the United States. These economies were found to have index values, respectively, of about

0.05 and 0.25. Hence, it may be expected that all states within the United States will produce values within this 0.05–0.25 region. Those that are relatively insulated from business fluctuations will, of course, be at the lower end of this range, while those that exhibit cyclical sensitivity will be near the upper bound. Having briefly described the derivation of the index and its region of regional values, its application to the economies of Texas, California, and Michigan will be examined.

IV. Application of the Business Cycle Index to Texas, California, and Michigan

The economies of Texas, California, and Michigan are diverse from one another in many respects and offer an excellent means of contrasting the sensitivity of individual regions to national business fluctuations. Initially, a brief insight into the performance of these areas is given in order to illustrate their heterogeneity. The historical patterns of cyclical movements in the United States, Texas, California, and Michigan, as depicted by quarterly percentage changes in real gross output, are graphically illustrated in figures 5-1–5-4, respectively. The shaded areas in these graphs represent periods designated by the National Bureau of Economic Research as recessions for the United States during the interval between 1958 and 1981.

Even a cursory examination of these graphs clearly reveals the overall strength of the Texas economy during recent years (figure 5-2). Over the entirety of the period being examined, Texas has enjoyed a mean quarterly increase of more than 1.3 percent in real output and an annual compounded growth rate of slightly over 5.25 percent. Moreover, Texas has never experienced a quarterly decline in gross state product as large as 1 percent and only once, during the mild contraction that accompanied the conclusion of the Vietnam buildup, did the state see a decline in production for two consecutive quarters. Moreover, Texas experienced positive growth rates throughout each of the major national recessions that occurred over the relevant time horizon.

California (figure 5-3), while not so prosperous as Texas during this period, has also enjoyed significant economic growth relative to the United States. The state has experienced a mean quarterly increase of more than 1.1 percent and a compounded annual growth rate of more than 4.5 percent over the twenty-four year span of the study. This performance compares with a mean quarterly increase in real gross national product of somewhat less than 1 percent and a compound growth rate of slightly more than 3 percent. California has, however, experienced consecutive quarterly down-

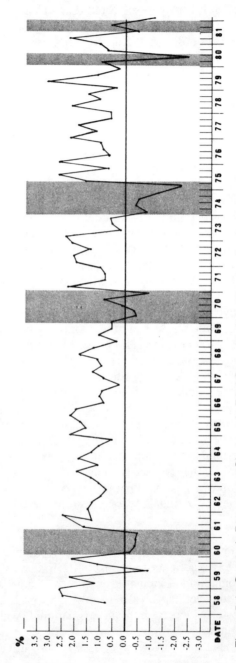

Figure 5-1. Quarterly Percentage Changes in Real Gross National Product for the United States: 1958–1981

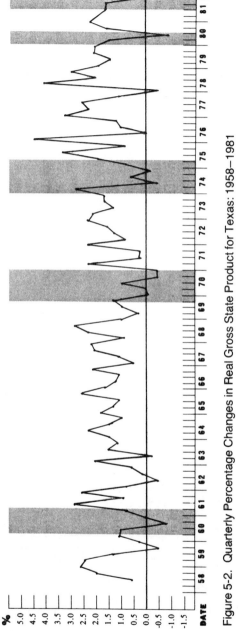

Figure 5-2. Quarterly Percentage Changes in Real Gross State Product for Texas: 1958–1981

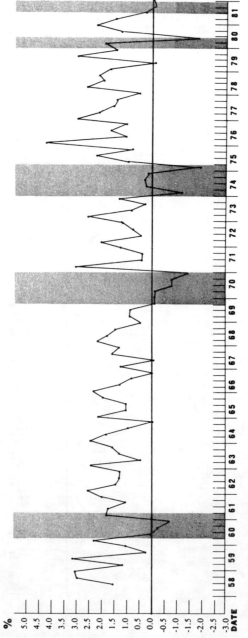

Figure 5-3. Quarterly Percentage Changes in Real Gross State Product for California: 1958–1981

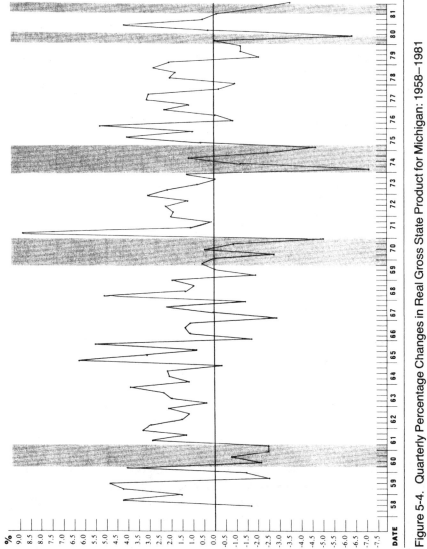

Figure 5-4. Quarterly Percentage Changes in Real Gross State Product for Michigan: 1958–1981

turns on several occasions and has generally seen declining output during major U.S. recessions.

The state of Michigan offers a marked contrast to both Texas and California. Its mean quarterly percentage growth has been about 0.75 percent and its compound rate of growth has been far below national norms. Moreover, as figure 5-4 clearly indicates, Michigan has experienced much greater variability than either Texas or California, with quarterly declines in excess of 7 percent and quarterly increases approaching 9 percent on occasion. Measured in terms of its standard deviation, the variability in the growth rate of the Michigan economy is more than twice that of Texas, California, or the United States. Additionally, during major national recessions, Michigan generally suffers downturns that far exceed those of the overall economy.

The reasons for the vast disparities observed across these regional economies can readily be traced to fundamental differences in industrial composition. As a means of emphasizing and illustrating this fact, the relative importance of the various productive sectors for Texas, California, and Michigan are summarized on a quarterly basis, respectively, in tables 5-1, 5-2, and 5-3 (all tables in this chapter appear at the end of the chapter). The state of Texas, for example, is endowed with natural resources and a favorable climate and tends to exhibit extreme diversity within its base of economic activity. Moreover, because Texas has come to prominence as an economically prosperous region rather late in the nation's history, it has not evolved a dependence upon durable goods manufacturing to the extent experienced by most industrialized areas of the country. Texas also has a large mining sector, which is dominated by oil and gas extraction and, which until the past few years, was not subject to significant cyclical patterns.

California, also, has rich natural endowments and has a reasonably diverse regional economy. Its period of rapid growth and maturity, however, came somewhat earlier than did that of Texas and to some extent corresponded with major industrialization of the Northeast near the turn of the century. Consequently, California has a base of durable manufacturing that is somewhat larger than that of Texas. It is not surprising, then, that the California economy appears from figure 5-3 to be somewhat more prone to experience adverse responses to national recessions.

As is well known, the economy of the state of Michigan is completely dominated by the production of automobiles and related durable goods. As table 5-3 indicates, these goods generally comprise approximately 30 percent of the state's total output. Consequently, it is to be expected that Michigan is highly susceptible to cyclical fluctuations and is capable of displaying dramatic ups and downs in its overall performance level.

Thus, the three states selected for this analysis provide an excellent basis for demonstrating the construction and application of a regional business cycle.

The results of an application of the methodology outlined in the preceding section for Texas, California, and Michigan are summarized in table 5-4. The values displayed within this table clearly confirm and quantify the results that were intuitively discussed at the outset of this analysis. Texas, which generally exhibits a high degree of insulation, exhibited values in the range from .083 to .106. These numbers correspond closely to those achieved by the "ideal" diversified economy that was created for testing purposes. California, on the other hand, consistently falls near the middle of the feasible range for the RBC index, while Michigan, with values reaching as high as .236, tends to approximate the highest reasonable levels that could be attained by a cyclically sensitive state. Hence, the index tends to confirm conventional wisdom and provides a good measure of the performance of a regional economy with respect to national economic fluctuations.

The Regional Business Cycle Index discussed in this paper has particular value in that, in addition to quantifying the degree of regional sensitivity and permitting comparisons of diverse areas in a concise manner, it also aids in the characterization of the evolution of a particular economy over time. For example, Michigan seems to be making some progress relative to the early 1970s in terms of building a more diverse economy, while California has generally exhibited a slight increase in its susceptibility to national events. On the whole, all of the states are more vulnerable at the present time than they were in the 1950s. This fact stems from a number of sources, the most significant of which is simply the much greater degree of integration of the various regions of the country which has emerged within the past two decades.

In the period from 1958 through 1981, the index of cyclical sensitivity for Texas increased by more than 27 percent, as compared to about 11 percent for California and less than 4 percent for Michigan. This fact suggests that, while Texas remains far less sensitive than the other two states, there has been a significant increase in the dependency of Texas on national economic conditions in both absolute and relative terms. This finding is further illustrated by certain aspects of our recent experience. In terms of both output and employment, the Texas economy has experienced the most recent two recessions to a much larger degree than was previously the case. In fact, the large downturn in the U.S. economy during the second quarter of 1980 was largely responsible for the largest single quarterly decrease in real output experienced by Texas during the entire twenty-four years examined in this study. Moreover, the substantial decline in the fourth quarter of 1981 for the

U.S. economy produced a modest reduction in business activity for Texas, and the state remained stagnant throughout the recent national contraction even prior to the world oil glut. Hence, it may be concluded that Texas has definitely entered a phase of development in which it is becoming more susceptible to national cyclical phenomena.

To fully understand the reasons behind this evolution of the Texas economy, it is necessary to examine the very process that produced the economic prosperity and relative insulation experienced by Texas in recent years. In examining the information in table 5-1, for example, it is seen that the percentage of Texas output generated by durable goods manufacturing has increased from about 8 percent to about 12 percent over the time period of this analysis. This gain of about 50 percent in relative share of state output for this most vulnerable of all productive sectors represents a significant movement toward cyclical sensitivity. Moreover, the increasing extent to which interest rates and levels of inflation are determined in national markets has also contributed significantly to recent fluctuations within the state's financial and construction sectors. Hence, there are distinct and irrefutable factors within the state which are generating a trend toward greater dependence between the Texas economy and the national business cycle. This finding, which confirms recent observations by many analysts in a more directly quantifiable manner, has significant implications for long-range planning of the industrial structure of the state. It also serves to reinforce the inevitable consequences that accompany the substantial benefits associated with a sustained period of rapid economic growth.

V. Forecasting Cyclical Sensitivity: An Application

Once the Regional Business Cycle Index is developed for a state, it may be projected into the future as follows:

1. With the aid of a regional econometric model, individual forecasts for gross state product must be generated for each industrial sector within the area, as well as an aggregate forecast for total real output.
2. Given these projected values, equation 5.21 may be solved for the ex ante values.

The application of this straightforward approach is summarized for the Texas economy in table 5-5. Specifically, this table provides projections for the Regional Business Cycle Index on a quarterly basis for the period through 1990. These values reveal that the index should remain essentially stable over the remainder of the decade. This result suggests that both (1) the recent trend toward growing sensitivity will not persist at its recent pace and (2) the Texas economy should experience future national recessions to approximately the same extent as observed during the contractionary phases in 1980 and 1981–1982. It is obvious, of course, that this particular application of the index is restricted to states that possess a functioning model with the capacity to generate sectoral output projections. Given the recent surge in the development of such systems, however, this impediment will generally not be highly significant.[8]

VI. Conclusion

The purposes of this paper have been (1) to describe a basic procedure that may be utilized in the construction of an index of the cyclical sensitivity of a regional economy; (2) to apply the resulting measure to the states of Texas, California, and Michigan; and (3) to illustrate the projection of the measure in a forecasting environment for the Texas economy. The analysis has involved both the development of the relevant gross state product series and its subsequent use in the derivation and calculation of the index. The interpretation of the series generated for the three states reveals that these areas conform in all respects to prior conceptions of their basic cyclical character. The time series forecasts for the Texas economy are also quite revealing in terms of the evolution of the cyclical character of a highly dynamic region.

Once an indicator of this nature is available, its potential pragmatic applicability for analyzing regional economic activity during business fluctuations in quite extensive. On a time series basis, it will permit measurement of the evolving cyclical sensitivity of a given area. For example, it was speculated earlier in this chapter that the economy of Texas may well experience more severe cyclical shocks in the future as a corollary to the rapid economic development that is presently occurring. The Regional Business Cycle Index suggested herein can be employed to assess this process and trace its development. Such information is quite useful for long-term policy planning for the state, particularly since its values are determinable irrespective of the present cyclical position of the national and regional economies. To further aid in this process, the measure may, as demonstrated in section V, be integrated with an econometric model to actually predict cyclical sensitivity. The Regional Business Cycle Index is also viable for cross-sectional analysis. As an illustration, a comparison of relative sensitivity across regions at a particular point seems in time quite viable. The resulting characterization would be extremely valuable in determining the impact of short-run countercyclical policies on various areas. It also provides a means of giving

Table 5-1. Percentage Composition of Quarterly Gross State Product by Industry for Texas: 1958–1981

Date	Mining	Construction	Transportation, Communication, & Public Utilities	Wholesale Trade	Retail Trade	Finance, Insurance, & Real Estate	Nondurable Manufacturing	Durable Manufacturing	Agriculture	Services	Government
1958:I	6.96	7.10	6.78	5.41	10.18	12.89	8.89	8.25	7.31	9.76	16.46
1958:II	7.19	6.70	6.89	5.48	10.26	13.45	9.60	7.99	6.26	9.53	16.66
1958:III	7.34	6.19	6.92	5.63	10.30	13.41	9.86	8.06	6.57	9.08	16.63
1958:IV	7.49	6.23	6.96	5.70	10.32	13.65	9.85	8.58	6.49	8.79	15.94
1959:I	6.75	6.58	7.08	5.70	10.01	13.38	10.28	8.88	6.87	8.75	15.72
1959:II	6.72	6.29	7.14	5.78	10.16	13.51	10.42	9.29	6.66	8.77	15.27
1959:III	7.01	6.12	7.12	5.85	10.26	13.89	10.36	8.61	6.59	8.97	15.32
1959:IV	6.94	6.05	7.26	5.78	10.18	13.98	10.29	8.46	6.80	8.96	15.29
1960:I	6.74	5.71	7.34	5.87	9.90	14.13	10.64	9.37	6.10	9.02	15.30
1960:II	6.76	6.07	7.24	5.77	9.68	14.06	10.30	8.99	6.50	9.12	15.40
1960:III	6.84	6.00	7.28	5.81	9.46	14.13	10.38	8.71	6.22	9.15	15.83
1960:IV	6.97	5.90	7.38	5.81	9.30	14.28	10.17	8.52	6.56	9.14	15.80
1961:I	7.19	5.96	7.43	5.83	9.17	14.52	10.88	7.81	6.34	8.93	15.61
1961:II	7.14	6.04	7.31	5.85	9.18	14.22	11.05	7.96	7.09	8.97	15.24
1961:III	7.09	6.15	7.40	5.93	9.32	14.40	10.84	8.23	6.73	8.91	15.08
1961:IV	7.01	5.97	7.43	5.93	9.37	14.20	10.89	8.60	7.02	8.96	14.88
1962:I	6.65	6.12	7.44	5.99	9.35	14.53	10.35	8.48	6.99	9.10	15.17
1962:II	6.75	5.80	7.52	6.10	9.20	14.87	10.54	8.57	6.03	9.21	15.34
1962:III	6.88	5.61	7.60	6.12	9.76	15.11	10.58	8.77	5.46	9.21	15.33
1962:IV	6.87	5.66	7.49	6.18	9.81	15.14	10.73	8.68	5.30	10.02	15.55
1963:I	6.67	5.72	7.32	6.24	9.73	13.62	11.04	8.44	5.94	10.11	15.24
1963:II	6.83	5.82	7.55	6.35	9.72	13.70	10.86	8.92	4.81	10.11	15.23
1963:III	6.98	5.93	7.52	6.41	9.73	13.56	10.83	9.12	4.74	10.13	15.05
1963:IV	6.97	5.71	7.63	6.52	9.72	13.64	10.57	9.40	4.76	10.05	15.04
1964:I	6.42	5.92	7.60	6.56	9.87	13.66	10.61	9.74	4.67	10.06	14.88
1964:II	6.57	6.19	7.40	6.56	9.89	13.54	10.57	9.80	4.78	9.99	14.64
1964:III	6.54	6.09	7.33	6.58	9.96	13.51	10.50	10.01	4.94	10.01	14.56
1964:IV	6.58	6.14	7.38	6.59	9.96	13.65	10.56	9.78	4.84	9.90	14.54
1965:I	6.36	6.18	7.37	6.63	9.95	13.58	10.68	9.96	5.00	10.01	14.37
1965:II	6.30	5.94	7.60	6.68	9.86	13.70	10.63	9.97	5.16	10.15	14.16
1965:III	6.21	5.82	7.67	6.72	10.03	13.83	10.66	10.08	4.94	10.11	13.89
1965:IV	6.16	5.67	7.70	6.66	9.96	13.88	10.78	10.20	4.63	9.72	14.25
1966:I	5.91	5.76	7.65	6.81	9.94	13.75	10.79	10.13	5.26	9.81	14.30
1966:II	5.99	5.86	7.78	6.84	9.92	13.64	10.98	10.24	4.53	10.05	14.59
1966:III	5.86	6.00	7.78	6.79	9.96	13.55	10.87	10.39	4.00	10.14	14.76
1966:IV	5.80	6.08	7.77	6.76	9.92	13.46	10.84	10.65	3.69	10.38	14.89
1967:I	5.88	6.00	7.79	6.80	9.87	13.59	11.15	9.90	3.58	10.51	15.05
1967:II	6.07	5.91	7.81	6.80	9.88	13.65	11.05	9.96	3.59	10.46	14.77
1967:III	6.44	5.71	7.73	6.78	9.75	13.58	10.81	9.97	4.02	10.37	14.75
1967:IV	6.55	5.45	7.78	6.80	9.59	13.55	10.86	10.29	4.09	10.42	14.69
1968:I	6.24	5.27	7.95	7.05	9.79	13.72	10.53	10.29	4.09	10.33	14.67
1968:II	6.09	5.35	7.84	7.13	9.74	13.74	10.48	10.68	4.16	10.25	14.46
1968:III	5.85	5.44	7.86	7.20	9.64	13.59	10.64	10.59	4.44	10.28	14.53
1968:IV	5.77	5.55	7.81	7.27	9.63	13.50	10.67	10.67	4.42	10.48	14.38
1969:I	5.31	5.63	7.81	7.33	9.80	13.91	10.74	10.51	3.99	10.48	14.48
1969:II	5.37	5.39	8.14	7.30	9.87	13.70	10.94	10.63	3.79	10.58	14.31

1969:III	5.27	5.50	8.10	7.36	9.71	13.36	11.11	10.87	3.57	10.57	14.56
1969:IV	5.26	5.26	8.09	7.45	9.55	13.16	11.26	10.73	3.86	10.88	14.50
1970:I	5.27	5.03	8.40	7.45	9.73	13.34	10.77	10.68	4.10	10.65	14.57
1970:II	5.13	5.23	8.39	7.48	9.66	13.18	10.80	10.36	4.70	10.63	14.50
1970:III	5.26	5.22	8.60	7.53	9.72	13.38	10.97	10.05	4.42	10.74	14.30
1970:IV	4.24	5.30	8.65	7.69	9.77	13.70	11.02	9.49	4.17	10.87	14.24
1971:I	4.30	5.34	8.60	7.72	9.97	13.60	11.39	9.83	4.37	10.70	14.28
1971:II	4.37	5.16	8.59	7.89	10.13	14.02	11.57	9.52	3.82	10.74	14.12
1971:III	4.89	4.93	8.51	7.85	10.17	14.36	11.49	9.69	3.60	10.76	14.11
1971:IV	4.94	4.88	8.41	8.04	10.17	14.23	10.57	10.22	3.98	10.60	13.83
1972:I	4.90	5.22	8.67	8.06	10.21	13.79	10.47	10.45	4.18	10.58	13.83
1972:II	4.85	5.15	8.79	8.22	10.20	13.78	10.75	10.49	3.48	10.58	13.48
1972:III	4.77	5.18	8.86	8.36	10.13	14.07	10.73	10.76	3.89	10.46	13.43
1972:IV	4.74	5.06	8.91	8.39	10.01	13.72	10.87	10.42	4.36	10.27	13.33
1973:I	4.84	5.01	9.01	8.38	10.09	13.61	10.96	10.48	4.69	10.36	13.07
1973:II	4.65	4.95	9.01	8.33	10.10	13.49	10.89	10.55	4.45	10.36	12.91
1973:III	5.74	5.19	9.18	8.45	9.99	13.38	11.28	10.45	4.36	10.37	12.73
1973:IV	5.54	5.24	9.21	7.87	10.17	13.30	12.70	10.60	3.77	10.37	12.59
1974:I	5.27	4.85	9.05	7.77	9.92	12.90	13.19	10.63	2.27	10.13	12.40
1974:II	5.06	5.16	9.31	7.56	9.58	13.11	13.07	10.64	2.24	10.36	12.47
1974:III	5.26	5.26	9.36	8.00	9.92	13.61	12.53	10.49	2.01	10.55	12.53
1974:IV	4.85	5.30	9.40	7.99	10.14	14.14	12.74	10.67	2.47	10.71	12.63
1975:I	4.73	5.22	9.25	7.78	10.02	13.80	12.74	10.85	2.79	10.84	12.68
1975:II	4.56	5.07	9.27	7.95	9.99	13.59	13.33	10.60	2.77	10.67	12.44
1975:III	5.03	5.05	9.36	7.85	10.09	13.40	13.43	10.53	2.78	10.44	12.11
1975:IV	4.89	5.26	9.46	8.11	10.13	13.37	12.74	10.45	3.11	10.41	12.30
1976:I	5.06	5.39	9.21	7.95	10.22	13.41	12.63	10.36	2.88	10.23	12.05
1976:II	4.75	5.56	9.31	7.96	10.17	14.05	12.39	10.23	2.87	10.34	12.15
1976:III	4.93	5.48	9.24	7.89	10.26	14.36	12.19	10.45	3.23	10.32	12.06
1976:IV	4.96	5.59	9.13	7.77	10.20	14.18	12.41	10.39	3.59	10.47	11.99
1977:I	4.72	5.48	9.09	8.12	10.29	14.21	12.57	10.43	3.30	10.33	11.51
1977:II	4.46	5.76	9.06	8.36	10.22	14.33	12.52	10.76	3.53	10.15	11.27
1977:III	4.21	5.73	9.16	7.80	10.40	14.67	12.47	10.91	3.40	10.16	10.77
1977:IV	4.59	5.77	9.36	7.96	10.24	14.39	12.54	10.98	3.42	10.14	10.95
1978:I	4.42	5.64	9.22	8.08	10.15	14.34	12.39	10.91	3.24	10.46	11.01
1978:II	4.61	5.96	9.35	8.30	10.07	14.77	12.32	11.57	2.99	10.36	10.55
1978:III	4.60	5.92	9.36	8.28	9.81	14.97	12.23	11.48	3.30	10.38	10.42
1978:IV	4.72	5.82	9.29	7.89	9.86	14.09	12.22	11.24	4.33	10.23	10.30
1979:I	4.82	5.59	9.39	7.93	9.93	13.97	12.18	11.03	4.73	10.27	10.25
1979:II	5.15	5.50	9.29	8.00	9.85	13.95	12.08	11.55	4.74	10.18	10.18
1979:III	5.31	5.37	9.42	8.19	9.55	14.07	12.01	11.03	4.77	10.38	10.06
1979:IV	5.14	5.27	9.46	7.93	9.90	14.21	12.06	11.45	4.30	10.51	10.04
1980:I	5.53	5.20	9.50	8.23	9.94	14.35	11.83	11.74	4.04	10.37	9.83
1980:II	4.78	5.06	9.60	7.86	9.78	14.45	11.62	12.38	3.89	10.58	9.85
1980:III	4.95	4.83	9.97	8.05	9.69	14.46	12.01	12.57	3.76	10.67	9.98
1980:IV	5.01	4.79	9.66	7.85	9.64	14.43	11.73	12.53	4.15	10.48	10.14
1981:I	5.24	4.89	9.61	7.81	9.55	14.09	11.96	12.52	4.54	10.24	9.97
1981:II		4.81	9.62	7.88	9.64	13.79	11.45		4.88	10.36	9.88
1981:III		4.74	9.65	7.88	9.55	13.88			4.82	10.26	9.75
1981:IV		4.80	9.86	7.92	9.41					10.31	9.79

Table 5-2. Percentage Composition of Quarterly Gross State Product by Industry for California: 1958–1981

Date	Mining	Construction	Transportation, Communication, & Public Utilities	Wholesale Trade	Retail Trade	Finance, Insurance, & Real Estate	Nondurable Manufacturing	Durable Manufacturing	Agriculture	Services	Government
1958:I	0.87	7.40	6.28	5.15	11.01	15.24	6.17	12.02	4.38	12.82	18.66
1958:II	0.87	7.20	6.18	5.18	10.87	15.70	6.69	11.99	4.34	12.51	18.47
1958:III	0.89	7.28	6.25	5.33	10.79	15.74	6.83	12.22	4.38	11.96	18.35
1958:IV	0.90	7.10	6.25	5.37	10.81	16.02	6.85	12.88	4.42	11.63	17.77
1959:I	0.85	7.29	6.41	5.48	10.81	15.90	7.07	12.09	4.80	11.67	17.62
1959:II	0.84	7.26	6.32	5.53	10.79	15.87	6.95	12.68	4.88	11.68	17.21
1959:III	0.87	7.12	6.32	5.57	10.83	16.27	7.01	11.71	4.91	11.99	17.40
1959:IV	0.87	7.20	6.45	5.50	10.77	16.29	6.83	11.51	5.23	12.19	17.17
1960:I	0.82	6.90	6.46	5.62	10.54	16.37	6.89	12.40	4.98	11.80	17.22
1960:II	0.82	6.92	6.49	5.62	10.63	16.47	6.75	12.07	4.97	11.81	17.45
1960:III	0.83	6.79	6.65	5.67	10.36	16.49	6.74	11.75	4.86	11.93	17.94
1960:IV	0.85	6.64	6.63	5.72	10.28	16.67	6.66	11.10	4.99	12.35	18.12
1961:I	0.91	6.86	6.56	5.71	10.23	17.03	6.47	11.44	4.64	12.55	17.61
1961:II	0.88	6.88	6.66	5.75	10.14	16.94	6.67	11.80	4.47	12.51	17.29
1961:III	0.88	6.81	6.61	5.80	10.10	16.93	6.47	12.04	4.45	12.59	17.31
1961:IV	0.89	6.74	6.62	5.85	10.22	16.95	6.48	12.05	4.42	12.55	17.24
1962:I	0.84	6.55	6.68	5.81	10.18	16.99	6.36	12.57	4.35	12.44	17.24
1962:II	0.85	6.39	6.66	5.83	10.06	17.00	6.40	12.76	4.45	12.53	17.06
1962:III	0.86	6.62	6.76	5.80	9.94	17.05	6.32	12.79	4.37	12.42	17.07
1962:IV	0.86	6.74	6.71	5.80	9.80	17.05	6.42	12.54	4.54	12.30	17.22
1963:I	0.83	6.83	6.52	5.83	10.47	15.40	6.18	13.13	4.32	13.48	17.00
1963:II	0.84	6.63	6.64	5.90	10.39	15.39	6.08	13.41	4.15	13.53	17.04
1963:III	0.84	6.69	6.73	5.93	10.40	15.39	6.04	13.48	4.10	13.55	16.84
1963:IV	0.85	6.83	6.83	5.95	10.48	15.34	5.91	13.25	4.10	13.56	16.90
1964:I	0.82	7.02	6.83	5.93	10.52	15.35	5.91	13.17	4.33	13.55	16.58
1964:II	0.85	7.01	6.77	5.91	10.69	15.27	5.93	12.94	4.62	13.58	16.44
1964:III	0.86	6.67	6.78	5.94	10.76	15.38	6.03	12.79	4.80	13.55	16.44
1964:IV	0.88	6.60	6.88	5.95	10.84	15.45	5.98	12.44	4.64	13.67	16.68
1965:I	0.84	6.51	7.02	6.04	10.83	15.75	6.11	12.55	4.35	13.58	16.42
1965:II	0.83	6.25	7.20	6.00	10.72	15.88	6.04	12.68	4.31	13.69	16.41
1965:III	0.85	6.07	7.20	5.97	10.84	15.97	5.97	12.79	3.91	13.79	16.64
1965:IV	0.85	5.80	7.41	5.90	10.78	15.94	6.04	12.95	3.70	13.75	16.87
1966:I	0.85	5.88	7.30	6.02	10.75	15.73	6.06	13.39	3.82	13.45	16.76
1966:II	0.87	5.91	7.55	6.01	10.67	15.43	6.17	13.64	3.59	13.33	16.82
1966:III	0.86	5.54	7.60	5.98	10.68	15.16	6.11	13.76	3.60	13.50	17.22
1966:IV	0.85	5.18	7.80	6.03	10.75	15.13	6.08	13.69	3.50	13.65	17.34
1967:I	0.81	4.92	7.86	6.03	10.54	15.11	6.02	14.23	3.47	13.58	17.43
1967:II	0.83	4.69	7.78	6.01	10.53	15.32	5.90	14.22	3.46	13.73	17.53
1967:III	0.86	4.88	7.82	6.99	10.42	15.39	5.81	14.05	3.67	13.67	17.43
1967:IV	0.88	4.72	7.79	6.00	10.35	15.42	5.93	14.16	3.75	13.49	17.52
1968:I	0.85	4.65	7.86	6.12	10.44	15.40	5.92	14.05	3.84	13.41	17.45
1968:II	0.85	4.62	7.89	6.19	10.38	15.56	5.98	14.03	4.01	13.31	17.19
1968:III	0.85	4.57	8.10	6.25	10.36	15.44	6.12	13.86	4.09	13.17	17.19
1968:IV	0.88	4.59	8.15	6.30	10.23	15.52	6.07	13.97	4.03	13.20	17.06
1969:I	0.78	4.33	8.42	6.23	10.37	15.53	6.24	14.04	3.66	13.46	16.95
1969:II	0.84	4.75	8.40	6.22	10.41	15.24	6.29	14.02	3.50	13.51	16.84

1969: III	0.85	4.49	8.46	6.29	10.30	15.01	6.46	14.01	3.30	13.45	17.40
1969: IV	0.86	4.79	8.51	6.36	10.15	14.76	6.49	13.73	3.28	13.84	17.23
1970: I	0.87	4.61	8.56	6.34	10.27	14.82	6.43	13.44	3.41	13.66	17.59
1970: II	0.84	4.56	8.65	6.40	10.42	14.78	6.45	13.24	3.48	13.71	17.49
1970: III	0.82	4.46	8.95	6.44	10.43	15.05	6.50	12.74	3.54	13.59	17.48
1970: IV	0.82	4.27	9.06	6.50	10.53	15.36	6.51	12.01	3.54	13.93	17.47
1971: I	0.73	4.39	8.82	6.52	10.46	15.15	6.64	12.94	3.85	13.50	16.99
1971: II	0.76	4.20	8.78	6.51	10.53	15.45	6.70	12.99	3.93	13.31	16.84
1971: III	0.77	4.18	8.78	6.65	10.74	15.83	6.68	12.71	3.72	13.21	16.73
1971: IV	0.83	4.14	8.71	6.70	10.59	15.64	6.69	12.95	4.09	13.13	16.53
1972: I	0.78	4.51	8.75	6.79	10.67	15.14	6.65	13.19	3.73	13.43	16.36
1972: II	0.79	4.29	9.01	6.81	10.57	15.09	6.68	13.56	3.73	13.36	16.12
1972: III	0.78	4.21	8.89	6.93	10.58	15.35	6.82	13.86	3.59	13.30	15.99
1972: IV	0.77	4.10	8.97	7.13	10.64	15.15	6.77	14.63	3.26	13.22	15.79
1973: I	0.78	4.06	9.04	7.30	10.52	14.86	6.75	14.72	3.34	13.54	15.25
1973: II	0.79	4.24	9.04	7.37	10.44	14.68	6.89	14.73	3.19	13.55	14.95
1973: III	0.80	4.35	9.11	7.40	10.56	14.56	6.92	14.56	3.33	13.49	14.89
1973: IV	0.89	4.28	9.09	7.42	10.49	14.36	7.15	13.48	3.53	13.53	15.04
1974: I	0.82	3.87	9.11	7.15	10.66	14.45	7.25	13.29	3.98	13.91	15.26
1974: II	0.73	3.91	9.25	6.97	10.76	14.59	7.34	13.22	3.89	13.92	15.29
1974: III	0.70	3.90	9.26	6.72	10.37	15.03	7.30	12.76	4.09	13.88	15.50
1974: IV	0.70	4.11	9.21	7.00	10.03	15.44	6.93	12.75	3.49	14.07	15.52
1975: I	0.74	3.82	9.36	7.07	10.63	15.25	6.40	12.77	3.58	14.44	16.06
1975: II	0.70	3.84	9.33	6.84	10.84	15.15	6.74	12.97	3.76	14.22	16.00
1975: III	0.69	3.80	9.28	7.01	10.73	15.02	7.04	12.54	3.84	13.99	15.71
1975: IV	0.67	3.79	9.55	7.00	10.64	15.13	7.18	12.94	4.51	14.03	15.63
1976: I	0.72	3.77	8.97	6.97	10.56	15.58	7.26	12.96	4.81	13.57	15.17
1976: II	0.69	3.81	9.07	6.89	10.45	15.72	6.98	12.73	4.83	13.66	15.01
1976: III	0.69	3.81	9.00	6.90	10.53	16.16	6.85	12.69	4.95	13.78	14.72
1976: IV	0.64	4.01	8.91	6.89	10.38	16.31	6.74	12.99	4.71	13.81	14.70
1977: I	0.63	4.00	8.59	6.81	10.50	16.98	6.81	12.92	4.56	13.50	14.17
1977: II	0.63	4.14	8.70	7.08	10.51	17.22	6.97	12.91	4.53	13.40	13.78
1977: III	0.62	4.08	8.73	7.16	10.61	17.35	6.93	12.90	4.09	13.59	13.69
1977: IV	0.57	4.18	8.77	6.75	10.45	18.02	6.94	12.89	4.31	13.75	13.75
1978: I	0.48	3.96	8.80	6.80	10.57	17.84	6.92	13.15	4.14	13.63	13.70
1978: II	0.55	4.22	8.85	6.87	10.38	18.01	6.91	13.25	4.38	13.56	13.29
1978: III	0.53	4.23	8.80	7.04	10.19	18.61	6.83	13.27	4.16	13.57	12.57
1978: IV	0.55	4.16	8.69	6.97	10.17	18.96	6.87	14.05	4.55	13.87	12.64
1979: I	0.55	4.06	8.82	6.64	10.00	18.00	6.92	14.03	4.75	14.02	12.54
1979: II	0.56	4.09	8.59	6.75	10.02	17.83	6.90	13.65	5.07	14.29	12.61
1979: III	0.56	4.00	8.82	6.72	10.15	17.88	6.80	13.42	5.18	14.06	12.46
1979: IV	0.54	3.87	8.73	6.71	10.01	18.00	6.80	13.63	6.25	14.17	12.22
1980: I	0.57	3.67	8.84	6.54	9.63	17.56	7.04	13.01	6.49	14.10	12.52
1980: II	0.59	3.64	8.83	6.79	10.00	17.29	6.68	13.31	6.52	13.93	12.36
1980: III	0.55	3.54	9.10	6.39	9.96	17.61	6.56	13.66	6.63	13.88	12.39
1980: IV	0.57	3.60	8.76	6.56	9.66	17.75	6.51	14.21	5.53	13.96	12.39
1981: I	0.51	3.65	9.04	6.63	9.70	17.66	6.81	14.39	5.75	14.01	12.40
1981: II	0.52	3.69	8.98	6.45	9.80	17.33	6.73	14.29	5.75	14.07	12.43
1981: III	0.51	3.52	9.07	6.59	9.85	17.20	6.77	14.29	6.15	14.07	12.58
1981: IV	0.52	3.38	9.13	6.57	9.53	17.16	6.61	14.29	6.15	14.07	12.58

Table 5-3. Percentage Composition of Quarterly Gross State Product by Industry for Michigan: 1958–1981

Date	Mining	Construction	Transportation, Communication, & Public Utilities	Wholesale Trade	Retail Trade	Finance, Insurance, & Real Estate	Nondurable Manufacturing	Durable Manufacturing	Agriculture	Services	Government
1958:I	0.79	6.69	5.47	4.56	10.36	12.30	6.73	27.62	2.55	10.18	12.74
1958:II	0.75	6.26	5.64	4.60	10.34	12.93	7.35	26.45	2.67	10.04	12.96
1958:III	0.78	5.71	5.60	4.63	10.06	12.65	7.33	29.30	2.56	9.46	11.91
1958:IV	0.87	5.53	5.70	4.73	10.23	12.92	7.64	28.67	2.53	9.20	11.99
1959:I	0.81	5.41	5.77	4.66	9.91	12.29	7.47	30.77	2.34	8.98	11.59
1959:II	0.84	5.73	5.69	4.58	9.64	11.95	7.33	32.16	2.36	8.83	10.89
1959:III	0.72	5.77	5.63	4.73	9.89	12.63	7.50	30.57	2.19	9.17	11.20
1959:IV	0.75	5.66	5.82	4.81	10.05	12.87	7.43	29.57	2.37	9.33	11.35
1960:I	0.86	5.43	5.92	4.70	9.58	12.47	7.43	31.13	2.28	9.08	11.12
1960:II	0.96	5.44	6.05	4.84	9.94	12.84	7.45	29.22	2.47	9.27	11.52
1960:III	0.99	5.70	6.07	4.88	9.74	13.02	7.48	28.47	2.47	9.30	11.87
1960:IV	1.01	5.50	6.20	4.96	9.70	13.36	7.46	27.50	2.67	9.40	12.23
1961:I	0.96	5.62	6.27	5.09	9.87	14.03	7.47	25.55	2.70	9.84	12.60
1961:II	0.90	5.57	6.21	5.01	9.57	13.65	7.66	26.64	2.74	9.50	12.56
1961:III	0.92	5.41	6.24	5.03	9.44	13.53	7.49	27.23	2.89	9.44	12.38
1961:IV	0.90	5.16	6.15	4.97	9.24	13.25	7.34	28.83	2.84	9.31	12.01
1962:I	0.83	4.87	6.20	4.95	9.26	13.01	7.33	29.97	2.65	9.09	11.85
1962:II	0.83	4.79	6.05	4.99	9.15	13.06	7.49	30.51	2.41	9.14	11.73
1962:III	0.83	4.82	6.13	4.93	8.98	12.98	7.28	31.00	2.28	9.18	11.60
1962:IV	0.82	4.80	5.98	4.89	8.73	12.85	7.33	31.65	2.29	9.09	11.59
1963:I	0.77	4.76	5.98	5.00	9.53	11.72	7.25	30.96	2.42	9.98	11.63
1963:II	0.80	5.02	5.96	4.99	9.34	11.55	7.01	31.44	2.46	9.93	11.48
1963:III	0.80	5.19	5.94	4.99	9.19	11.29	6.97	31.74	2.55	9.92	11.42
1963:IV	0.79	5.10	5.91	4.96	9.25	11.10	6.72	32.73	2.50	9.83	11.12
1964:I	0.78	5.20	5.89	4.98	9.17	11.03	6.83	32.79	2.44	9.75	11.13
1964:II	0.80	5.15	5.95	5.02	9.22	10.98	6.86	32.70	2.51	9.81	11.00
1964:III	0.78	5.17	5.86	5.08	9.36	10.74	6.73	33.14	2.48	9.81	10.86
1964:IV	0.81	5.48	5.88	5.21	9.55	11.19	6.78	31.75	2.31	10.09	10.95
1965:I	0.75	5.34	5.86	5.23	9.13	10.52	6.66	34.72	2.14	9.37	10.28
1965:II	0.73	5.47	5.84	5.18	9.11	10.63	6.52	34.80	2.03	9.54	10.15
1965:III	0.75	5.30	5.91	5.21	9.36	10.77	6.54	34.33	1.88	9.71	10.24
1965:IV	0.75	5.41	5.81	5.11	9.31	10.60	6.40	35.34	1.75	9.66	9.86
1966:I	0.77	5.45	6.05	5.31	9.26	10.87	6.33	34.18	2.02	9.57	10.18
1966:II	0.79	5.40	6.02	5.34	9.26	10.99	6.36	33.96	1.98	9.67	10.24
1966:III	0.76	5.34	6.14	5.37	9.27	11.00	6.28	33.58	2.01	9.82	10.42
1966:IV	0.76	4.95	6.10	5.42	9.26	11.04	6.31	33.83	1.88	9.82	10.63
1967:I	0.73	5.32	6.28	5.60	9.54	11.60	6.55	31.04	1.83	10.02	11.00
1967:II	0.75	5.44	6.35	5.63	9.68	11.57	6.47	31.04	1.77	10.18	11.13
1967:III	0.72	5.23	6.29	5.71	9.57	11.60	6.41	31.24	1.80	10.13	11.30
1967:IV	0.76	5.09	6.40	5.75	9.55	11.61	6.53	30.60	1.86	10.23	11.66
1968:I	0.69	5.12	6.29	5.72	9.58	11.24	6.24	31.97	1.78	10.01	11.38
1968:II	0.70	4.45	6.32	5.78	9.53	11.20	6.28	32.62	1.83	9.92	11.34
1968:III	0.71	4.75	6.52	5.85	9.57	11.15	6.49	31.93	1.82	9.94	11.28
1968:IV	0.73	5.00	6.53	5.84	9.31	10.77	6.45	32.67	1.83	9.73	11.28
1969:I	0.67	5.26	6.73	5.92	9.78	11.22	6.61	31.11	1.95	10.06	11.14
1969:II	0.69	5.17	6.74	5.96	9.86	11.08	6.61	30.96	1.93	10.27	10.73

Quarter											
1969: III	0.74	5.26	6.75	6.03	9.67	10.86	6.60	31.05	1.84	10.24	10.97
1969: IV	0.72	4.97	6.88	6.16	9.74	10.83	6.83	30.54	1.86	10.54	10.94
1970: I	0.73	4.89	6.94	6.37	9.91	10.97	6.84	29.29	1.93	10.69	11.44
1970: II	0.72	4.76	7.07	6.28	9.85	10.93	6.88	29.84	1.83	10.57	11.29
1970: III	0.73	4.52	7.13	6.61	9.93	11.17	6.93	29.13	1.86	11.00	11.43
1970: IV	0.75	4.78	7.35	6.80	10.33	12.18	7.07	25.66	1.99	10.16	12.09
1971: I	0.64	4.45	7.00	6.63	9.83	10.89	6.83	30.51	1.85	10.22	11.19
1971: II	0.66	4.58	7.00	6.61	9.98	11.03	6.99	30.06	1.85	10.13	11.02
1971: III	0.65	4.58	6.97	6.77	10.13	11.38	6.91	29.68	1.69	10.02	11.13
1971: IV	0.71	4.48	6.74	6.79	9.96	11.11	6.89	30.45	1.85	10.20	11.00
1972: I	0.71	4.53	6.94	6.83	10.00	10.57	7.09	30.43	1.80	10.02	10.89
1972: II	0.69	4.56	6.93	6.71	9.78	10.45	6.96	31.40	1.94	10.07	10.55
1972: III	0.70	4.45	7.00	6.77	9.83	10.45	7.14	31.33	1.80	9.76	10.44
1972: IV	0.68	4.36	6.93	6.77	9.76	10.15	7.15	32.36	1.78	10.09	10.29
1973: I	0.70	4.33	7.06	6.80	9.74	9.96	7.01	32.68	1.66	10.04	9.97
1973: II	0.70	4.20	6.99	6.79	9.59	9.89	6.95	33.39	1.46	10.12	10.00
1973: III	0.74	4.13	7.12	6.74	9.70	9.84	6.97	33.14	1.44	10.13	9.97
1973: IV	0.71	4.03	7.25	6.87	9.74	9.84	7.09	32.76	1.55	10.99	9.93
1974: I	0.86	4.10	7.42	6.95	10.47	10.55	7.11	28.86	1.86	11.11	10.91
1974: II	0.78	4.15	7.62	6.81	10.53	10.83	7.22	28.20	1.80	11.11	11.00
1974: III	0.70	4.07	7.44	6.45	10.02	10.97	7.09	28.90	2.04	11.33	11.13
1974: IV	0.69	3.77	7.63	6.94	9.72	11.68	6.76	28.13	2.02	11.93	11.04
1975: I	0.76	3.57	7.49	6.72	10.73	12.11	6.90	26.15	1.60	11.71	11.84
1975: II	0.69	3.34	7.64	6.43	10.74	11.95	7.19	26.44	1.76	11.29	11.88
1975: III	0.70	3.33	7.71	6.37	10.41	11.32	7.38	28.21	1.85	11.30	11.43
1975: IV	0.68	3.23	7.91	6.26	10.23	11.44	7.52	28.11	1.78	10.86	11.44
1976: I	0.62	3.38	7.55	6.08	10.07	11.23	7.51	30.07	1.89	10.87	10.89
1976: II	0.59	3.39	7.49	5.79	9.98	11.25	7.36	30.87	1.74	10.76	10.69
1976: III	0.64	3.45	7.55	5.80	10.07	11.54	7.38	30.53	1.60	10.97	10.63
1976: IV	0.58	3.42	7.40	5.72	9.86	11.52	7.11	31.43	1.61	10.72	10.55
1977: I	0.58	3.73	7.26	5.69	10.01	11.54	7.25	31.26	1.80	10.65	10.23
1977: II	0.49	3.72	7.17	5.96	9.87	11.56	7.29	31.19	1.94	10.67	10.02
1977: III	0.45	3.76	7.33	6.09	9.95	11.59	7.16	31.35	1.99	10.97	9.71
1977: IV	0.47	3.94	7.32	5.63	9.87	11.75	7.20	31.61	2.11	10.85	9.78
1978: I	0.49	3.89	7.38	5.88	10.05	11.95	7.33	30.28	2.00	10.85	9.94
1978: II	0.49	3.90	7.50	6.00	9.91	11.73	7.40	30.73	1.82	10.64	9.67
1978: III	0.51	3.84	7.46	6.13	9.66	12.06	7.35	30.72	1.91	10.71	9.60
1978: IV	0.50	3.72	7.43	6.06	9.53	11.56	7.51	31.11	1.79	10.98	9.51
1979: I	0.50	3.64	7.48	5.83	9.29	11.54	7.42	32.24	1.78	11.46	9.48
1979: II	0.53	3.66	7.51	6.05	9.46	11.85	7.45	30.97	2.12	11.85	9.78
1979: III	0.52	3.61	7.53	6.20	9.75	11.93	7.42	29.11	2.38	11.90	10.18
1979: IV	0.53	3.45	7.78	6.24	9.78	11.94	7.46	28.14	2.71	12.45	10.31
1980: I	0.53	3.08	7.50	5.90	9.47	12.56	7.64	28.66	2.90	12.41	10.30
1980: II	0.44	2.86	7.93	6.24	9.95	12.64	7.37	25.81	3.03	11.88	11.18
1980: III	0.47	2.92	8.25	5.84	10.00	12.21	7.17	26.35	3.06	11.75	11.00
1980: IV	0.40	2.99	7.99	5.81	9.59	11.73	7.07	28.44	2.86	11.63	10.56
1981: I	0.40	2.80	7.74	5.76	9.49	11.45	7.27	29.46	2.90	11.98	10.74
1981: II	0.40	2.65	7.46	5.69	9.39	11.38	7.23	30.31	3.08	12.34	11.02
1981: III	0.40	2.64	7.63	5.82	9.49	11.64	7.44	29.11	3.53		11.37
1981: IV			7.87	5.96	9.37		7.14	27.74			

Table 5-4.   Quarterly Values for the Regional Business Cycle Index for Selected
States: 1958–1981

Date	Texas	Michigan	California
1958: I	.083	.207	.149
1958: II	.083	.204	.151
1958: III	.084	.214	.153
1958: IV	.086	.214	.156
1959: I	.087	.221	.154
1959: II	.089	.225	.156
1959: III	.087	.220	.152
1959: IV	.086	.217	.151
1960: I	.089	.222	.155
1960: II	.088	.216	.153
1960: III	.086	.213	.152
1960: IV	.086	.210	.148
1961: I	.084	.203	.155
1961: II	.084	.207	.152
1961: III	.085	.209	.153
1961: IV	.087	.213	.153
1962: I	.086	.217	.155
1962: II	.087	.219	.155
1962: III	.087	.220	.155
1962: IV	.087	.222	.154
1963: I	.087	.221	.155
1963: II	.088	.222	.156
1963: III	.089	.223	.156
1963: IV	.090	.225	.155
1964: I	.091	.226	.155
1964: II	.091	.226	.154
1964: III	.092	.228	.154
1964: IV	.091	.223	.152
1965: I	.092	.234	.154
1965: II	.092	.233	.154
1965: III	.093	.232	.154
1965: IV	.093	.235	.155
1966: I	.093	.231	.157
1966: II	.094	.230	.158
1966: III	.094	.229	.158
1966: IV	.095	.230	.158
1967: I	.093	.223	.159
1967: II	.093	.222	.159
1967: III	.092	.222	.158
1967: IV	.093	.220	.158

Table 5-4.   (Cont.)

Date	Texas	Michigan	California
1968: I	.094	.224	.158
1968: II	.095	.226	.159
1968: III	.095	.225	.159
1968: IV	.095	.228	.159
1969: I	.095	.225	.160
1969: II	.096	.224	.160
1969: III	.097	.224	.160
1969: IV	.096	.224	.159
1970: I	.096	.220	.158
1970: II	.095	.222	.157
1970: III	.095	.220	.156
1970: IV	.094	.209	.153
1971: I	.096	.225	.158
1971: II	.096	.224	.158
1971: III	.096	.222	.158
1971: IV	.095	.224	.159
1972: I	.097	.226	.160
1972: II	.098	.229	.161
1972: III	.099	.230	.162
1972: IV	.100	.233	.164
1973: I	.099	.234	.167
1973: II	.099	.236	.168
1973: III	.099	.236	.169
1973: IV	.100	.236	.168
1974: I	.099	.222	.163
1974: II	.100	.220	.163
1974: III	.100	.221	.162
1974: IV	.100	.217	.159
1975: I	.099	.210	.158
1975: II	.100	.212	.159
1975: III	.101	.219	.161
1975: IV	.101	.219	.159
1976: I	.100	.225	.161
1976: II	.100	.227	.160
1976: III	.100	.226	.160
1976: IV	.099	.227	.159
1977: I	.100	.227	.161
1977: II	.100	.228	.163
1977: III	.101	.229	.163
1977: IV	.102	.229	.163
1978: I	.102	.225	.163

Table 5-4. (Cont.)

Date	Texas	Michigan	California
1978: II	.102	.228	.164
1978: III	.103	.227	.165
1978: IV	.103	.229	.166
1979: I	.104	.232	.167
1979: II	.103	.228	.167
1979: III	.103	.222	.165
1979: IV	.102	.219	.164
1980: I	.103	.220	.164
1980: II	.102	.210	.160
1980: III	.103	.211	.161
1980: IV	.104	.217	.162
1981: I	.106	.221	.166
1981: II	.106	.223	.166
1981: III	.106	.220	.166
1981: IV	.106	.214	.165

Table 5-5.   Quarterly Projections for the Texas Business Cycle Index: 1982–1990

Date	Business Cycle Index
1982: I	.1047
1982: II	.1042
1982: III	.1051
1982: IV	.1051
1983: I	.1052
1983: II	.1052
1983: III	.1051
1983: IV	.1051
1984: I	.1050
1984: II	.1049
1984: III	.1050
1984: IV	.1049
1985: I	.1049
1985: II	.1049
1985: III	.1048
1985: IV	.1049
1986: I	.1047
1986: II	.1047
1986: III	.1047
1986: IV	.1047
1987: I	.1046
1987: II	.1046
1987: III	.1046
1987: IV	.1046
1988: I	.1046
1988: II	.1046
1988: III	.1046
1988: IV	.1046
1989: I	.1046
1989: II	.1046
1989: III	.1046
1989: IV	.1047
1990: I	.1047
1990: II	.1046
1990: III	.1046
1990: IV	.1046

precise empirical content to notions such as the sensitivity of Michigan to economic fluctuations in comparison with the relative insulation of Texas. Finally, a pooled cross-section and time series analysis would provide a detailed assessment of the evolution of cyclical patterns across regions on a temporal basis. This information would serve to greatly enhance overall understanding of the recent economic history and to improve the ability to identify and forecast regional migrations. In summary, it is reasonable to assert that (1) an index of the cyclical sensitivity of a subnational economy is potentially a most useful tool for regional analysis and planning and (2) the derivation (and projection) of such a measure for all regions of the United States would provide a significant enhancement to the current system of knowledge for policy formulation and evaluation.

Notes

[1] Systematic analysis of business cycles may be traced at least as far as the work of Clement Juglar in the mid-nineteenth century, with "exogenous" cycle theories dating much earlier. Recent work in the area of business cycle analysis is typified by Lucas (1981).

[2] A comprehensive summary of many existing models and approaches is given in Knapp, Fields, and Jerome (1977).

[3] In fact, an earlier Commerce Department study found Michigan to be the state most sensitive to national cycles. The measure utilized in that study, however, is not as broad and applicable as the index proposed herein. See Bretzfelder (1973).

[4] A complete and unified set of these accounts for the United States is presently under development by the Center for the Advancement of Economic Analysis under the general direction of the authors.

[5] This approach follows the general framework of a value-added computational process.

[6] Negligible indirect business taxes and capital consumption allowances sometimes occur due to the inclusion of government enterprises in this category.

[7] In the case of a simple first-differenced trend process, of course, the detrended variables would not be "massaged" prior to estimation for temporal purposes.

[8] For more information on this predictive process, see Perryman (1983).

References

Andersen, L., and Jordan, J. L. 1968. Monetary and fiscal actions: a test of their relative importance in economic stabilization. *Federal Reserve Bank of St. Louis Review* 50.

Box, G. E. P., and Jenkins, G. M. 1976. *Time Series Analysis: Forecasting and Control*. San Francisco: Holden Day.

Bretzfelder, R. B. 1973. Sensitivity of state and regional income to national business cycles. *Survey of Current Business* 53:22.

Glickman, N. J. 1977. *Econometric Analysis of Regional Systems: Explorations in Model Building and Policy Analysis*. New York: Academic Press.

Kendrick, J. W., and Jaycox, C. M. 1965. The concept and estimation of gross state product *Southern Economic Journal* 32:144–159.

Knapp, J. L., Fields, T. W., and Jerome, R. T. 1977. *A Survey of State and Regional Econometric Models*. Charlottesville: Tayloe Murphy Institute.

L'Esperance, W. L., Nestel, G., and Fromm, D. 1969. Gross state product and an econometric model of a state. *Journal of the American Statistical Association* 64:787–807.

Lucas, R. E. 1981. *Studies in Business-Cycle Theory*. Cambridge: MIT Press.

Niemi, A. W. 1972. A reexamination of the Kendrick-Jaycox method of estimating gross state product. *Review of Regional Studies* 2:14–22.

Perryman, M. R. 1980. The supply side of regional econometric models. *Modeling and Simulation* 11:1309–1316.

Perryman, M. R. 1981a. A quarterly temporal index for measuring the cyclical sensitivity of a regional economy: Theory and an application to the Texas economy. Conference of the Western Economic Association, San Francisco, California.

Perryman, M. R. 1981b. Toward a comprehensive index of cyclical patterns and interrelationships within the U.S. economy. Conference of the Atlantic Economic Society, New York.

Perryman, M. R. 1982. On the measurement of regional business activity. *Atlantic Economic Journal* 10:61.

Perryman, M. R. 1983. Forecasting cyclical patterns in regional economies: An integrated econometric modeling approach. *Modeling and Simulation* 14:763–768.

Weber, R. E. 1979. Estimating quarterly gross state product. *Business Economics* 14:38–43.

6 A METHOD FOR ANALYZING THE CHANGING IMPACT OF THE BUSINESS CYCLE ON REGIONAL ECONOMIES

Jerald R. Barnard
and James E. Kennedy

The views expressed in this paper are solely those of the authors and do not reflect the views of the Federal Reserve Board.

I. Introduction

During the last ten years, the sensitivity ranking of U.S. regions and states to the U.S. business cycle has changed markedly (Bretzfelder, 1973; Bretzfelder and Friedenberg, 1980; Bretzfelder and Brown, 1982). For example, the New England and Southeast regions have become less sensitive to fluctuations in U.S. business activity. In contrast, the Plains region has become much more sensitive to the U.S. business cycle.

For regional analysts and policy makers such changes present some difficulties. In particular, the large structural models typically employed as analytical tools by regional analysts are neither a reliable nor a convenient framework within which to study structural change. The models are unreliable for this task due to the plethora of identifying restrictions built into them, as well as the simple and convenient specification of the equations.[1] This is not to say that such models are not useful for forecasting employment and income in a given state or region. Indeed, many analysts use such models in preparing forecasts for state and regional economies. The restrictions imposed on such models, however, limit their usefulness in the task of structural analysis. Furthermore, the large number of equations typically included in such models make them unwieldy vehicles within which to study structural change.

In this paper we discuss and apply a method that can be used to identify general changes in the relationship between a regional economy and the U.S. business cycle. The method involves specifying a vector-autoregressive (VAR) model of the regional economy. This model includes variables from both the regional (or state) and U.S. economies. The VAR model is a reduced-form model, where each of the variables in the model is explained by its own past, and by past realizations of all of the other variables in the model. In the application of this technique presented below, we examine the hypothesis that the Iowa economy has become more sensitive to the U.S. business cycle during recent years. The Iowa economy is represented by nonagricultural employment in Iowa, and the U.S. economy by the index of industrial production and the ninety-day Treasury bill rate.

The VAR model is much less detailed than the large-scale model we use to forecast employment and income in Iowa. The VAR includes only one variable from the Iowa economy (we have experimented with VARs that included up to five variables from the Iowa economy), whereas about fifty Iowa variables are included as nonidentities in the forecasting model. Through the use of submodels, the VAR could be expanded to offer the disaggregated detail of the structural model. However, this is not necessary for the purpose at hand, which is to demonstrate how the hypothesis of a change in the relationship between a regional economy (in this case, the Iowa economy) and the U.S. economy can be analyzed in a reduced-form model.

In section II, the properties and specification of the model are discussed. The results of tests for Granger causality from the U.S. variables to Iowa employment for the full sample period (1947:III to 1983:IV) are presented. Then the sample is split between 1968 and 1969, and the results of tests for Granger causality conducted on data from the two subperiods are compared in order to provide a preliminary indication as to whether or not either the interest rate or the index of industrial production is more significant in the tests on data from the latter part of the sample. Second, the null hypothesis that the U.S. economy (as represented by the interest rate and the index of industrial production) is exogenous to the Iowa economy (as represented by Iowa employment) is tested. Third, tests for the appropriate lag length of the VAR are performed. Fourth, two different types of tests are used in order to gauge the stability of the coefficients of the Iowa employment equation for a variety of different splits in the sample. These tests are included here, in part, because they are in the vein of standard hypothesis testing. However, these test results indicate only whether or not the null hypothesis of stable coefficients is acceptable. If the null hypothesis is rejected, the usual tests for stable coefficients provide little information as to the nature of whatever changes have occurred.

In section III, we begin by discussing how the estimated VAR is transformed to its moving average (MA) representation. The MA form of the model is used in deriving the decomposition of forecast error variance and impulse response functions for Iowa employment. This technique is not new. Sims (1980a) used it in comparing the coherence of a number of time series in interwar and postwar business cycles. Sims (1980b) also used this technique in a study of postwar business cycles. Litterman (1979) and Litterman and Weiss (1985) discussed the technical features of this method and applied it in studies using macroeconomic time series data. The VAR model is estimated for the full sample, as well as for the two subperiods given by a split in the sample between 1968 and 1969. The conjecture of a change in the relationship between Iowa employment and the two U.S. variables is examined by comparing the decomposition of variance and impulse response functions of Iowa employment for the subperiods.

The results presented in section III demonstrate the usefulness of this technique in identifying the nature of changes that have occurred between state and regional economies and the U.S. economy. Rather than simply providing a basis for rejecting or failing to reject the hypothesis of stable coefficients, the decomposition of variance and impulse response functions provides information that is useful in evaluating the nature of changes that have occurred in the relationship between Iowa employment and the U.S. business cycle.

II. The Model

The following model was postulated in order to examine the relationship between the Iowa economy and the U.S. economy:

$$EP_t = A(L)EP_{t-1} + B(L)Z_{t-1} + e_{1t} \qquad (6.1a)$$

$$Z_t = D(L)Z_{t-1} + e_{2t} \qquad (6.1b)$$

where EP denotes nonagricultural employment in Iowa; Z is a vector of variables of U.S. economic activity; $A(L)$, $B(L)$, and $D(L)$, are polynomial matrices defined on the lag operator L (L is defined by the following expression: $Z_{t-i} = L^i Z_t$); and e_1 and e_2 are stochastic processes with the following properties: (i) $E(e_{jt}e_{jt-i}) = 0, j = 1,2$ and $i \neq 0$; and (ii) $E(e_{1t}e_{2t-i}) = 0, i \neq 0$. That is, e_1 and e_2 are white-noise error processes that may only be correlated contemporaneously with each other. The model assumes that Z is exogenous to EP. The validity of this assumption is tested below.

In the results reported below, Z includes only two variables: the ninety-day Treasury bill rate (IN) and the total index of industrial production (IP). These two variables include information pertaining to both real and nominal fluctuations in U.S. economic activity. We experimented with larger models that included other variables from the U.S. economy—the money supply, manufacturers' shipments, personal income, and real GNP. The results reported below were essentially the same as those obtained from models that included various combinations of these additional variables.[2]

Before proceeding, it should be noted that the sample was split between 1968 and 1969 to examine the stability of the coefficients of the EP equation given as equation 6.1a. Although our prior belief is that the relationship between the Iowa and U.S. economy changed, for the most part, after the early 1970s, we chose to work with the 1968/1969 split in order to increase the number of observations in the latter part of the sample.

The data used in this analysis are quarterly and span the period from 1947:III to 1983:IV. All of the series were deseasonalized, lagged, and detrended prior to estimation. The data series are discussed in chapter appendix A. As is noted in appendix A, the main conclusions of this paper held for a variety of alternative representations of the variables in the estimation of the VAR models.

We now turn to the results used in specifying the empirical model. First, the results of tests for Granger causality from IN and IP to EP are reported. Second, the exogeneity assumption is tested. Third, tests are performed to establish the appropriate number of lags to use in estimating equations 6.1. Fourth, before estimating the three-equation model, the results of tests for the stability of the coefficients of the EP equation are discussed.

In table 6-1 the results of tests for Granger causality from IN and IP to EP are reported.[3] The results reported in the first two rows of table 6-1 indicate that both IN and IP Granger-cause EP when applied to data from 1949 to 1983. When the sample is split between 1968 and 1969, the results suggest that the influence both IN and IP have on EP is greater in the latter part of the sample. In particular, at the conventional critical level (CL) of 0.05, IN is not significant in the test on data from the first subperiod, but the null hypothesis that IN does not Granger-cause EP is rejected in the second subperiod. IP is highly significant in the tests on data from both of the

Table 6-1. Results of Tests for Granger Causality

Null Hypothesis	1949–1983	1949–1968	1969–1983
H_0: $IN \nrightarrow EP$	$F(6,127) = 5.14(0.00)$	$F(6,67) = 1.95(0.09)$	$F(6,47) = 3.15(0.01)$
H_0: $IP \nrightarrow EP$	$F(6,127) = 9.05(0.00)$	$F(6,67) = 3.77(0.00)$	$F(6,47) = 6.27(0.00)$
H_0: $IN \nrightarrow (EP/IP)$	$F(6,121) = 4.75(0.00)$	$F(6,61) = 2.06(0.07)$	$F(7,41) = 3.02(0.02)$
H_0: $IN \nrightarrow (EP/IN)$	$F(6,121) = 8.45(0.00)$	$F(6,61) = 3.75(0.00)$	$F(6,41) = 5.81(0.00)$
H_0: $(IN,IP) \nrightarrow EP$	$F(12,121) = 7.7(0.00)$	$F(12,61) = 3.1(0.00)$	$F(12,41) = 5.4(0.00)$

Note: The symbol $\nrightarrow$ denotes "does not Granger-cause." Six lags of each variable were used in both the bivariate and trivariate tests. The test in row 1, for example, was conducted by regressing EP on six lags of its own past as well as six lagged values of IN. The null hypothesis $IN \nrightarrow EP$ is equivalent to the statement "none of the coefficients on lagged IN are significantly different from zero." That is, past IN is not significant in explaining the component of EP that cannot be explained on the basis of its own past. The data span the interval from 1947: III to 1983: IV, and as six lags were used in the tests reported above, data from 1947: III to 1948: IV were used as initial values for the series. The marginal significance levels of the test statistics are reported in parentheses.

Table 6-2. Tests for Exogeneity of *IN* and *IP*

	1949–1983	1949–1968	1969–1983
H_0: $EP \nrightarrow IN$	$F(6,127) = 1.02(0.42)$	$F(6,67) = 1.83(0.11)$	$F(6,47) = 1.58(0.18)$
H_0: $EP \nrightarrow IP$	$F(6,127) = 1.59(0.16)$	$F(6,67) = 1.74(0.13)$	$F(6,47) = 1.55(0.18)$
H_0: $EP \nrightarrow (IN, IP)$	$\chi^2(12) = 7.27(0.89)$	$\chi^2(12) = 14.85(0.25)$	$\chi^2(12) = 15.60(0.21)$

Note: The symbol $\nrightarrow$ denotes "does not Granger-cause." All of the tests were conducted by regressing on a constant term and six lags of each variable. The test of the null hypothesis $EP \nrightarrow (IN, IP)$ was conducted by regressing both IN and IP on lagged IN and IP, and then lagged EP was added to each equation. The test statistics are likelihood ratio tests computed as follows: $L = (T - K) \cdot \log_e (\det \Sigma_R / \det \Sigma_u)$, where L is the test statistic, T is the sample size, K is the number of parameters estimated in each equation of the unrestricted system, and Σ_R and Σ_u are the variance-covariance matrices of the restricted and unrestricted systems, respectively.

Table 6-3. Tests for Lag Length of the System

	1949–1983	1949–1968	1969–1983
4 lags vs. 6 lags	$\chi^2(14) = 76.60(0.00)$	$\chi^2(14) = 43.28(0.00)$	$\chi^2(14) = 36.59(0.00)$
6 lags vs. 8 lags	$\chi^2(14) = 10.90(0.69)$	$\chi^2(14) = 16.70(0.27)$	$\chi^2(14) = 5.37(0.98)$

Note: The first row tests a four-lag model against a six-lag model, and the second row tests a six-lag model against an eight-lag model. Exogeneity of (IN, IP) to EP is assumed in the three-equation system. The test statistics are likelihood ratio tests of the restricted versus the unrestricted system, computed as discussed in the footnote for table 6-2.

subperiods, although the marginal significance level (MSL) of the test statistic from data in the second subperiod is much lower than the one obtained from the first subperiod.[4]

The results of tests of the null hypothesis that *IN* does not Granger-cause *EP* given past *EP* and *IP* are reported in row 3 of table 6-1. Similarly, the results of tests of the null hypothesis that *IP* does not Granger-cause *EP* given past *EP* and *IN* are given in row 4. The results of these tests are similar to those reported in the first two rows of table 6-1, as both *IN* and *IP* are more significant in the conditional tests for Granger-causality in the second subperiod (although *IP* is highly significant in all three tests). The results reported in rows 3 and 4 of table 6-1 indicate that (relative to the information set given by *IN*, *IP*, and *EP*) the significant results reported in the bivariate tests are not spurious, in the sense discussed by Hsiao (1979, 1980). That is, the results indicate that in the instances where both *IN* and *IP* are significant in the bivariate tests, each variable contains unique information that helps to explain the component of *EP* that cannot be explained on the basis of past *EP*. The fifth row of table 6-1 contains results of tests of the null hypothesis that past *IN* and *IP*, together, do not Granger-cause *EP*. The hypothesis is rejected in all three tests.

The validity of the exogeneity assumption was evaluated by testing whether or not *EP* Granger-causes *IN* and *IP*. The results of these tests are reported in table 6-2. At a critical level of 0.1, *EP* is not significant in any of the bivariate tests for Granger-causality (reported in the first two rows of table 6-2). Moreover, the null hypothesis that *EP* does not Granger-cause *IN* and *IP* together is rejected (the third row of table 6-2) for all three periods. Thus, the data indicate the exogeneity assumption is reasonable.[5]

Results of tests for the appropriate lag length of the system are reported in table 6-3. The four-lag model is soundly rejected in favor of the six-lag specification. However, the test fails to reject the six-lag model in favor of the eight-lag model for each of the three periods.

As noted in section I, the change in the relationship between *EP* and *Z* is examined by comparing the decomposition of variance and impulse response functions for *EP* between the two subperiods. Before discussing these results, however, the results of tests for the stability of the coefficients of the *EP* equation are discussed. These results provide some information as to when the data suggest that the hypothesis of stable coefficients in the *EP* equation becomes unreasonable.

The results of sample-split tests applied to the *EP* equation are given in table 6-4. These tests (described in more detail below table 6-4) were performed by estimating the *EP* equation in unrestricted form with six lags of *EP*, *IN*, and *IP*, a constant term, and dummy variables that account for all of

Table 6-4.   Sample Split Tests Applied to the *EP* Equation

Sample Split	Test Statistic
74/75	$F(36,85)\ = 1.38(0.12)$
75/76	$F(32,89)\ = 1.49(0.08)$
76/77	$F(28,93)\ = 1.63(0.04)$
77/78	$F(24,97)\ = 1.80(0.02)$
78/79	$F(20,101) = 1.86(0.02)$
79/80	$F(16,105) = 1.82(0.04)$

Note: The sample split tests were conducted by including dummy variables in the *EP* equation to account for all of the variation in the shorter of the two parts (the latter part) of the split sample. In the first test, for example, 36 dummy variables are included in order to explain all of the variation in *EP* from 1975 to 1983. The *F* statistic is then computed for the null hypothesis that none of these dummy variables are significantly different from zero.

Table 6-5.   Sample Split Tests Applied to the Three-Equation Restricted System

Sample Split	Estimation	Test Statistic
49–68/69–83		
	Stability of *IN* and *IP* equations	$\chi^2(26) = 36.70(0.08)$
	Stability of *EP* equation	$\chi^2(19) = 16.97(0.59)$
	Stability of all three equations	$\chi^2(45) = 59.20(0.08)$
49–72/73–83		
	Stability of *IN* and *IP* equations	$\chi^2(26) = 43.55(0.02)$
	Stability of *EP* equation	$\chi^2(19) = 15.75(0.67)$
	Stability of all three equations	$\chi^2(45) = 67.49(0.02)$

Note: The test results were computed by estimating the three-equation system separately for each of the subperiods (the unrestricted model), and then estimating the system for the full sample (the restricted model). The chi-square statistics were computed in the same way as those presented in table 6-3.

the variation within the period being tested, which is always the shorter (or latter) part of the sample. The *EP* equation was then estimated in restricted form without these dummy variables. The restricted form was tested against the unrestricted form using the standard *F* test. The test results indicate that the coefficients of the *EP* equation are not stable for splits in the sample in the mid to late 1970s. For example, at a critical level of 0.05, the null hypothesis is not rejected for either the 1974/1975 or the 1975/1976 sample split. However, the null hypothesis is rejected in all of the tests for sample splits from 1976/1977 to 1979/1980.[6]

Table 6-6. Summary of Results of the Estimated System

	1949–1983	1949–1968	1969–1983
IN equation:	$R^2 = 0.808$	$R^2 = 0.800$	$R^2 = 0.868$
	se = 0.123	se = 0.125	se = 0.115
	$Q(33) = 21.02(0.95)$	$Q(24) = 13.66(0.95)$	$Q(21) = 3.55(0.99)$
IP equation:	$R^2 = 0.917$	$R^2 = 0.928$	$R^2 = 0.917$
	se = 0.019	se = 0.019	se = 0.020
	$Q(33) = 16.89(0.99)$	$Q(24) = 21.92(0.58)$	$Q(21) = 6.01(0.99)$
EP equation:	$R^2 = 0.983$	$R^2 = 0.967$	$R^2 = 0.991$
	se = 0.0071	se = 0.0074	se = 0.0070
	$Q(33) = 36.94(0.29)$	$Q(24) = 19.15(0.74)$	$Q(21) = 23.14(0.34)$

Note: In the above table, se denotes the standard error. The Box-Pierce statistic is denoted by $Q(i)$, where i is the number of residual autocorrelations used in computing the test statistic. Under the null hypothesis that a given series is a white-noise process, $Q(i)$ is distributed as a chi-square random variable with i degrees of freedom.

Tests for the stability of the three-equation model (assuming the exogeneity of Z and a lag length of six) are reported in table 6-5. The system was estimated using generalized least squares with three iterations of the two-step estimation procedure. Some summary statistics of the model estimated on the interval from 1949 to 1983, as well as models estimated for the sample split between 1968 and 1969, are reported in table 6-6. The tests for stability were performed by first estimating the system separately for the two subperiods, providing the residuals of the unrestricted model. Next, the residuals from the restricted model were obtained by estimating the model over the full-sample period. The test for stability is a likelihood ratio test (described in more detail in the footnote to table 6-5), based upon the ratio of the determinant of the variance-covariance matrix from the restricted model to that of the unrestricted model. For the sample split between 1968 and 1969, the chi-square statistic for the null hypothesis that the coefficients of all three equations in the model are stable is equal to 59.2 with MSL of 0.08. For the sample split between 1972 and 1973, the statistic is equal to 67.5 with MSL of 0.02. Both tests provide evidence that the coefficients of the model are not stable over time although the null hypothesis is less tenable for the later split in the sample.

The coefficients of the IN and IP equations appear to be more unstable than those of the EP equation. For the split between 1972 and 1973, for example, the chi-square statistic for the null hypothesis that the coefficients of the *IN* and *IP* equations are stable is 43.55 with MSL of 0.02, whereas the statistic for the EP equation is 15.75 with MSL of 0.67.

These tests provide no evidence that the *EP* equation is unstable for either the 1968/1969 or 1972/1973 splits in the sample. Nor do the *F* tests conducted on the *EP* equation for these sample splits indicate that the sum of squared residuals from the fit of this equation is significantly reduced in the unrestricted fit of the equation. However, as we shall discuss in section III, the decomposition of variance and impulse response functions for *EP* indicate that the relationships between *EP* and the two U.S. variables changed in a pronounced manner between the first and second parts of the sample. This discrepancy may arise because the *F* and chi-square tests are not powerful enough to detect the change in the coefficients of the *EP* equation. Furthermore, our prior conjecture, as was mentioned above, is that the way in which realizations of *IN* and *IP* affect *EP* did not change significantly until the mid 1970s. The more detailed information provided by the decomposition of variance and impulse response may be more capable of detecting this change when the sample is split prematurely (between 1968 and 1969).

III. Decomposition of Variance and Impulse Response Functions

In this section, the decomposition of variance and impulse response functions of the estimated model are discussed. The stability of the coefficients in the model is analyzed by first comparing the decomposition of forecast error variance (FEV) in *EP* given by estimating the model on the first subperiod (1949–1968) to that provided by fitting the model to the second subperiod (1969–1983). The impulse response functions of the system for the two subperiods are then examined. Before discussing these results, details are provided on how the results reported in this section were obtained, as well as how they should be interpreted.

The system of equations 6.1 can be represented as

$$\begin{pmatrix} EP_t \\ Z_t \end{pmatrix} = \begin{pmatrix} A(L) \ B(L) \\ C(L) \ D(L) \end{pmatrix} \begin{pmatrix} EP_{t-1} \\ Z_{t-1} \end{pmatrix} + \begin{pmatrix} e_{1t} \\ e_{2t} \end{pmatrix} \tag{6.2}$$

where $C(L) = 0$ is equivalent to the assumption that Z is exogenous to EP. An alternative representation of the model, with current and past EP and Z moved over to the left-hand side of the equal sign in equation 6.2 is as follows:

$$\begin{pmatrix} EP_t \\ Z_t \end{pmatrix} = \begin{pmatrix} A(L) \, B(L) \\ C(L) \, D(L) \end{pmatrix} \begin{pmatrix} EP_{t-1} \\ Z_{t-1} \end{pmatrix} + \begin{pmatrix} e_{1t} \\ e_{2t} \end{pmatrix} \quad (6.2)$$

where I represents an Identity Matrix. Multiplying both sides of equation 6.3 by the inverse of the coefficient matrix gives us the moving-average or impulse-response representation of the system:

$$\begin{pmatrix} EP_t \\ Z_t \end{pmatrix} = \begin{pmatrix} I - A(L) & -B(L) \\ 0 & I - D(L) \end{pmatrix}^{-1} \begin{pmatrix} e_{1t} \\ e_{2t} \end{pmatrix} \quad (6.4)$$

The moving-average model expresses current EP and Z as a function of current and past realizations of the error processes e_1 and e_2. Specifically, the equations are as follows:

$$EP_t = [I - A(L)]^{-1} e_{1t} + B(L)[I - A(L)]^{-1}[I - B(L)]^{-1} e_{2t} \quad (6.5)$$

$$Z_t = [I - D(L)]^{-1} e_{2t} \quad (6.6)$$

Note that Z_t is expressed only as a function of current and past e_2, which follows from the exogeneity assumption. EP_t is expressed as a function of current and past realizations of both e_1 and e_2. The estimated autoregressive system (given in equation 6.2). That is, the estimated coefficient matrix of the autoregressive form of the model was inverted, providing estimates of the parameters of the moving-average model.

The K-step FEV in a variable can be unambiguously decomposed into components attributable to innovations in each of the variables when the variance-covariance matrix of residuals is transformed to lower diagonal form.[7] This transformation is accomplished by choosing an ordering of the variables and then orthogonalizing the error processes according to this ordering.[8] Different orderings of the variables were used to decompose the forecast error variance in EP, however only the results of the ordering (IN, IP, EP) are reported below. The main conclusions from the discussion that follows are not altered appreciably when different orderings of the variables are assumed.

Table 6-7 provides a summary of the decomposition of variance of the three variables in the model for each of the three periods to which the model was fitted: A: 1949 to 1983; B: 1949 to 1968; and C: 1969 to 1983. A change in the relationship between the U.S. variables and EP is strongly suggested by the reduction in the forty-quarter FEV in EP explained by its own innovations: In the first subperiod (B: 1949 to 1968), innovations to EP explain 48.7 percent of its forty-quarter FEV but only 12.2 percent in the second subperiod (C: 1969 to 1983). This change is largely due to the increase in the percentage of the forty-quarter FEV in EP explained by innovations to IN: 18 percent in the first subperiod, and 63.9 percent in the second subperiod.

Table 6-7. Decomposition of Variance of Iowa Employment

	IN			IP			EP		
Step	A	B	C	A	B	C	A	B	C
1	1.5	2.9	7.4	3.8	5.6	7.6	94.7	91.5	85.0
2	1.3	2.6	8.3	21.3	21.2	37.0	77.4	76.1	54.7
3	2.4	2.7	5.2	30.6	32.8	51.4	67.0	64.6	43.4
4	5.8	4.7	6.1	32.9	37.6	54.8	61.3	57.7	39.1
5	7.7	4.3	7.4	27.3	36.1	44.7	65.0	59.6	47.8
6	13.5	6.9	15.7	22.8	33.8	38.0	63.6	59.3	46.3
7	21.9	12.0	27.9	19.4	31.3	33.0	58.7	56.7	39.0
8	27.7	15.2	36.1	16.8	29.0	30.1	55.5	55.9	33.8
9	30.7	16.0	40.9	14.7	27.4	26.4	54.5	56.7	32.7
10	33.9	16.7	46.3	13.6	27.0	24.2	52.5	56.3	29.5
11	37.2	17.9	51.5	13.3	27.4	23.2	49.5	54.6	25.2
12	39.2	18.5	54.9	13.1	28.2	22.7	47.7	53.4	22.4
13	40.0	18.3	56.7	13.0	29.1	21.8	46.9	52.6	21.5
14	40.9	18.2	58.7	13.1	30.1	21.2	46.0	51.7	20.1
15	41.8	18.3	60.7	13.3	31.0	21.0	44.9	50.8	18.3
16	42.3	18.3	61.9	13.4	31.6	21.1	44.4	50.2	17.0
17	42.4	18.2	62.4	13.5	32.1	21.0	44.1	49.7	16.5
18	42.6	18.1	62.9	13.6	32.6	21.2	43.8	49.3	15.9
19	42.8	18.1	63.5	13.7	32.9	21.5	43.5	48.9	15.0
20	42.9	18.1	63.7	13.8	33.2	21.9	43.2	48.6	14.4
21	42.9	18.1	63.8	13.9	33.4	22.2	43.1	48.4	14.1
22	43.0	18.2	63.8	14.0	33.6	22.5	43.0	48.2	13.7
23	43.1	18.2	63.9	14.1	33.7	22.8	42.8	48.1	13.3
24	43.1	18.2	63.9	14.1	33.7	23.1	42.7	48.1	12.9
25	43.2	18.2	63.9	14.2	33.7	23.4	42.7	48.1	12.7
26	43.2	18.2	63.9	14.2	33.7	23.6	42.6	48.1	12.5
27	43.2	18.1	63.9	14.2	33.7	23.8	42.7	48.2	12.3
28	43.1	18.1	64.0	14.2	33.7	23.9	42.7	48.2	12.2
29	43.1	18.1	64.0	14.2	33.6	24.0	42.7	48.3	12.1
30	43.0	18.1	64.0	14.1	33.6	24.0	42.8	48.4	12.0
31	43.0	18.0	64.0	14.1	33.5	24.1	42.9	48.4	11.9
32	42.9	18.0	64.1	14.1	33.5	24.1	43.0	48.5	11.9
33	42.8	18.0	64.1	14.0	33.5	24.1	43.1	48.5	11.9
34	42.8	18.0	64.1	14.0	33.4	24.1	43.3	48.6	11.8
35	42.7	18.0	64.1	13.9	33.4	24.0	43.3	48.6	11.9
36	42.7	18.0	64.0	13.9	33.4	24.0	43.4	48.6	11.9
37	42.7	18.0	64.0	13.8	33.4	24.0	43.5	48.6	12.0
38	42.7	18.0	64.0	13.8	33.4	24.0	43.5	48.7	12.0
39	42.7	18.0	63.9	13.8	33.4	24.0	43.6	48.7	12.1
40	42.7	18.0	63.9	13.7	33.4	24.0	43.6	48.7	12.2

Note: In the above table, the percentage of the K-step ($K = 1$ to 40) forecast error variance in Iowa employment (EP) explained by each of the variables in the model is given. Under the subheading A, the decomposition of variance for the fit of the model from 1949–1983 is given. Subheadings B and C give the decomposition for fits of the model from the subperiods 1949 to 1968 and 1969 to 1983, respectively.

Innovations to *IP* explain less of the forty-quarter FEV in Iowa employment in the second subperiod than in the first; however, for forecasting horizons between one and nine quarters, innovations to *IP* explain a larger percentage of the FEV in *EP* in the second subperiod. In both subperiods, the largest percentage of the *K*-step FEV in *EP* explained by innovations to *IP* occurs at the four-quarter forecasting horizon: 37.6 percent in the first subperiod and 54.8 percent in the second.

In summary, the decomposition of variance for *EP* indicates that the relationship between employment in Iowa and the U.S. business cycle is markedly different between the two subperiods. In particular, innovations to *IP* and *IN* together explain 36.5 percent more of the forty-step FEV in *EP* in the second subperiod. Innovations to *IP* explain a larger percentage of the FEV in *EP* than innovations to *IN* for forecasting horizons of less than two years. This result holds in both subperiods. For horizons between two and five quarters, the percentage of FEV in *EP* explained by innovations to *IP* is substantially greater in the second subperiod that in the first. For forecasting horizons greater than two years, innovations to *IN* are marginally significant in explaining the FEV in *EP* in the first subperiod. In the second subperiod, however, innovations to *IN* explain over 60 percent of the FEV in *EP* for horizons greater than fourteen quarters.

The impulse response functions of *EP* given in table 6-8 provide more specific information as to the change in the relationship between the two U.S. variables and *EP* between the first and second subperiods, as they allow us to trace out the dynamic responses of the system to innovations in any of the variables. The response functions are dynamic in the sense that the inertial properties of each of the variables are taken into account, as well as the lagged relationships that exist between them. The estimated impulse response functions reported in table 6-8 were computed by feeding innovations of typical size (one orthogonalized standard deviation) into the moving-average representation of the system. For ease of interpretation, each of the response functions was scaled to the standard error of the residual series corresponding to the variable whose response is being mapped. As Litterman (1979) has argued, one must be careful in interpreting the responses since shocks to the variables do not, in general, occur independently. The correlations between the residuals of the estimated models (reported in appendix B) indicate which innovations are most likely to occur together. Because the model is linear, the response of *EP* at time *K*, for example, to simultaneous shocks in *IP* and *IN* is equal to the sum of their separate contributions.

The response of Iowa employment to a one-standard-deviation innovation in the nominal interest rate is much more pronounced in the second

Table 6-8. Scaled Responses of Iowa Employment to Innovations in Each of the Variables in the System

	IN			IP			EP		
Step	A	B	C	A	B	C	A	B	C
1	0.1	0.2	0.3	0.2	0.2	0.3	1.0	1.0	0.9
2	0.1	0.2	0.4	0.7	0.7	1.0	1.0	0.9	0.8
3	−0.2	−0.2	−0.1	0.8	0.8	1.2	0.9	0.7	0.7
4	−0.5	−0.4	−0.4	0.9	1.0	1.1	1.0	0.9	0.7
5	−0.6	−0.3	−0.5	0.7	0.9	0.8	1.5	1.3	1.4
6	−1.0	−0.6	−1.2	0.6	0.7	0.9	1.5	1.1	1.3
7	−1.4	−0.9	−1.8	0.6	0.6	1.0	1.3	1.0	1.0
8	−1.5	−0.9	−1.9	0.6	0.6	1.1	1.5	1.1	1.1
9	−1.5	−0.7	−2.1	0.6	0.6	1.1	1.7	1.1	1.5
10	−1.7	−0.6	−2.6	0.7	0.6	1.3	1.6	0.9	1.4
11	−1.8	−0.7	−2.9	0.8	0.7	1.6	1.4	0.8	1.1
12	−1.8	−0.7	−2.9	0.9	0.8	1.6	1.5	0.8	1.1
13	−1.6	−0.5	−2.9	0.8	0.8	1.5	1.5	1.7	1.4
14	−1.5	−0.4	−3.1	0.8	0.7	1.6	1.3	0.6	1.3
15	−1.5	−0.4	−3.3	0.8	0.7	1.7	1.2	0.5	1.0
16	−1.3	−0.3	−3.1	0.7	0.6	1.7	1.1	0.4	0.9
17	−1.1	−0.2	−2.8	0.7	0.5	1.6	1.1	0.3	1.2
18	−1.0	−0.2	−2.9	0.6	0.5	1.6	0.9	0.2	1.0
19	−1.0	−0.2	−2.9	0.6	0.4	1.7	0.7	0.1	0.7
20	−0.8	−0.2	−2.6	0.5	0.4	1.6	0.7	0.1	0.6
21	−0.6	−0.2	−2.3	0.4	0.3	1.5	0.5	0.0	0.8
22	−0.6	−0.2	−2.2	0.4	0.3	1.5	0.4	−0.1	0.7
23	−0.5	−0.2	−2.2	0.3	0.2	1.5	0.3	−0.1	0.3
24	−0.4	−0.1	−1.9	0.3	0.2	1.4	0.2	−0.1	0.3
25	−0.2	−0.1	−1.6	0.2	0.1	1.2	0.1	−0.2	0.4
26	−0.2	−0.1	−1.6	0.1	0.1	1.2	−0.1	−0.2	0.3
27	−0.1	−0.0	−1.6	0.1	0.1	1.1	−0.2	−0.2	0.0
28	0.0	0.0	−1.3	0.1	0.1	1.0	−0.2	−0.2	−0.0
29	0.1	0.0	−1.1	0.0	0.1	0.8	−0.3	−0.2	0.1
30	0.2	0.0	−1.1	−0.0	0.1	0.7	−0.4	−0.2	0.0
31	0.2	0.0	−1.1	−0.1	0.0	0.7	−0.4	−0.2	−0.2
32	0.3	0.1	−0.8	−0.1	0.0	0.5	−0.4	−0.2	−0.3
33	0.3	0.0	−0.6	−0.1	0.0	0.3	−0.5	−0.2	−0.1
34	0.4	0.0	−0.6	−0.2	−0.0	0.3	−0.5	−0.2	−0.2
35	0.4	0.0	−0.5	−0.2	−0.0	0.3	−0.5	−0.1	−0.4
36	0.5	0.0	−0.3	−0.2	−0.0	0.1	−0.5	−0.1	−0.4
37	0.5	0.0	−0.1	−0.2	−0.0	−0.0	−0.5	−0.1	−0.2
38	0.5	0.0	−0.1	−0.2	−0.0	−0.0	−0.5	−0.1	−0.3
39	0.5	0.0	−0.0	−0.2	−0.0	−0.0	−0.5	−0.1	−0.5
40	0.5	0.0	0.2	−0.2	−0.0	−0.1	−0.5	−0.0	−0.4

Note: The above table gives the scaled responses of *EP* to innovations of typical size (one orthogonalized standard deviation) in *IN*, *IP*, and *EP*, respectively. Under subheading A, the response of *EP* given by the coefficients from the model estimated over 1949–1983 are provided. Under subheadings B and C, the responses from the model estimated over 1949 to 1968 and 1969 to 1983, respectively, are given. The standard errors of the *EP* residuals from each of the three estimations of the model were used in scaling the responses under A, B, and C, respectively. Because the standard errors did not differ materially for the three estimation periods, this did not introduce a distorting influence.

subperiod compared to the first. In both subperiods, the *IN* and *IP* residuals are correlated positively, although the correlation in the second subperiod is about 60 percent larger than that in the first subperiod (0.271 as opposed to 0.170). The response of *EP* turns negative after two quarters in both subperiods. In the first subperiod, the maximum negative response of *EP* occurs after twelve quarters, and is about 70 percent as large as the standard deviation of the *EP* residuals. *EP* returns to trend (or its steady-state value) after about two years. In the second subperiod, in contrast, the largest response of *EP* to a shock of typical size in *IN* occurs after fifteen quarters, and is 3.3 times as large as the standard deviation of the *EP* residuals. The effect of the innovation damps out slowly, with Iowa employment returning to trend after about three years. These results indicate that Iowa employment was much more sensitive to interest rate innovations in the second subperiod than in the first.

The response of Iowa employment to innovations of typical size to the index of industrial production indicates that *EP* also was more sensitive to shocks to *IP* in the second subperiod. The correlation between the *IP* and *EP* residuals is 0.282 in the first subperiod and 0.376 (about 30 percent greater) in the second subperiod. In both subperiods, *EP* moves above trend in response to an *IP* innovation. In general, the magnitude of the subsequent responses is greater in the second subperiod. For example, the maximum response of *EP* in the first subperiod occurs after four quarters and is about as large as the standard deviation of the *EP* residuals. In contrast, the largest response in the second subperiod occurs after about nineteen quarters and is 1.7 times as large as the standard error of the *EP* residual series. The response functions also indicate that *IP* shocks had a much more persistent effect on *EP* in the second subperiod, as *EP* returns to trend more slowly in the second subperiod than in the first.

The response of *EP* to its own innovations dies out more slowly in the second subperiod than in the first—*EP* returns to trend about 21 quarters after the innovation in the first subperiod but the effect persists for about another year in the second subperiod. The undulating pattern of the response function of *EP* to itself in the second subperiod is apparently due to a seasonal pattern in the transformed *EP* series. This conjecture is based upon the autoregressive coefficients of the model estimated from the data in the second subperiod; the coefficient on the fourth lag of *EP* in the *EP* equation is much larger than the coefficients for the third and fifth lags. It is possible that the seasonality in the *EP* series is not stable over time. If this is the case, then the regression on seasonal dummy variables (done prior to estimating the model) would not have sufficiently smoothed out the seasonal fluctuations in the raw series. In order to establish whether or not this was a serious

problem, the restricted VAR given in equations 6.1 was estimated using series
that were not seasonally adjusted. The model was estimated both with and
without seasonal dummy variables included in each equation. The decomposition of variance and impulse response results were virtually identical in
each case to those reported in tables 6-7 and 6-8. In the model where seasonal dummy variables were included in equations 6.1a and 6.1b, the response
function of EP to innovations in itself exhibited a similar, though less pronounced, seasonal pattern.

In summary, the impulse response functions indicate that EP was more
sensitive to innovations in each of the three variables in the second subperiod
than in the first. The most pronounced difference is in how EP responds to
innovations in IN. The magnitude and duration of the response is much
greater in the second subperiod. One must be careful in interpreting the
results discussed above. For instance, the pronounced change in the response
pattern of EP to IN innovations cannot be attributed solely to changes in
the direct relationship between IN and EP. Indeed, the response function
for IP (which is not reported in the tables) shows that IN shocks had a
more pronounced effect on IP in the second subperiod than in the first. In
both subperiods, the response of IP is positive for about three quarters and
then falls below trend for about fourteen quarters. In the second subperiod,
however, the absolute value of the negative deviations from trend are on
average about 30 percent greater than those in the first subperiod. The
observed increase in the sensitivity of EP to IN shocks is thus partly due to
the more pronounced response of IP to IN in the second subperiod.

IV. Conclusions

In this chapter we have used data from the Iowa economy to demonstrate
how decompositions of variance and impulse response functions can be used
to examine the nature of changes in relationships between a regional economy and the U.S. economy. Our results indicate that Iowa employment is
much more sensitive to both interest rate and industrial production innovations in the subperiod of 1969–1983 versus 1949–1968. These results suggest
that the Iowa economy, once characterized as relatively insensitive to the
U.S. business cycle, is now strongly influenced by fluctuations in the U.S.
economy. The growth of traditional sectors—especially farm and construction machinery, other durable goods, and agricultural exports—during the
last decade markedly changed the sensitivity of the Iowa economy to external forces.

The method we have employed can be useful in providing regional analysts with information as to how they should modify their large-scale forecasting models in order to account for structural changes. For example, it is clear that it would be inappropriate to estimate an Iowa employment equation with fixed coefficients over 1949 to 1983. Rather, a varying-parameters model should be employed. Finally, the impulse response functions are enlightening to regional analysts in that they show the magnitude and time path of change in regional variables as a result of changes in key variables at the national level.

Appendix A

The series used in this chapter were obtained from Data Resources Incorporated.

$IN(RMGBS3NS)$: The ninety-day yield on U.S. government Treasury bills
$IP(JQIND)$: The total (including manufacturing, mining, and utilities industries) industrial production index
$EP(EEANS@IA)$: Iowa nonagricultural employment

The series were transformed as follows:

$$IN_t = \log(IN_t/IN_I) \cdot 100$$
$$IP_t = \log(IP_t) \cdot 100$$
$$EP_t = \log(EP_t/EP_I) \cdot 100$$

where the subscript I denotes the 1968:IV value of the IN and EP series, respectively, used in indexing the series.

Each of the log-indexed series was then regressed on constant, trend, and trend squared. The IN and EP regressions also included seasonal dummy variables. The residuals from these models were then used to represent IP, IN, and EP in the estimated VAR models. This representation of the variables in the estimated models gave well-behaved results (for example, none of the impulse response functions were explosive) and provided reasonable out-of-sample forecasts. It is noteworthy, however, that other representations of the variables (for example, log, log-index, log-detrend, log-seasonally adjusted) provided essentially the same results as those reported in section III. Thus, our main conclusions are not dependent on the transformation applied to the raw data.

Appendix B

The K-step forecast error variance (FEV) in EP is equal to

$$E[EP_{t+k} - E_t(EP_{t+k})]^2 \qquad K = 1, 2, \ldots$$

where E_t is the expectational operator defined on all information available at time t.

The K-step FEV in EP can be unambiguously decomposed into components attributable to innovations in IN, IP, and EP (that occur from $t + 1$ to $t + K$) when the variance-covariance matrix of innovations is transformed to lower triangular form. The method used in this chapter, suggested by Sims (1980b) and also discussed by Litterman (1982), is to choose an ordering of the variables and then transform the variance-covariance matrix to lower diagonal form using a Choleski transformation. Although we experimented with a number of different orderings, we report only the results of the ordering (IN, IP, EP) here. The transformed variance-covariance matrix thus includes the variance of the IN residuals in its first diagonal element. The second diagonal element is the variance of the component of the IP residuals orthogonal to the IN residuals. The third diagonal element is the variance of the component of the EP residuals orthogonal to both the IN and IP residuals. For example, the variance of the EP residuals for the fit of the model from 1949 to 1983 was 0.4396×10^{-4}. The variance of the component of these residuals orthogonal to both the IN and IP residuals was 0.4165×10^{-4}, which is a reduction of about 5.3 percent from the untransformed variance.

The unorthogonalized correlations of the innovations were as follows:

	IN			IP		
	A	B	C	A	B	C
IP	0.33	0.36	0.43	—	—	—
EP	0.12	0.17	0.27	0.22	0.28	0.37

Notes

[1] The equations therefore are not "structural," in the sense that they explain the inner workings of markets and sectors of the regional economy. The models are referred to as "structural" partly because of convention, and partly because of what they purport to capture.

[2] A proxy for the agricultural cycle was also considered for inclusion in Z since many of Iowa's industries produce goods and services related to agriculture. We experimented with a number of proxies for the state of agricultural markets such as cash receipts from crops and livestocks. In general, the agricultural variables were not significant in explaining the compo-

nent of *EP* that could not be explained on the basis of past realizations of *EP*, *IN*, and *IP*. Perhaps this is because the information contained in the agricultural variables is captured adequately in the past history of *EP*.

[3] The notes below table 6-1 include a definition of Granger causality, and also description of how these tests were performed.

[4] The marginal significance level is the probability of obtaining a value equal to or larger than the value of the test statistic, assuming that the null hypothesis is true.

[5] The model in equations 6.1 also was estimated in unrestricted form where past realizations of *EP* were included in both the *IN* and *IP* equations. The results reported in section III (on the difference between how innovations to *IN* and *IP* affect *EP* in the two parts of the sample) were not materially affected by dropping the exogeneity assumption. We mention this because the MSL's of some of the test statistics reported in the first two rows of table 6-2 are possibly small enough to raise some doubt as to the validity of the exogeneity assumption (for example, the test of the null hypothesis, $EP \nrightarrow IN$, for the period from 1949 to 1989 generates an MSL of 0.11). The exogeneity assumption also was supported by other types of tests, such as the Akaike final prediction error criterion.

[6] A variety of other tests were performed in order to test the hypothesis of stable coefficients in the *EP* equation. These alternative tests were performed in order to assuage some doubts we had as to the reliability of split sample tests of this sort where, as Sims (1980a) points out, some of the parameters are not estimated consistently. Moreover, as the period being tested becomes longer, the degrees of freedom in the numerator of the test statistic increase relative to those in the denominator, thus rendering the power of the test suspect. Because of this problem, we did not perform tests of this sort for sample splits in the late 1960s. The other tests, such as the standard Chow test for structural stability (see, for example, Intrilligator, 1978), suggested the same conclusion—the coefficients of the *EP* equation are not stable for sample splits in the mid to late 1970s.

[7] In the time series literature, the error terms are often times referred to as innovations, as the error in *EP*, for example, at time *t*, is the part of EP_t that cannot be explained given all relevant information available at $t - 1$. Thus, e_{1t} represents the new information (in the sense that this information is not related to any past information), or the innovation to *EP* at time *t*.

[8] Appendix B provides a brief discussion of how the decomposition of variance is computed. This method was suggested by Sims (1980a, 1980b).

References

Bretzfelder, R. B. 1973. Sensitivity of state and regional income to national business cycles. *Survey of Current Business* 53: 22–40.

Bretzfelder, R. B., and Brown, R. L. 1982. Sensitivity of states to the national business cycle, first quarter 1980 to third quarter 1981. *U.S. Department of Commerce News*, February.

Bretzfelder, R. B., and Friedenberg, H. 1980. Sensitivity of states to the national business cycle, 1973–79. *U.S. Department of Commerce News*, June.

Hsiao, Cheng. 1979. Causality tests in econometrics. *The Journal of Economic Dynamics and Control* 1: 321–346.

Hsiao, Cheng. 1980. Autoregressiveness modelling and causal ordering of economic variables. Research Monograph 274. Princeton, N5: Princeton University.

Intrilligator, M. D., 1978. *Econometric Models, Techniques, and Applications*. Englewood Cliffs, NJ: Prentice Hall.

Litterman, R. B. 1979. Techniques of forecasting using vector autoregressions. Working Paper #115, PACS File #2700, November.

Litterman, R. B., and Weiss, L. 1985. Money, real interest rates, and output: A reinterpretation of postwar U.S. data. *Econometrica* 53(1): 129–156.

Sims, C. A. 1980a. Comparison of interwar and postwar business cycles: Monetarism reconsidered. *American Economic Review* 70(2): 250–257.

Sims, C. A. 1980b. Macroeconomics and reality. *Econometrica* 48(1): 1–48.

III DATA AND MODEL EVALUATION ISSUES

7 A GENERAL FRAMEWORK FOR INTERPOLATION, DISTRIBUTION, AND EXTRAPOLATION OF A TIME SERIES BY RELATED SERIES

James R. Schmidt

I. Introduction

Analyses and performance summaries of economies can be limited by the frequency (level of temporal aggregation) at which variables in the form of time series are reported. There are at least two aspects of this problem. First, and most obvious, is the situation in which a time series is available at a low reporting frequency, say annual, while the desired frequency is higher, say quarterly. Having estimates of the time series at the frequency higher than that reported may allow for more detailed analyses to be made. For example, key economic activity accounts or econometric models could be extended to higher frequencies. Second, the reporting lags of some important time series can be quite long, thereby diminishing the ability of such a series to contribute to descriptions of current, or reasonably recent, economic activity.

The incidence of low reporting frequencies for economic time series becomes more pronounced as the level of geographic aggregation represented by an economic area decreases. Broadly defined time series of economic activity at the county and city levels on less than an annual frequency are few in number. However, it is precisely those geographic levels that are of

181

interest to private and public enterprises as they attempt to develop market profiles, assess policy impacts, and formulate economic models for their market areas. Efficient estimation of time series at higher frequencies than reported can contribute to the above goals.

The general problem posed in the preceding paragraphs can be broken into three cases termed *interpolation*, *distribution*, and *extrapolation* of discrete time series. For interpolation, the task is to estimate values of a time series for the beginning of calendar periods of a desired frequency (e.g., months) when the observed values of the series are reported only at the beginning of the leading subperiod having the desired frequency within less frequent calendar periods (e.g., quarters). The interpolation problem can be changed slightly and also apply to the situation where the observed values of the series are reported only at the end of the last subperiod within less frequent calendar periods. The quarterly earnings totals of a firm reported at the end of the last month within successive quarters is a convenient example. Asset stocks and balance sheet items in general provide other examples where the interpolation problem may be of interest. The two cases of the interpolation problem shall be distinguished below by referring to the former as "beginning-of-period" and the latter as "end-of-period." For distribution, the task is to allocate the values of a time series pertaining to entire calendar periods (e.g., years or quarters) among more frequent calendar periods (e.g., quarters or months). Economic series measured as flows during a calendar period and various index numbers fall within the context of the distribution problem. A recent example of applied work under the distribution problem is provided in Gordon (1982) where quarterly values of real GNP and the GNP deflator for the United States are estimated from annual values over the span 1890–1946. Finally, the extrapolation problem involves predicting values of the series for calendar periods of the desired higher frequency which are outside the sample used in either the interpolation or distribution effort.

Chow and Lin (1971) developed the basic regression approach to the above problems. Their method is based upon the specification of a regression model relating the series being constructed or extrapolated to other series which are observed at the desired higher frequency. The series estimators are best linear unbiased and also ensure that the corresponding averages of estimated high-frequency values of the series match the observed low-frequency values in the distribution problem. In the interpolation problem, the estimated high-frequency values of the series will match the observed value of the series in time periods when the latter is available. The series estimators in both problems are generalized least squares estimators and therefore depend upon the structure of the error terms in the regression model. First, we shall extend the regression approach by developing the series estimators for the general case where the number of high-frequency periods within a low-frequency period is an arbitrary integer. Any combination of common frequencies such as annual, biannual, quarterly, and monthly are special cases. Since the estimators are based upon generalized least squares, the involved covariance matrixes of the error terms are developed in terms of general autocorrelations among the errors. Special cases associated with some popular error structures are also noted. The results may also be of use in regression models where observations on an exogenous variable are reported on a lower frequency than are the observations on the endogenous and remaining exogenous variables. Dagenais (1973) and Hsiao (1979) have utilized the regression approach to distribution and interpolation of exogenous variables in this context. Second, we present an illustration of the distribution problem using personal income of regions. Quarterly personal income of a state is estimated and compared to known values. The technique is then applied to the personal incomes of a set of counties.

II. The Estimators

Consider a low-frequency time series of n values observed in consistently spaced periods. Also consider a set of p time series of kn values observed in consistently spaced periods of higher frequency within the span of the low-frequency time series. The following linear model is assumed to describe the relationship between the hypothetical kn values of the arbitrarily chosen low-frequency series, $\mathbf{y}$, and the kn values of the set of p high-frequency series

$$\mathbf{y} = X\boldsymbol{\beta} + \mathbf{u} \qquad (7.1)$$

where X is the $kn \times p$ data matrix of the p-related series, $\boldsymbol{\beta}$ is the $p \times 1$ vector of parameters, and $\mathbf{u}$ is the $kn \times 1$ vector of error terms for the model with $kn \times kn$ covariance matrix

$$E(\mathbf{uu'}) = V = \sigma_u^2 \begin{bmatrix} \rho_0 & \rho_1 & \rho_2 & \cdots & \rho_{kn-1} \\ \rho_1 & \rho_0 & \rho_1 & \cdots & \rho_{kn-2} \\ \rho_2 & \rho_1 & \rho_0 & \cdots & \rho_{kn-3} \\ \cdot & \cdot & \cdot & \cdots & \cdot \\ \cdot & \cdot & \cdot & \cdots & \cdot \\ \cdot & \cdot & \cdot & \cdots & \cdot \\ \rho_{kn-1} & \rho_{kn-2} & \rho_{kn-3} & \cdots & \rho_0 \end{bmatrix}$$

By definition, σ_u^2 is the finite variance of any individual error term u_t, $t = 1$, ..., kn, ρ_r is the autocorrelation between u_t and $u_{|t-r|}$ with $\rho_r = \rho_{-r}$, and E ( ) is the standard expectations operator.

The linear regression model of equation 7.1 can be transformed with a $n \times kn$ matrix C to give a model that relates the observed low-frequency series of interest to the corresponding low-frequency values of the set of related high-frequency series,

$$C\mathbf{y} = CX\beta + C\mathbf{u} \tag{7.2}$$

or

$$\mathbf{y}_* = X_*\beta + \mathbf{u}_* \tag{7.3}$$

The $n \times n$ covariance matrix of $\mathbf{u}_*$ is therefore

$$E(\mathbf{u}_*\mathbf{u}_*') = V_* = CVC' \tag{7.4}$$

In the beginning-of-period case of the interpolation problem, C takes the form

$$C_1 = [I \quad \otimes \quad \iota_1'] \tag{7.5a}$$

where I is the $n \times n$ identity matrix and ι_1' is the $1 \times k$ vector $[1 \quad 0 \quad \ldots \quad 0]$. For the end-of-period case, C is

$$C_2 = [I \quad \otimes \quad \iota_2'] \tag{7.5b}$$

where ι_2' is the $1 \times k$ vector $[0 \quad \ldots \quad 0 \quad 1]$. In the distribution problems, C is

$$C_D = [I \quad \otimes \quad \iota_D'] \tag{7.6}$$

where ι_D' is the $1 \times k$ vector $[1/k \quad \ldots \quad 1/k]$. The $n \times 1$ vector $\mathbf{y}_*$ in model 7.3 . contains the observed values of the low-frequency series while X_* contains the observed low-frequency values of the set of related high-frequency series. For the distribution problem, the above framework assumes that the observed low-frequency values of the set of related high-frequency series are simple averages of the k constituent subperiods. This is a common convention for the measurement of economic flows as in, for example, the National Income Accounts.

From the results of Chow and Lin (1971), the generalized least squares estimator of β in model 7.3 is

$$\hat{\beta} = (X_*'V_*^{-1}X_*)^{-1}X_*'V_*^{-1}\mathbf{y}_* \tag{7.7}$$

and the best linear unbiased estimator of the kn values in $\mathbf{y}$ is

$$\hat{\mathbf{y}} = X\hat{\beta} + VC'V_*^{-1}\hat{\mathbf{u}}_* \tag{7.8}$$

where $\hat{\mathbf{u}}_* = \mathbf{y}_* - X_*\hat{\boldsymbol{\beta}}$, the vector of generalized least squares residuals from the model employing the respective low-frequency series in model 7.3. It is easy to show that $C\hat{\mathbf{y}} = \mathbf{y}_*$. In the interpolation problem, this result is

$$\hat{y}_t = y_t \qquad t = 1, k+1, 2k+1, \ldots, (n-1)k+1$$

for the beginning-of-period case and

$$\hat{y}_t = y_t \qquad t = k, 2k, 3k, \ldots, nk$$

for the end-of-period case, i.e., the estimated values of the series at the low-frequency time periods match the observed values. In the distribution problem, the result is

$$y_{*i} = \sum_{j=1}^{k} \hat{y}_{(i-1)k+j}/k \qquad i = 1, \ldots, n$$

i.e., the simple average of the estimated high-frequency values of the series within low-frequency periods equals the corresponding low-frequency values.

In the extrapolation problem, the general predictor of an $m \times 1$ vector of contiguous out-of-sample values, $\mathbf{y}_m$, is

$$\hat{\mathbf{y}}_m = X_m\hat{\boldsymbol{\beta}} + E(\mathbf{u}_m\mathbf{u}'_*)V_*^{-1}\hat{\mathbf{u}}_*$$

or

$$\hat{\mathbf{y}}_m = X_m\hat{\boldsymbol{\beta}} + E(\mathbf{u}_m\mathbf{u}')C'V_*^{-1}\hat{\mathbf{u}}_* \tag{7.9}$$

where X_m is the $m \times p$ matrix of corresponding out-of-sample values of the respective p related series and $\mathbf{u}_m$ is the vector of model errors for the out-of-sample periods. The predictor differs between the interpolation and distribution problems by virtue of the differing forms of the C matrix in each.

III. Covariance Matrices and Alternative Error Processes

The generalized least squares estimator (equation 7.7) of $\boldsymbol{\beta}$, the series estimator (equation 7.8) of $\mathbf{y}$, and the extrapolation predictor (equation 7.9) of $\mathbf{y}_m$ involve various matrixes of error covariances. In this section, we develop expressions for the contents of these matrices that can be manipulated in computer applications. First, consider the covariance matrix V_* in the beginning-of-period case of the interpolation problem. From equation 7.4 we have

$$V_* = C_1VC_1' = [I \otimes \iota_1']V[I \otimes \iota_1]$$

Since V_* is persymmetric (symmetric with respect to both main diagonals), the elements in the first column of V_* will completely specify the matrix. Each element in the first column of V_* is a quadratic form in V given by $\mathbf{a}_i V \mathbf{a}'_1$, $i = 1, \ldots, n$, where $\mathbf{a}_i$ is row i of the matrix C_1. Negative subscripts in the upper triangle of V are maintained during the simplification of these quadratic forms. The i, j element of V_* is thus

$$v_{*i,j} = \sigma_u^2 \rho_{(|i-j|)k} \qquad i, j = 1, \ldots, n$$

The form of V_* in the beginning-of-period and end-of-period cases of the interpolation problem are identical. Derivation of V_* in the distribution problem involves quadratic forms in a similar manner and leads to the typical i, j element

$$v_{*i,j} = (\sigma_u^2/k^2) \sum_{\omega=0}^{k-1} \sum_{\tau=0}^{k} \rho_{(|i-j|+1)k-\tau-\omega} \qquad i, j = 1, \ldots, n$$

where it is understood that $\rho_r = \rho_{-r}$ for the negative subscripts that occur in $v_{*1,1}$. VC' and $E(\mathbf{u}_m \mathbf{u}')C'$ are the other matrices of error covariances necessary for implementing estimator equations 7.7, 7.8, and 7.9. We summarize the contents of these matrices, along with the contents of V_*, in table 7-1. The factor of proportionality σ_u^2 is explicitly included in the descriptions of the matrices for the purpose of clarity although it cancels within equations 7.7, 7.8, and 7.9.

The matrices in table 7-1 clearly show the dependence of the respective estimators (7.7, 7.8, and 7.9) upon the autocorrelations of the error terms in model 7.1. Whatever assumption is made concerning the form of serial correlation in the error terms of model 7.1 will dictate the specific contents of the involved matrices. Specifications of the autocorrelations among the respective error terms in $\mathbf{u}$ need only be substituted into the expressions in table 7-1 to completely specify V_*, VC', and $E(\mathbf{u}_m \mathbf{u}')C'$. Table 7-2 contains the autocorrelation structures associated with some popular error processes. The special fourth-order autocorrelation process discussed by Thomas and Wallis (1971) and the combined first-order and fourth-order process discussed by Wallis (1972) are included in the table because of potential application to the case where the low-frequency series is annual and the set of related high-frequency series are quarterly ($k = 4$).

Previous authors have addressed certain special cases of the parameter estimator $\hat{\beta}$ (equation 7.7) and the series estimator $\hat{y}$ (equation 7.8). Chow and Lin (1971) discussed the case of $k = 3$ while assuming a first-order autoregressive AR(1) process with no initial conditions for the error terms in $\mathbf{u}$. Their discussion of the contents of V_* was limited to the leading two elements of the first row. Fernandez (1981) discussed the distribution prob-

Table 7-1. Element i,j of Error Covariance Matrixes

Matrix	Dimension	Context	Interpolation		Distribution
			Beg. of Period	End of Period	
V_*^a	$n \times n$	$\hat{\beta}, \hat{y}, y, \hat{y}_m$	$\sigma_u^2 \rho_{(|i-j|)k}$	$\sigma_u^2 \rho_{(|i-j|)k}$	$(\sigma_u^2/k^2) \sum\limits_{\omega=0}^{k-1} \sum\limits_{\tau=1}^{k} \rho_{(|i-j|+1)k-\tau-\omega}$
VC'	$kn \times n$	$\hat{y}$	$\sigma_u^2 \rho_{|(j-1)k+i-1|}$	$\sigma_u^2 \rho_{|jk-i|}$	$(\sigma_u^2/k) \sum\limits_{\tau=1}^{k} \rho_{|i-jk+\tau-1|}$
$E(\mathbf{u}_m \mathbf{u}')C'$	$m \times n$	$\hat{y}_m$	$\sigma_u^2 \rho_{(n-j+1)k+i-1}$	$\sigma_u^2 \rho_{(n-j)k+i}$	$(\sigma_u^2/k) \sum\limits_{\tau=1}^{k} \rho_{(n-j)k+i+\tau-1}$

[a] V_* is persymmetric so each element in upper and lower minor diagonal i of V_* is element i, 1, the leading element of the respective minor diagonals.

Table 7-2. Autocorrelations Under Various Error Processes

Process[a]	Form[b]	Autocorrelations	Parameter Restrictions
Random	$u_t = \varepsilon_t$	$\rho_o = 1$ $\rho_r = 0$ $r = 1, \ldots, kn - 1$	—
AR(1)	$u_t = \phi u_{t-1} + \varepsilon_t$	$\rho_r = \phi^r$ $r = 0, \ldots, kn - 1$	$|\phi| < 1$
AR(2)	$u_t = \phi_1 u_{t-1} + \phi_2 u_{t-2} + \varepsilon_t$	$\rho_0 = 1$ $\rho_1 = \phi_1/(1 - \phi_2)$ $\rho_2 = \phi_2 + \phi_1^2/(1 - \phi_2)$ $\rho_r = \phi_1 \rho_{r-1} + \phi_2 \rho_{r-2}$ $r = 3, \ldots, kn - 1$	$\phi_1 + \phi_2 < 1$ $\phi_2 - \phi_1 < 1$ $|\phi_2| < 1$
AR(4)	$u_t = \phi u_{t-4} + \varepsilon_t$	$\rho_r = \phi^{r/4} \quad r = 0, 4, 8, \ldots, 4(n-1)$ $= 0 \qquad$ otherwise	$|\phi| < 1$
Combined AR(1), AR(4)	$u_t = \phi_1 u_{t-1} + \phi_4 u_{t-4}$ $- \phi_1 \phi_4 u_{t-5} + \varepsilon_t$	$\rho_0 = 1$ $\rho_1 = (\phi_1 + \phi_1^3 \phi_4)/(1 + \phi_1^4 \phi_4)$ $\rho_2 = \phi_1^2 (1 + \phi_4)/(1 + \phi_1^4 \phi_4)$ $\rho_3 = (\phi_1 - \phi_1 \phi_4) \rho_2 + \phi_4 \rho_1$ $\rho_4 = \phi_1 \rho_3 - \phi_1 \phi_4 \rho_1 + \phi_4$ $\rho_5 = \phi_1 \rho_4 + \phi_4 \rho_1 - \phi_1 \phi_4$ $\rho_r = \phi_1 \rho_{r-1} + \phi_4 \rho_{r-4} - \phi_1 \phi_4 \rho_{r-5}$ $r = 6, \ldots, kn - 1$	$|\phi_1| < 1$ $|\phi_4| < 1$
MA(1)	$u_t = \varepsilon_t + \theta \varepsilon_{t-1}$	$\rho_0 = 1$ $\rho_1 = \theta/(1 + \theta^2)$ $\rho_r = 0$ $r = 2, \ldots, kn - 1$	$|\theta| < 1$

[a], [b] ε_t represents a random error term.

lem for an arbitrary value of k and considered a random-walk process for the error terms in $\mathbf{u}$ with the initial condition of $u_0 = 0$ imposed. Litterman (1983) considered the distribution problem for the case of $k = 3$ with a restricted second-order autoregressive AR(2) process for the errors $(\phi_2 = 1 - \phi_1)$ and the initial conditions of $u_0 = 0$ and $u_1 = \varepsilon_1$ imposed, where ϕ_1 and ϕ_2 are the parameters and ε_t is the random error term in the AR(2) process.

In practice, the values of the elements in V_* will not be known and will need to be estimated to obtain a feasible estimator of β, as in equation 7.7. The descriptions of the forms of V_* in table 7-1 in conjunction with the error processes outline in table 7-2 indicate that the estimate of V_* is determined by the estimate(s) of the parameter(s) in the respective processes. Popular scanning procedures can be employed to search over the admissible values of the error process parameter(s) in those cases where the number of parameters is manageable. The objective in this approach to generalized least squares estimation of β is, as usual, minimization of $\hat{\mathbf{u}}_*'\hat{\Omega}^{-1}\hat{\mathbf{u}}_*$ where $V_* = \sigma_u^2 \Omega$ and Ω is the variance-covariance matrix. The parameter estimates obtained at the conclusion of the search can then be used to form estimates of the error covariances present in VC' and $E(\mathbf{u}_m \mathbf{u}')C'$. Calculation of the high-frequency series, $\hat{\mathbf{y}}$, and extrapolation of the series on the high-frequency basis, $\hat{\mathbf{y}}_m$, then follows in a straightforward manner via equations 7.8 and 7.9.

Certain simple forms of V_* appear under several of the error processes listed in table 7-2. In the interpolation problem, V_* under the special AR(4) process with $k = 4$ is $\sigma_u^2[\phi^{|i-j|}]$, while V_* under the AR(1) process is given by $\sigma_u^2[\phi^{|i-j|k}]$. Both inverses are easily obtained. V_* under the assumption of randomness in the errors is of course $\sigma_u^2 I$ and the same form is implied by a moving average MA(1) process for the errors where k exceeds 1. This equivalence rules out the use of an MA(1) process in the interpolation problem since the parameter θ will not appear in the estimator of β. If an MA process is to be assumed for the model errors, then the order of the process must be at least equal to k. Turning to the distribution problem, V_* under the special AR(4) process with $k = 4$ is $(\sigma_u^2/k)[\phi^{|i-j|}]$ which differs from a standard AR(1) covariance matrix only by the multiplicative constant. Under the randomness assumption for the errors, V_* is $(\sigma_u^2/k)I$ within the distribution problem.

IV. Application to Regional Personal Income

The personal incomes of states and counties are key indicators of economic conditions prevailing in those regions. State personal income is routinely reported at a quarterly frequency in table 2A of the Regional Economic Information System, while county personal incomes are reported only at an annual frequency in the April issue of *The Survey of Current Business*. The method outlined in preceding sections will be used to estimate a quarterly personal income series for the state of Nebraska. Since the series is officially reported, it provides a test case for demonstrating the applicability and accuracy of the method in a regional setting. The method will then be applied to the personal income of several counties within the state which have diverse land area and population sizes. The county level results serve to illustrate an application of the method to a practical situation where a series of higher frequency than reported is desired.

The span of observations in analyses at both the state and county level is 1970–1982. Two related series were chosen for the state personal income model: state retail sales (taxable) and U.S. personal income. Both series were in seasonally adjusted form. In principle, the sales series introduces a state specific cyclical pattern into the estimated quarterly income series. The national income series will account for the state's tendency (however strong) to follow national economic trends and cycles. Use of the national series in the model is consistent with the so called top-down strategy employed in other regional econometric methods. Arguments could be advanced for the inclusion of other state or national series in the models or for the specification of certain distributed lag schemes. The latter alternative is not addressed here. Series measuring employment- and farm-sector conditions were considered in the course of developing the model but they performed poorly in contrast to state retail sales and U.S. personal income.

An AR(1) process was used for the quarterly error terms of the model. In the context of the general framework and tables 7-1 and 7-2, the distribution case at hand is $k = 4$, $n = 13$, and $\rho_r = \phi^r$ for $r = 0, \ldots, 51$. The estimate of the full model appears on the third line of table 7-3. Estimates of models obtained after deleting the sales and national income series, respectively, appear on the first two lines of table 7-3. Two prediction statistics, mean absolute percentage error and Theil U (MAPE and U in table 7-3), were computed from the estimated and known quarterly series of state personal income. Both statistics are quite low, indicating a very close correspondence between the estimated and known series. The full model (line 3 of table 7-3) does not provide any improvement in the prediction statistics when compared to the model that utilizes only U.S. personal income as a related

Table 7-3. Distribution Models of Quarterly Personal Income: Nebraska and Selected Counties: 1970–1982

Area	Population	Square Miles	% of Pop. Rural	Constant[a]	RS[a,b]	NPI[a,c]	$USPI$[a,d]	R^2[e]	ϕ[f]	$MAPE$[g]	U[h]
State	1,569,825	76,644	21.7	−757.04 (−0.78)	1.737 (12.340)	—	—	.921	.77	1.7	.012
State	—	—	—	825.80 (2.89)	—	—	6.340 (35.381)	.990	.63	.7	.005
State	—	—	—	494.75 (1.49)	0.278 (1.680)	—	5.385 (9.141)	.992	.59	.7	.005
Douglas County	397,038	333	3.8	−16.84 (−0.15)	0.362 (1.412)	0.228 (5.792)	—	.992	.55	—	—
Lancaster County	192,884	839	7.5	−103.39 (−2.96)	0.446 (2.437)	0.102 (7.960)	—	.994	.60	—	—
Lincoln County	36,455	2,525	24.3	−33.68 (−3.60)	0.550 (3.754)	0.017 (8.868)	—	.987	.70	—	—
Cherry County	6,758	5,961	49.0	1.49 (0.31)	0.058 (0.132)	0.003 (3.554)	—	.863	.79	—	—

[a] T ratios appear in parentheses.
[b] RS = retail sales (state total or county total in millions).
[c] NPI = Nebraska personal income (in millions).
[d] $USPI$ = United States personal income (in billions).
[e] R^2 = Buse's (1973) measure of R^2 for generalized least squares.
[f] ϕ = Estimated parameter of the AR(1) process.
[g] $MAPE$ = Mean absolute percentage error.
[h] U = Theil inequality coefficient.

series. However, the sales series (*RS* in table 7-3) can be judged to be marginally significant in the full model under asymptotic criteria. In addition, the role of the sales series in introducing regional cyclical behavior into the model would seem to justify its presence.

The distribution model of county personal income was specified in a manner similar to the model for state personal income. County retail sales (taxable) and state personal income were selected as the related series and both were in seasonally adjusted form. This specification is essentially the same as was used for the state-level model but merely applied to the county level. An AR(1) process was assumed for the error terms.

Estimates of the model for four Nebraska counties appear in table 7-3. There is wide variation in the character of these counties in terms of population, area, and the percentage of population that is rural. Rural is defined here as areas other than urban areas or incorporated places. Douglas and Lancaster are the two counties of Nebraska having the largest populations and highest densities with the latter having a density one-fifth that of the former. Lincoln county comprises an area that is substantially larger than Douglas or Lancaster but has one city, North Platte, which dominates the region in terms of population concentration and trade activity. Cherry county comprises a very large area (roughly equal to the combined areas of Connecticut and Rhode Island) and has a corresponding low density (1.1 persons per square mile); half of the residents are dispersed over the rural areas of the county.

The models of the four counties all contain significant coefficients on the state personal income series but the coefficient on the sales series is not significant in the models for Douglas and Cherry counties. Douglas county has accounted for about 30 percent of state personal income in the years of the sample period 1970–1982. Movements in state personal income through the period would be expected to be closely matched by movements in Douglas county personal income, thereby leaving little influence to be ascribed to local sales. In contrast, Cherry county has a very low population density with half the of residents being classified as rural. These rather extreme characteristics of population, area, and dispersion weaken the relationship between personal income and sales activity in the county.

The quarterly income series for a given county over the 1970–1982 period would be formed using the estimator in equation 7.8. Income for quarters in the post-1982 period would be formed using the predictor in equation 7.9. Thus, a complete quarterly series can be generated through the last quarter for which the selected related series have been officially reported.

V. Summary

A general framework has been provided for the approach to interpolation, distribution, and extrapolation of a time series by related series. The basic models, parameter estimators, series estimators, and contents of the involved error covariance matrixes have been developed for the general case where the desired number of high-frequency periods within a low-frequency period is an arbitrary integer. Of particular interest are the error covariance matrixes whose contents were described in terms of autocorrelations among the high-frequency error terms. A variety of popular processes may be incorporated into the analysis by substituting the implied autocorrelation structure into the formulas developed for the contents of the respective error covariance matrixes. The framework should prove useful in light of the differing levels of temporal aggregation observed across sets of discrete time series. One need only specify the desired number of high-frequency periods within a low-frequency period and the error process of the high-frequency errors.

An illustration of the distribution problem in a regional economic setting was given. Quarterly personal income for counties is a series that is not officially reported but could prove useful in economic analyses confined to substate areas. Distribution models were estimated for four counties in the state of Nebraska. A model was also estimated for the state personal income series; and the accuracy of the estimated quarterly series was checked against the officially reported series. The results are encouraging and indicate that the general framework outlined for allocating a low-frequency series to periods of higher frequency can be a useful tool in regional econometric work.

References

Buse, A. 1973. Goodness of fit in generalized least squares estimation. *The American Statistician* 27:106–108.

Chow, G. C., and Lin, A. 1971 Best linear unbiased interpolation, distribution, and extrapolation of time series by related series. *The Review of Economics and Statistics* 53:372–375.

Dagenais, M. G. 1973. The use of incomplete observations in multiple regression analysis: A generalized least squares approach. *Journal of Econometrics* 1:317–328.

Fernandez, R. B. 1981. A methodological note on the estimation of time series. *The Review of Economics and Statistics* 63:471–476.

Gordon, R. J. 1982. Price inertia and policy ineffectiveness in the United States. *Journal of Political Economy* 90:1087–1117.

Hsiao, C. 1979. Linear regression using both temporally aggregated and temporally disaggregated data. *Journal of Econometrics* 10:243–252.

Litterman, R. B. 1983. A random walk Markov model for the distribution of time series. *Journal of Business and Economic Statistics* 1:169–173.

Thomas, J. J., and Wallis, K. F. 1971. Seasonal variation in regression analysis. *Journal of the Royal Statistical Society* ser. A 134:67–72.

U.S. Department of Commerce, Bureau of Economic Analysis. *Survey of Current Business*.

Wallis, K. F. 1972. Testing for fourth-order autocorrelation in quarterly regression equations. *Econometrica* 40:617–636.

8 NEW TECHNIQUES FOR DETERMINING IF A TIME SERIES CAN BE SEASONALLY ADJUSTED RELIABLY

David F. Findley
and Brian C. Monsell

The opinions expressed in this paper are those of the authors and do not necessarily reflect Census Bureau policy or practice.

I. Introduction

Deciding when a series is a good candidate for seasonal adjustment can be difficult. There are situations where a series may show evidence of seasonality, but because of a dominating irregular component, for example, or a volatile seasonal component, many of its seasonal factors cannot be estimated reliably. In these circumstances, the estimates of a given month's seasonal factor can change substantially when more data are added to the series and earlier data are deleted. Some seasonal adjustment programs, such as X-11 and X-11-ARIMA, provide diagnostics that can be used to help the analyst make this decision. However, the diagnostics provided by X-11 and X-11-ARIMA are sometimes inadequate. In this article, we will discuss two new sets of measures that help to determine when a series can be seasonally adjusted reliably by a proposed seasonal adjustment methodology.

The first set, described in section III, compares seasonal (and trading-day) adjustments performed on sliding spans of data. These enable the analyst to see how stable the estimates of seasonal factors and month-to-month changes are in the seasonally adjusted data. If too many months have unstable estimates, it is an indication that the adjustment method used cannot reliably adjust the series being examined.

The second set, described in section V, uses the revisions history of a series to provide measures of how much the initial seasonal adjustments are revised in later years and how rapidly these adjustments converge to their final value. These measures help determine whether the seasonal adjustments of the series being analyzed are subject to excessive amounts of revision and help ascertain if the final adjustments are merely artifacts of the finite lengths of the adjustment filters used. In either of these situations, the seasonal adjustments are likely to be unreliable.

In the remaining sections, these methods are used in conjunction with others to analyze a number of Census Bureau series. In sections IV and VI, a Census Bureau series called XU3 (exports of mineral fuels, lubricants, and related materials) serves as an example for a detailed illustration of the use of the new techniques to determine if a series is a candidate for seasonal adjustment using X-11 (or X-11-ARIMA without the ARIMA forecasts). Then, in section VII, thirty foreign trade series are analyzed with these new techniques and with some conventional diagnostics. The reader who is chiefly interested in our conclusions regarding the adjustment of these series can proceed directly to sections III, VII, and VIII. Although X-11 and X-11-ARIMA are used in this study, the techniques presented here can be adapted for use with other seasonal adjustment methods.[1]

II. Conventional Analysis of XU3

The graph of the series XU3, given in figure 8-1, does not indicate any persistent seasonal pattern, apart from a trough each December. Also, it suggests that the series undergoes a significant change around 1974. The analyst should carefully consider the question of what data span to use. For illustrative purposes, we begin with an analysis of the full series (January 1966 to December 1983) and later give a summary of an analysis performed on the abridged series (January 1974 to December 1983).

X-11-ARIMA was used, without forecasting, to seasonally adjust the full series using 3×9 seasonal filters. Some of the diagnostics from X-11-ARIMA support seasonally adjusting the series, but others are cautionary. A summary of conventional diagnostics is given in table 8-1. The F tests used

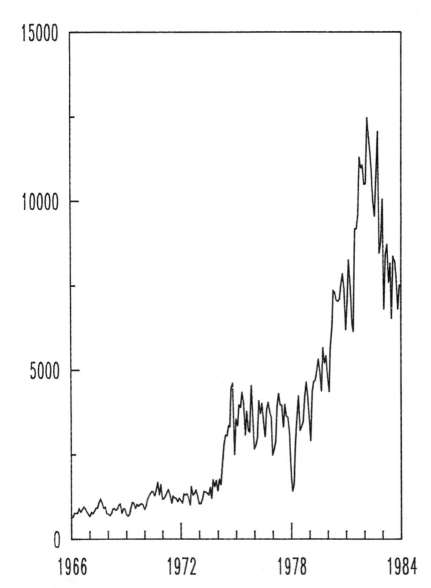

Figure 8-1. Graph of XU3

Table 8-1.   Diagnostics from X-11-ARIMA Adjustment of XU3

	Full Series (1966–1983)	*Abridged Series (1974–1983)*
F test for stable seasonality, performed on XU3	11.1	5.8
F test for stable seasonality, performed on final unmodified SI ratios	15.2	7.7
F test for moving seasonality, performed on final unmodified SI ratios	1.6	2.5
F test for trading day	4.1	7.7
Relative contribution of the irregular component to the sum of squared percent changes at lag one	59.0	58.7
Relative contribution of the irregular component to the sum of squared percent changes at lag three	27.6	27.2

to detect stable seasonality tentatively suggest that there is significant seasonal variation in this series. The F test for (linearly) moving seasonality indicates that there is no linear movement in the pattern of seasonality that would prevent its reliable estimation. (For more information on these F tests, see Shiskin et al., 1967; Dagum, 1983; and Morry and Lothian, 1978.)

However, there are also indications that XU3 may not be a good candidate for seasonal adjustment. There are several signs that the series is highly irregular. The proportion of the sum of squared percent changes attributed to the irregular component is high for this adjustment: 59.0 percent at lag one and 27.6 percent at lag three.[2] A graph of the SI ratios for the last six years of data (given in figure 8-2) shows how this irregularity is reflected in the spread of the values of the SI ratios for the individual calendar months. This kind of spread can lead to degraded estimates of seasonal factors obtained as weighted averages of the SI ratios.[3]

Trading-day adjustment was also performed on this series using X-11-ARIMA.[4] While this adjustment was accepted by X-11-ARIMA because of a significant F statistic for trading-day variation, the irregularity in the series causes concern about its reliability. Young (1965) states that "[trading-day] estimates made from highly irregular series cannot be expected to be useful."

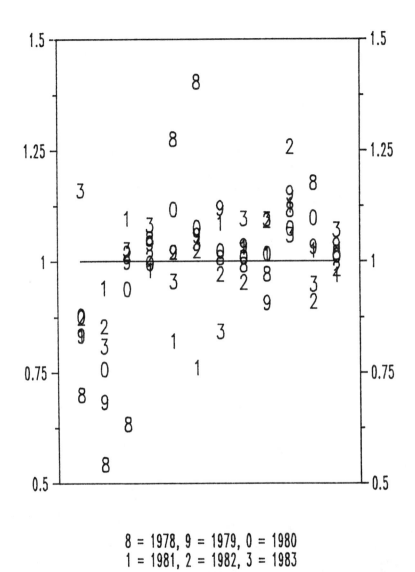

8 = 1978, 9 = 1979, 0 = 1980
1 = 1981, 2 = 1982, 3 = 1983

Figure 8-2. Year over Year Plot of SI Ratios of XU3

Finally, the quality control statistics of X-11-ARIMA are not encouraging. Eleven quality control statistics are provided to help the user evaluate the acceptability of a seasonal adjustment performed by X-11-ARIMA. These eleven statistics are combined in a weighted average to derive Q, an overall measure of the acceptability of the seasonal adjustment. See Lothian and Morry (1978) for more details. If Q is less than 1, the adjustment is deemed acceptable by X-11-ARIMA's criterion. If Q is greater than 1, the adjustment is unacceptable.[5] For XU3, the value of Q is 1.08, casting some doubt on the adjustability of the series. The authors have revised this measure due to an anomaly found in one of the eleven quality control statistics.[6] The value of the original Q is 0.87 for XU3.

III. Sliding-Spans Analysis

A technique that is particularly helpful for testing the reliability of a seasonal adjustment of a series is the examination of the results of seasonal adjustment for months common to a sequence of "sliding spans" within the series. These reveal how the seasonal (and trading-day) adjustments vary according to which span is used.

To obtain these sliding spans, an initial span is selected on the basis of the criteria described below. Then a second span is obtained by deleting the earliest year of data from the first span and appending the year of data succeeding the last year of the first span. A third span is obtained from the second in like manner and the process continues until there is no "future" data with which to create a new span. For example, consider a monthly series that begins in January 1974 and ends in December 1983. Three eight-year sliding spans can be formed: one from 1974 to 1981, another from 1975 to 1982, and a third from 1976 to 1983. The number and length of these sliding spans will depend upon the length of the series being examined and on the length of the seasonal adjustment filter chosen by the analyst, as explained in section IV below. Each span is seasonally adjusted as though it were a complete series and each month common to more than one span is examined to see if its seasonal adjustments vary excessively from span to span. In the above example, three estimates would be available for the seasonal factor of the observation occurring in January of 1981. By comparing these three estimates, evidence is obtained on how reliably the seasonal adjustment method is able to adjust January 1981.

Such a comparison is made in the following manner: let

$S_t(k)$ = the seasonal factor estimated from span k for month t

$A_t(k) =$ the seasonally (and, usually also, trading-day) adjusted value from span k for month t

$N_t \quad = \{k:$ month t is in the kth span$\}$.

The time series value associated with month t is flagged as having an unreliable seasonal factor if

$$\frac{\max_{k\varepsilon N_t} S_t(k) - \min_{k\varepsilon N_t} S_t(k)}{\min_{k\varepsilon N_t} S_t(k)} > 0.03 \tag{8.1}$$

and as having an unreliable estimate of month-to-month percentage change of the seasonally adjusted data if

$$\max_{k\varepsilon N_t} \frac{A_t(k) - A_{t-1}(k)}{A_{t-1}(k)} - \min_{k\varepsilon N_t} \frac{A_t(k) - A_{t-1}(k)}{A_{t-1}(k)} > 0.03 \tag{8.2}$$

Equation 8.1 tests whether the maximum percentage difference in the seasonal factors for month t is greater than 3 percent. When no trading-day adjustment is done, this can be interpreted as testing whether the estimates of the level of the seasonally adjusted data vary substantially. Equation 8.2 tests whether the largest difference in the month-to-month percentage change in the seasonally (and trading-day) adjusted data is greater than 3 percent for a month t. Often, analysts will seasonally adjust series mainly to get a percentage change. With this test, we assess the reliability of the estimate of month-to-month percentage change obtained from the seasonal adjustment method. Based on our experience, the threshold values of 0.03 used above seem adequate for use with X-11 or X-11-ARIMA on most series. It may be appropriate to use different threshold values if other seasonal adjustment methods are used. Also, varying requirements of reliability might dictate different values.

Once all months common to more than one span have been analyzed in the above manner, the results can be summarized in a series of tables. One table is designed to give a summary, for each category (seasonal factors, month-to-month percentage changes), of how many months were flagged as having excessive variability as well as the percentage of months flagged. Another table shows how many times each calendar month was flagged and how many months in each calendar year were flagged for each category. A further breakdown (histogram) of the values of the test statistics that exceed the threshold is also given for each statistic.

If too many months are flagged (see below), it means that enough of the seasonal adjustments are unreliable to cast doubt upon the wisdom of seasonally adjusting the series. Note that an unreliable estimate of a month's

seasonal factor can give rise to unreliable estimates of the two associated
month-to-month changes. For this reason, there are almost always more
months flagged for unreliable month-to-month changes than for the unreliable seasonal factors. One should look for frequent unreliable adjustments
associated with certain calendar months and years as well. For example,
problems with early years can sometimes be a sign that seasonal adjustments
should be calculated from a segment of the series that does not include those
years.

Trading-day factors can also be analyzed in a similar manner. Let

$TD_t(k)$ = the trading-day factor estimated from span k for month t
N_t = {k: month t is in the kth span}

A month t is flagged as having an unreliable trading-day factor if

$$\frac{\max\limits_{k\varepsilon N_t} TD_t(k) - \min\limits_{k\varepsilon N_t} TD_t(k)}{\min\limits_{k\varepsilon N_t} TD_t(k)} > 0.02 \qquad (8.3)$$

Equation 8.3 tests to see if the maximum percentage variation in the trading-
day factor estimates associated with a given month t is greater than 2 percent. Again, summaries of the months flagged can be produced and broken
down by year, by calendar month, and by magnitude, as will be illustrated in
section IV.

If a large number of months have estimated trading-day factors that have
been deemed unstable, the results of the trading-day regression must be
considered suspect. Another frequent sign of a troublesome trading-day
adjustment is a high number of unacceptable month-to-month changes relative to the number of unacceptable seasonal factors. This is because the
trading-day factors are used to obtain the (seasonally and trading-day) adjusted data, and their irregularities will usually be reflected in unstable
estimates of month-to-month changes in the adjusted series. In this study,
only two series were found (XUASIA and XUUK, see section VII below),
both not amenable to seasonal adjustment, in which a disproportionately
large number of erratic month-to-month changes were observed and this
number could not be significantly reduced by eliminating the trading-day
adjustment.

In our investigations, series that seemed to have good characteristics for
seasonal adjustment usually had fewer than 15 percent of their months
flagged for erratic seasonal factors, while series that had more than 25 percent of their months flagged could not be reliably adjusted. A "gray area"
exists, between 15 and 25 percent, where a small proportion of the series in

question probably could be adequately adjusted. These same threshold values are tentatively used for the percentage of months flagged for erratic trading-day factors pending further investigation. Varying data-user requirements make it difficult to determine analogous threshold values for erratic estimates of adjusted month-of-month changes, but we recommend that seasonal adjustment not be performed if more than 40 percent of the estimates are flagged. Analysts may decide to change any of the threshold values, depending upon their judgement of how much variability can be tolerated in the adjustment; but caution is advised in raising the upper limits without careful study of the type of series being adjusted.

IV. Sliding-Spans Analysis of XU3

In this section, the export series XU3 is analyzed using the sliding-spans methodology. The length of the spans was chosen to be 11 years, this being the length of the 3 × 9 seasonal filters selected for the X-11-ARIMA adjustment (ARIMA model forecasts were not used, so the adjustment procedure is essentially that of X-11). The length of the sliding spans should be at least as great as the length of the seasonal adjustment filter, since X-11 and X-11-ARIMA can produce poor adjustments even for a good series if the length of the filter selected exceeds the series length. Four sliding spans were used for XU3. Table 8-2 shows the January 1970–December 1973 section of a month-by-month analysis of the estimates of seasonal factors of XU3 for months common to the several spans. The maximum percentage differences are given, along with symbols flagging those months where the maximum percentage difference exceeds the limit set for reliability. Different symbols correspond to the different levels of excess described in the breakdowns given in the analysis summary in Table 8-3.

Table 8-3 shows the results of the first analysis, which was done using the four spans. Trading-day adjustment was performed if significant residual trading-day variation was found in the irregulars, using an F test. First of all, note that the total number of months tested is not the same for the seasonal factors (144), the month-to-month changes (143), and the trading-day factors (135). Since we are testing all months common to two or more spans, the set of months that can be examined begins after the first year of the first span and ends before the last year of the last span. For this example, the months common to more than one span fall between 1971 and 1982, a total of 144 months. There are at least two seasonal factor estimates for every month in this set. There is not, however, a month-to-month change for January 1971 in the span covering 1971 to 1981, since one cannot calculate a previous

Table 8-2. Sliding-Spans Analysis of Seasonal Factors for XU3

Month	1970–1980	1971–1981	1972–1982	1973–1983	Maximum % Diff.
1–70	83.62	—	—	—	—
2–70	84.78	—	—	—	—
3–70	96.20	—	—	—	—
4–70	102.82	—	—	—	—
5–70	107.40	—	—	—	—
6–70	105.29	—	—	—	—
7–70	93.46	—	—	—	—
8–70	105.01	—	—	—	—
9–70	99.85	—	—	—	—
10–70	113.69	—	—	—	—
11–70	104.95	—	—	—	—
12–70	103.41	—	—	—	—
1–71	83.48	84.57	—	—	1.30
2–71	84.27	84.04	—	—	0.27
3–71	95.37	94.49	—	—	0.94
4–71	103.03	104.03	—	—	0.97
5–71	107.80	109.98	—	—	2.02
6–71	105.78	105.21	—	—	0.54
7–71	93.65	91.88	—	—	1.93
8–71	104.74	106.20	—	—	1.39
9–71	99.60	99.72	—	—	0.12
10–71	114.05	112.54	—	—	1.34
11–71	106.00	107.59	—	—	1.49

12–71	103.16	100.61	—	—	2.53	% %ᵃ
1–72	82.90	83.90	80.34	—	4.42	% %
2–72	83.51	83.40	79.90	—	4.51	
3–72	94.30	93.83	92.62	—	1.81	
4–72	103.73	104.45	103.79	—	0.69	
5–72	108.32	110.12	109.79	—	1.66	
6–72	106.11	105.69	106.24	—	0.52	%
7–72	94.18	92.56	95.73	—	3.43	
8–72	103.62	105.07	103.33	—	1.68	
9–72	100.29	100.27	98.94	—	1.36	
10–72	114.08	112.76	116.94	—	3.71	%
11–72	107.12	108.46	112.23	—	4.78	% %
12–72	103.30	101.14	100.66	—	2.62	% % % %
1–73	81.90	82.68	79.79	77.95	6.06	% % %
2–73	82.51	82.47	79.57	78.12	5.62	% % % %
3–73	92.94	92.73	91.84	86.60	7.31	% % % %
4–73	104.49	105.08	104.40	104.88	0.65	
5–73	109.23	110.45	110.42	109.54	1.12	
6–73	106.36	106.08	106.45	108.91	2.67	% % % %
7–73	95.10	93.77	96.30	99.69	6.31	
8–73	102.27	103.50	101.97	101.23	2.24	
9–73	100.94	101.00	99.82	98.26	2.79	
10–73	114.02	112.78	116.36	117.71	4.37	% %
11–73	108.27	109.45	112.73	113.51	4.83	% %
12–73	103.47	101.69	100.99	103.65	2.64	

ᵃSee text.

Table 8-3. Sliding-Spans Analysis for XU3—With Trading-Day Adjustments

	S		M–M		TD	
Total	51	(out of 144) (35.4 percent)	116	(out of 143) (81.1 percent)	84	(out of 135) (62.2 percent)
January	6		9		7	
February	7		7		2	
March	9		9		7	
April	0		11		8	
May	6		9		7	
June	3		8		8	
July	6		9		8	
August	0		12		8	
September	2		11		7	
October	4		8		8	
November	6		12		7	
December	2		11		7	
1971	0		5		0	
1972	5		7		5	
1973	9		11		7	
1974	8		11		9	
1975	4		10		8	
1976	1		12		9	
1977	2		7		7	
1978	3		9		7	
1979	5		11		7	
1980	7		12		9	
1981	6		12		9	
1982	1		9		7	

S   : Number of months flagged for erratic seasonal factors
M–M: Number of months flagged for erratic month-to-month changes in the seasonally adjusted data
TD : Number of months flagged for erratic trading-day factors

Breakdown of maximum percentage difference in seasonal factors:
    18 months between 3 and 4 percent
    16 months between 4 and 5 percent
    10 months between 5 and 6 percent
     7 months greater than or equal to 6 percent

Breakdown of maximum difference in month-to-month change:
    40 months between 3 and 5 percent
    26 months between 5 and 7 percent
    35 months between 7 and 10 percent
    15 months greater than or equal to 10 percent

Breakdown of maximum percentage difference in trading-day factors:
    61 months between 2 and 3 percent
    23 months between 3 and 4 percent

month-to-current-month change for the first observation of a series. Therefore, one month fewer is tested for unreliable adjustment of month-to-
month change.

While there are at least two trading-day factor estimates for every month
between 1971 and 1982, the occurrence of nonleap-year Februaries must be
taken into account. Such months have the same number of Mondays, Tues-
days, Wednesdays, etc. Therefore, the trading-day factor produced by X-11
(and X-11-ARIMA) for a nonleap-year February will be the same no matter
what the coefficients are in the trading-day regression. We adjust the total
number of months tested by subtracting the number of nonleap-year Februaries, since the maximum percentage difference in the trading-day factors
for these months will always be zero.

One sees from table 8-3 that a large number of months are flagged for
unstable trading-day factors, and an even larger number of months are
flagged for unstable month-to-month changes. This immediately suggests
a problem with the estimation of the trading-day factors. An examination
of the F statistic used to identify the presence of trading-day effects by X-
11-ARIMA shows that in two of the four spans, 1971–1981 and 1973–1983,
the residual trading-day variation was deemed not significant enough to
warrant adjustment.

The spectrum of the final irregular series, modified for outliers, from an
X-11-ARIMA run of XU3 without trading-day adjustment was also estimated. (See Cleveland and Devlin, 1980, and Cleveland, 1983, for more
information about this analysis.) The spectrum revealed no relatively strong
peaks at either of the primary trading-day (alias) frequencies, 0.348 and
0.432. Combining this fact with the information from the F tests and sliding
spans, it appears that there is not enough trading-day variation present in
the series for X-11-ARIMA to estimate trading-day factors reliably. The
sliding-spans analysis was then repeated without incorporating a trading-day
adjustment. The results are summarized in table 8-4. Note that although
there is improvement, especially in the adjusted month-to-month changes,
the percentage of erratic seasonal factor estimates is still too high (32.6
percent being greater than the threshold value of 25 percent mentioned
earlier).

It was noted before that an abridged version of XU3 might have better
characteristics for adjustment. Some X-11-ARIMA diagnostics from a run
done on the abridged series, using 3×5 seasonal filters, are given in the
second column of table 8-1. A sliding-spans analysis was done on the
abridged series, using three eight-year spans starting in January of 1974.
However, the percentages of months flagged for erratic seasonal factors (35
percent) and erratic trading-day factors (49 percent) were still too high to

Table 8-4. Sliding-Spans Analysis for XU3—Without Trading-Day Adjustments

	S		M–M	
Total	47	(out of 144) (32.6 percent)	66	(out of 143) (46.2 percent)
January	7		8	
February	6		3	
March	8		4	
April	0		8	
May	5		5	
June	2		2	
July	6		3	
August	0		8	
September	3		5	
October	3		5	
November	7		9	
December	0		6	
1971	1		4	
1972	5		6	
1973	8		9	
1974	6		7	
1975	5		6	
1976	0		2	
1977	0		1	
1978	3		3	
1979	5		6	
1980	7		9	
1981	6		10	
1982	1		3	

S   : Number of months flagged for erratic seasonal factors
M–M: Number of months flagged for erratic month-to-month changes in the seasonally adjusted data

Breakdown of maximum percentage difference in seasonal factors:
    17 months between 3 and 4 percent
    15 months between 4 and 5 percent
     9 months between 5 and 6 percent
     6 months greater than or equal to 6 percent

Breakdown of maximum difference in month-to-month change:
    29 months between 3 and 5 percent
    19 months between 5 and 7 percent
     7 months between 7 and 10 percent
     1 month greater than or equal to 10 percent

recommend adjusting the abridged series. For a more complete version of the analysis of the abridged series, see Monsell and Findley (1984).

V. Revisions-History Analysis

In the second method for determining the reliability of an adjustment of a series, the revisions histories of a span of individual months of the series provide the data needed for computing two measures called CPREV and CONRAT. While this method has certain limitations that are not present in the sliding-spans method, the measures can be quite informative.

To make it possible to produce full revisions histories for some of the months in the time interval over which the series is measured, this interval must be long enough that some (nearly) final seasonal adjustments can be calculated. Such adjustments are only available for months that are far enough away from the ends of the series that their seasonal adjustments are obtained by use of the symmetric versions of the type of moving average (filter) specified. Hence, a start up period is required, which for XU3 was chosen to be the first eleven years of the series because of the length of the 3×9 seasonal filter. Thereafter, for each month following the start-up period for which a final adjustment can be obtained, successive seasonal adjustments are calculated as later data are added to the series, one observation at a time.

Let $X_{i,t}$ be the seasonal adjustment for month i obtained from X-11 or X-11-ARIMA using data up through month $i + t$. For example, $X_{i,0}$ is the concurrent adjustment for month i. Because of the finite length of the filters used, as t increases these $X_{i,t}$ converge to a final value. The number of months N until the final adjustment $X_{i,N}$ is reached depends upon the length of the seasonal filter used to adjust the data. With X-11 and X-11-ARIMA, truly final values are obtained only when N is twice the length of the seasonal filter used, but adequate final values can usually be obtained by choosing N to be the filter length. For the analysis of XU3, N is set at 60. The revisions history $X_{i,0}, \ldots, X_{i,N}$ for each month that falls within a preselected span after the start-up period will be considered. This span is called the experimental period.

This first quantity ($CPREV$) defined below measures the cumulative amount of revision undergone by the seasonal adjustment of a given month in the experimental period, expressed as a percentage of the concurrently adjusted value for that month. Let $NOBS$ be the number of observations in the experimental period. Then

$$CPREV(i) = \frac{1}{X_{i,0}} \sum_{t=0}^{N-1} |X_{i,t+1} - X_{i,t}|(60/N) \qquad (8.4)$$

where $i = 1, \ldots, NOBS$.

The factor $(60/N)$ at the end of equation 8.4 is applied to make it easier to set threshold values for $CPREV$, which do not change with the length of the seasonal filters used. Lengthier filters take longer to produce a final estimate, and if no compensating factor were used to normalize $CPREV$, adjustments obtained from shorter filter lengths would usually have smaller $CPREV$ values.

If $CPREV(i)$ is large for a particular month i, this usually means that the seasonally adjusted value for month i undergoes frequent substantial revisions as more data become available. This is what one observes when seasonal adjustment is performed on a nonseasonal or erratically seasonal series. It is usually a sign that none of that month's adjustments can be counted upon to be reliable. If too many months have large values of $CPREV(i)$, the series cannot be adequately adjusted by the methodology being used.

Another indication of the reliability of the final (and presumably best) seasonal adjustment of a given month's datum can be obtained by assessing how erratically or slowly the preliminary seasonal adjustments converge to the final value. The intuitive reasoning goes as follows: The finite length of the adjustment filter ensures that the adjustments obtained for a given month will always converge to a final value as future data are added to the series. This occurs even if there is no seasonality in the series, there is a seasonal pattern which is changing too rapidly to be accurately estimated, or there is a regular seasonal pattern which is too weak to measure relative to the noise background (irregular). In each of these three situations, the final adjustment is merely an artifact of the adjustment procedure and the manner in which preliminary adjustments converge to it should be noticeably more erratic than in a series having strong and regular seasonality.

The measure $CONRAT$, used to assess the rate or manner of convergence to the final seasonal adjustment, is defined as follows. Let $NOBS$ and N be the same as in equation 8.4. Then

$$CONRAT(i) = \frac{\sum_{t=0}^{N-1} \beta^{N-1-t} \left| \dfrac{X_{i,t} - X_{i,N}}{X_{i,N}} \right|}{\sum_{t=0}^{N-1} \beta^t} \qquad (8.5)$$

where $i = 1, \ldots, NOBS$, and $0 < \beta < 1$. The weights β^{N-1-t} give more weight to deviations from the final seasonal adjustment occurring closer in time to the final value.

The authors have examined the value of these measures for a number of series regarded as candidates for both seasonal and trading-day adjustment. Based on this experience, values of $CPREV > 0.18$ or $CONRAT > 0.01$ are considered to be signs of a series that cannot be reliably seasonally adjusted with the X-11 procedure. The choice of β for CONRAT is described below.

VI. Revisions-History Analysis of XU3

Table 8-5 contains the results of a revisions history analysis of XU3 using X-11 with 3×9 seasonal filters and trading-day adjustment. Rather than examine each value of $CPREV$ and $CONRAT$, we consider only the minimum, maximum, and mean value of these measures over the experimental period, and the number of months whose values exceed the threshold levels specified above.

In $CONRAT$, β was selected so that

$$\beta^{N/2} = 1/2$$

which ensures that the earlier terms in equation 8.5 are weighted substantially less than the later ones. Since $N = 60$, solving $\beta^{30} = 0.5$ leads to $\beta = (0.5)^{1/30} = 0.97716$.

In table 8-5, the averages of $CPREV$ and $CONRAT$ for XU3 (0.2851 and 0.0188) are higher than the threshold values given in section V, so X-11's seasonal adjustment of XU3 is not acceptable, the same conclusion reached earlier on the basis of the sliding-spans analysis. Histograms of the individual values of $CPREV$ and $CONRAT$ are also given in table 8-5. The values for a substantial majority of the months in the experimental period are higher than the threshold values.

While the revisions-history analysis gives valuable information, there are two drawbacks to its use. One is that it requires a series with a large number of observations in order for the experimental period to have sufficient length for a meaningful analysis. The second is the fact that the most recent months are excluded from the experimental period because final adjustments are unavailable for them. With XU3, the latest month in our experimental period was December 1978. Direct information about the adjustment of data closer to the present is not obtainable, but would ordinarily be the data of greater interest. Because of these drawbacks, the revisions history should probably be used only when the sliding-spans analysis is inconclusive. In section VII below, we will show that the measured values from the sliding-

Table 8-5.　Revisions-History Analysis for XU3

Month	CPREV	CONRAT
1	.370	.025
2	.234	.018
3	.418	.015
4	.319	.027
5	.225	.021
6	.270	.016
7	.266	.014
8	.287	.009
9	.293	.011
10	.290	.006
11	.236	.011
12	.342	.012
13	.273	.025
14	.250	.023
15	.369	.031
16	.257	.007
17	.325	.027
18	.289	.024
19	.276	.013
20	.281	.009
21	.268	.007
22	.211	.016
23	.234	.013
24	.240	.005
AVE	.284	.016
MAX	.418	.031
MIN	.211	.005

24 out of 24 months tested (100.0 percent) had $CPREV > 0.18$
18 out of 24 months tested (75.0 percent) had $CONRAT > 0.01$

Histogram of CPREV for XU3				Histogram of CONRAT for XU3		
(.180,	.195)	0		(.000,	.002)	0
(.195,	.210)	0		(.002,	.005)	0
(.210,	.225)	1	*	(.005,	.007)	3 ***
(.225,	.240)	4	****	(.007,	.009)	3 ***
(.240,	.255)	2	**	(.009,	.011)	2 **
(.255,	.270)	3	***	(.011,	.014)	3 ***
(.270,	.285)	4	****	(.014,	.016)	4 ****
(.285,	.300)	4	****	(.016,	.018)	1 *

Table 8–5 (*contd.*)

(.300,	.315)	0		(.018,	.020)	0	
(.315,	.330)	2	**	(.020,	.023)	1	*
(.330,	.345)	1	*	(.023,	.025)	3	***
(.345,	.360)	0		(.025,	.027)	2	**
(.360,	.375)	2	**	(.027,	.029)	1	*
(.375,	.390)	0		(.029,	.032)	1	*
(.390,	.405)	0					
(.405,	.420)	1	*				

spans and revisions-history analyses are quite highly correlated for a group of series.

VII. Analysis of Thirty Regional Foreign Trade Series

In this section, results from analyzing 30 U.S. foreign trade series with the sliding-spans and revisions-histories methods are presented. The two techniques are compared with each other and with some commonly used measures found in X-11 or X-11-ARIMA. The series investigated are a diverse set of 15 import and 15 export series. Definitions of the series are given in the chapter appendix.

Table 8-6 gives a summary of the sliding-spans analyses performed on the 15 export series, nine of which were also adjusted for trading-day factors. All but two of the 15 series begin in 1966. The exceptions, XUCOME and XUCOMEA, both begin in 1968. For each of these series the sliding-spans analysis utilized four spans having lengths of 11 years. X-11-ARIMA (without forecasts) was used to adjust the series, with 3 × 9 seasonal filters used in each span (as in the analysis of XU3).

From the table, a fairly clear dichotomy emerges between series that should and should not be seasonally adjusted. Series such as XUAFR, XUCOME, XUCOMEA, and XUSASIA have a high percentage of seasonal and trading-day factors flagged, while most others (XUASIA, XUDEVC, XULAR, XUOECD, XUOEEC, XUWEUR, and XUWH) have a low percentage flagged. XUASIA, however, has a high percentage of unreliable estimates of adjusted month-to-month change. Only four series (XUANEC, XUJAP, XUUK, XUWGER) have erratic seasonal or trading-day factor percentages in the gray areas between 15 and 25 percent.

Seasonal adjustments using all of the available observations were also calculated for these series. A summary of the X-11-ARIMA diagnostics is

Table 8-6. Results of Sliding-Spans Analysis on Foreign Trade Export Series

Series	TD?	S	S(%)	M–M	M–M(%)	TD	TD(%)	Adjust?
XUAFR	yes	62	43.1	123	86.0	73	54.1	no
XUANEC	yes	22	15.3	71	49.7	15	11.1	no
XUANEC	no	25	17.4	44	30.8	—	—	no(?)
XUASIA	yes	8	5.6	57	39.9	10	7.4	no(?)
XUASIA	no	22	15.3	46	32.2	—	—	no(?)
XUCOME	yes	112	77.8	133	93.0	109	80.7	no
XUCOMEA	yes	94	65.3	122	85.3	110	81.5	no
XUDEVC	yes	0	0.0	6	4.2	0	0.0	yes
XUJAP	yes	25	17.4	82	57.3	31	23.0	no
XUJAP	no	28	19.4	48	33.6	—	—	no(?)
XULAR	yes	3	2.1	42	29.4	17	12.6	yes*
XULAR	no	1	0.7	4	2.8	—	—	yes*
XUOECD	yes	3	2.1	24	16.8	0	0.0	yes
XUOECD	no	3	2.1	11	7.7	—	—	yes
XUOEEC	yes	5	3.5	61	42.7	7	5.2	no
XUOEEC	no	8	5.6	27	18.9	—	—	yes*

	TD?	S	S(%)	M–M	M–M(%)	TD	TD(%)	Adjust?
XUSASIA	yes	118	81.9	134	93.7	117	86.7	no
XUUK	yes	27	18.8	87	60.8	36	26.7	no
XUUK	no	32	22.2	72	50.3	–	–	no
XUWEUR	yes	4	2.8	21	14.7	1	0.7	yes
XUWEUR	no	3	2.1	14	9.8	–	–	yes
XUWGER	yes	20	13.9	75	52.4	38	28.1	no
XUWGER	no	22	15.3	33	23.1	–	–	yes(?)*
XUWH	yes	0	0.0	2	1.4	0	0.0	yes

TD? : Are trading-day factors estimated?
S : Number of months flagged for erratic seasonal factors
S(%) : Percentage of months flagged for erratic seasonal factors
M–M : Number of months flagged for erratic month-to-month changes in the seasonally adjusted data
M–M(%) : Percentage of months flagged for erratic month-to-month changes in the seasonally adjusted data
TD : Number of months flagged for erratic trading-day factors
TD(%) : Percentage of months flagged for erratic trading-day factors
Adjust? : Based on our interpretation of series (2)–(7) only, would we accept the X-11 seasonal adjustment (and trading-day adjustment if (1) is yes) of this series? (?) indicates uncertainty. * indicates conflict with a decision based solely on our interpretation of X-11-ARIMA's quality control statistics (table 8-7)

Table 8-7. X-11-ARIMA Diagnostics for Foreign Trade Export Series

Series	TD?	F ST	F TD	OLDQ	NEWQ	C-1	C-3	Adjust?
XUAFR	yes	6.8	8.7	1.28	1.36	61.46	52.63	no
XUANEC	yes	14.5	6.5	1.02	1.18	61.16	37.76	no
XUANEC	no	14.2	—	1.06	1.21	64.76	38.33	no
XUASIA	yes	7.0	23.8	1.06	1.25	55.36	48.69	no
XUASIA	no	7.2	—	1.06	1.26	68.38	48.62	no
XUCOME	yes	12.3	11.9	0.88	1.13	61.41	31.01	no
XUCOMEA	yes	11.6	8.8	0.87	1.13	65.22	36.61	no
XUDEVC	yes	40.3	5.0	0.51	0.76	30.57	11.56	yes
XUJAP	yes	6.6	7.4	1.08	1.30	66.57	46.66	no
XUJAP	no	6.1	—	1.14	1.35	73.84	48.01	no
XULAR	yes	11.1	5.6	0.82	1.09	50.76	36.68	no(?)*
XULAR	no	11.0	—	0.82	1.09	53.77	37.51	no(?)*
XUOECD	yes	23.0	8.0	0.78	1.00	47.11	23.68	yes
XUOECD	no	21.7	—	0.86	1.07	52.77	23.72	yes(?)
XUOEEC	yes	19.3	3.4	0.89	1.10	53.00	26.97	no(?)

	TD?	F ST	F TD	OLDQ	NEWQ	C-1	C-3	Adjust?
XUOEEC	no	18.6	—	0.88	1.08	54.56	27.91	no*
XUSASIA	yes	2.2	1.0	1.57	1.57	77.28	67.29	no
XUUK	yes	9.0	11.4	1.14	1.28	59.18	43.23	no
XUUK	no	7.6	—	1.33	1.43	67.48	52.45	no
XUWEUR	yes	23.2	7.9	0.78	1.00	46.21	23.41	yes
XUWEUR	no	21.9	—	0.85	1.06	51.53	23.56	yes(?)
XUWGER	yes	12.6	10.7	1.06	1.19	61.48	32.49	no
XUWGER	no	11.7	—	1.12	1.24	69.33	36.66	no*
XUWH	yes	57.9	9.9	0.40	0.61	21.16	8.97	yes

TD? : Are trading day factors estimated?

F ST : F statistic for stable seasonality

F TD : F statistic for trading-day variation

OLDQ : Conventional X-11-ARIMA Q statistic

NEWQ : Revised X-11-ARIMA Q statistic

C-1 : Relative contribution of the irregular component to the variance of the original series at lag one

C-3 : Relative contribution of the irregular component to the variance of the original series at lag three

Adjust? : Based on X-11-ARIMA's quality control statistics alone, mainly those of this table (see text for others), would we accept X-11's seasonal adjustment (and trading-day adjustment if TD? is yes) of this series? (?) indicates uncertainty. * indicates conflict with a decision based soley on our interpretation of the sliding-spans analysis (table 8-6) given in table 8-7. By rather lax standards, X-11's F test for stable seasonality should exceed 7.0; the new Q statistic should be less than 1.20; and the contribution of the irregular components to the sum of squares of the series of percentage changes in the original data at lags one and three (C-1 and C-3) should be less than 50 and 30 percent, respectively, before seasonal adjustment should be contemplated.[7] In comparing the conclusions one would draw from just examining this table with those suggested by the sliding-spans analysis, two of the series, XUCOME and XUCOMEA, have acceptable values for some of the X-11-ARIMA diagnostics listed in table 8-7 despite the striking instability of their adjustments. A further examination of table 8-7 shows, however, that these two series both suffer from a high degree of irregularity. For example, C-1 for XUCOME is calculated to be 60.71. These high values indicate that this series should not be seasonally or trading-day adjusted with X-11-ARIMA. Thus, examination of only a limited set of conventional measures could lead to an incorrect conclusion. Finally, the X-11-ARIMA diagnostics strongly suggest that the four series for which the sliding-spans analysis was inconclusive—XUANEC, XUJAP, XUUK and XUWGER—should not be seasonally adjusted and this verdict is accepted.

Now we turn to the analysis of the 15 import series using the sliding-spans methodology. Most of these series start in 1974, the exceptions being FUDEVC and FULAR, which both begin in 1971. Three eight-year sliding spans (the first starting in 1974) were used in the analysis of these series, applying 3×5 seasonal filters for the adjustment of each span. Note that these span lengths and filter specifications differ from those used with the export series. The results of the analysis are presented in table 8-8.

Many more of the import series experience problems with the trading-day factors estimated by X-11-ARIMA than did the export series. Even when seasonally adjusted again without adjusting for trading-day effects, some of the series (FUAFR, FUCACM, FUCOME, and FUSA) do not improve enough to encourage seasonal adjustment. In addition, other series (FUOECD, FUWEUR, FUWGER, and FUWH), which already have acceptable values for the percentage of seasonal factors flagged when trading-day adjustments are included but have an unacceptable trading-day adjustment, show a dramatic drop in the number of months flagged for erratic month-to-month changes and little increase of erratic seasonal factors when seasonal adjustments are recalculated without trading-day adjustments. Only two series (FUASIA and FUOEEC) have acceptably low values of both percentages, erratic seasonal factors, and erratic trading-day factors; and even these series show substantially more stable estimates of adjusted month-to-month change when trading-day adjustment is not performed.

Table 8-8. Results of Sliding-Spans Analysis on Foreign Trade Import Series

Series	TD?	S	S(%)	M–M	M–M(%)	TD	TD(%)	Adjust?
FUAFR	yes	49	51.0	72	75.8	54	60.0	no
FUAFR	no	39	40.6	54	56.8	—	—	no
FUANEC	yes	22	22.9	45	47.4	1	1.1	no*
FUANEC	no	17	17.7	27	28.4	—	—	no*(?)
FUASIA	yes	9	9.4	45	47.4	11	12.2	no*
FUASIA	no	9	9.4	19	20.0	—	—	yes
FUCACM	yes	48	50.0	75	78.9	50	55.6	no
FUCACM	no	37	38.7	50	52.6	—	—	no
FUCOME	yes	57	59.4	74	77.9	64	77.1	no
FUCOME	no	56	58.3	63	66.3	—	—	no
FUDEVC	yes	23	24.0	39	41.1	5	5.6	no
FUDEVC	no	17	17.7	28	29.5	—	—	no(?)
FUJAP	yes	16	16.7	46	48.4	32	35.6	no
FUJAP	no	15	15.6	30	31.6	—	—	no(?)
FULAR	yes	21	21.9	51	53.7	33	36.7	no
FULAR	no	18	18.8	38	40.0	—	—	no*
FUOECD	yes	11	11.5	43	45.3	28	31.1	no*
FUOECD	no	7	7.3	19	20.0	—	—	yes
FUOEEC	yes	11	11.5	42	44.2	11	12.2	no
FUOEEC	no	13	13.5	21	22.1	—	—	yes*
FUSA	yes	54	56.3	78	82.5	53	58.9	no
FUSA	no	45	46.9	56	58.9	—	—	no
FUUK	yes	24	25.0	37	38.9	20	22.2	no
FUUK	no	20	20.8	20	21.1	—	—	no(?)
FUWEUR	yes	12	12.5	36	37.9	20	22.2	no*(?)
FUWEUR	no	6	6.3	17	17.9	—	—	yes
FUWGER	yes	9	9.4	47	49.5	33	36.7	no*
FUWGER	no	5	5.2	11	11.6	—	—	yes
FUWH	yes	5	5.2	38	40.0	23	25.6	no*
FUWH	no	2	2.1	9	9.5	—	—	yes

Note: See table 8-6 for definition of headings.

This leaves five series (FUANEC, FUDEVC, FUJAP, FULAR, and FUUK) having values for the percentage of the months flagged for extreme seasonal factors which fall in the gray area of 15 to 25 percent. Two of these series, FUANEC and FUDEVC, have trading-day factor estimates that are acceptably stable; but unless trading-day adjustment is omitted, FUANEC has too many erratic estimates of month-to-month change. For four of these five series, there is sufficient evidence from the X-11-ARIMA application to recommend against seasonally adjustment. FULAR and FUDEVC have a high degree of irregularity, coupled with a lack of stable seasonality (reflected by the F test for stable seasonality). FUUK also is very irregular. FUJAP exhibits a deleterious amont of linearly moving seasonality—reflected by the moving seasonality F test of the X-11-ARIMA program (Morry and Lothian, 1978). Therefore, we recommend that these four series not be adjusted. If stringent reliability requirements are not needed, an examination of the SI ratios suggests that FUANEC can be seasonally but not trading-day adjusted. The summary measures from X-11-ARIMA for these and the other import series can be found in table 8-9.

Now we turn to the results from the revisions-history analysis of the foreign trade series. Only 13 of the 30 series, the set of export series excluding XUCOME and XUCOMEA, are long enough to permit a revisions-history analysis. (The experimental period was required to contain at least two years of data.) Results for these series are given in table 8-10. The X-11 applications used to produce the revision histories used 3×9 seasonal filters and included a trading-day adjustment if the F test from X-11 did not reject it.

The experimental period for the series runs from January 1977 through December 1978. Using the criteria given in section V, five series (XUAFR, XUOEEC, XUSASIA, XUUK, and XUWGER) are found to be unsuitable for seasonal adjustment. Two of the remaining series (XUANEC and XUJAP) have mean values of $CONRAT$ equal to 0.009, near enough to the 0.01 threshold value to suggest careful examination of other measures. The values of CPREV and CONRAT for all other remaining series are acceptable. Except for XUASIA, whose revisions histories give no hint of difficulty with the seasonal adjustment, these results are quite similar to those obtained from the sliding-spans analysis. However, a sliding-spans analysis of XUASIA restricted to the time interval 1966–1978 containing the revisions-history start-up and experimental period finds very few erratic estimates of level (1.5 percent), month-to-month change (6.1 percent), or trading-day effect (0.0 percent), and a graph of XUASIA suggests that the character of the series changes around 1978. Diagnostics from X-11-ARIMA ($FST = 4.3$, $NEWQ = 1.30$) indicate that there is little seasonality

Table 8-9. X-11-ARIMA Diagnostics for Foreign Trade Import Series

Series	TD?	F ST	F TD	OLDQ	NEWQ	C-1	C-3	Adjust?
FUAFR	yes	2.3	6.7	1.24	1.51	55.44	43.07	no
FUAFR	no	2.3	—	1.26	1.52	61.83	45.78	no
FUANEC	yes	10.5	4.7	0.85	0.97	46.46	20.64	yes*
FUANEC	no	9.8	—	0.89	1.01	48.86	21.96	yes*
FUASIA	yes	8.2	5.0	0.77	0.92	36.16	20.18	yes*
FUASIA	no	8.3	—	0.82	0.96	33.96	21.09	yes
FUCACM	yes	5.6	2.5	1.22	1.35	55.34	37.06	no
FUCACM	no	5.7	—	1.25	1.38	55.09	37.07	no
FUCOME	yes	2.5	9.9	1.36	1.44	55.70	47.64	no
FUCOME	no	2.4	—	1.41	1.48	70.35	53.86	no
FUDEVC	yes	2.6	7.6	1.26	1.41	46.46	29.92	no
FUDEVC	no	2.8	—	1.21	1.37	46.17	32.82	no
FUJAP	yes	7.7	7.1	1.06	1.18	35.48	25.96	no
FUJAP	no	7.5	—	1.02	1.17	38.32	25.57	no
FULAR	yes	2.9	3.3	1.27	1.38	50.33	41.43	no
FULAR	no	2.9	—	1.27	1.38	55.58	45.22	no
FUOECD	yes	8.6	6.0	0.95	1.14	30.91	27.00	yes*
FUOECD	no	9.1	—	0.95	1.14	35.73	25.00	yes
FUOEEC	yes	4.7	3.8	1.19	1.29	42.20	39.05	no*
FUOEEC	no	4.6	—	1.21	1.30	47.42	40.70	no*
FUSA	yes	2.4	6.8	1.56	1.56	57.79	41.99	no
FUSA	no	2.5	—	1.59	1.59	65.35	41.82	no
FUUK	yes	5.5	6.3	1.13	1.23	44.35	40.38	no
FUUK	no	5.4	—	1.17	1.26	49.42	42.32	no
FUWEUR	yes	9.9	5.4	0.91	1.10	30.94	25.29	yes*
FUWEUR	no	10.2	—	0.96	1.15	35.18	24.30	yes(?)
FUWGER	yes	10.7	6.2	0.92	1.11	34.66	26.95	yes*
FUWGER	no	11.2	—	0.95	1.15	31.17	28.42	yes
FUWH	yes	7.2	3.4	1.05	1.12	43.47	23.82	yes*
FUWH	no	7.4	—	1.02	1.14	46.44	25.51	yes

Note: See table 8-7 for definition of headings.

Table 8-10. Results of Revision-History Analysis of Export Series

Series	CPREV				CONRAT			
	AVE	MAX	MIN	NOM	AVE	MAX	MIN	NOM[a]
XUAFR	.389	.629	.166	23	.015	.006	.031	18
XUANEC	.144	.213	.104	1	.009	.005	.022	9
XUASIA	.099	.146	.066	0	.005	.014	.001	1
XUDEVC	.142	.211	.074	4	.006	.012	.003	5
XUJAP	.154	.262	.090	6	.009	.005	.020	8
XULAR	.151	.359	.072	6	.008	.020	.002	5
XUOECD	.114	.163	.074	0	.006	.013	.003	4
XUOEEC	.194	.361	.096	12	.009	.029	.003	5
XUSASIA	.435	.619	.274	24	.029	.052	.015	24
XUUK	.211	.390	.132	16	.013	.029	.004	15
XUWEUR	.120	.184	.080	1	.006	.014	.003	3
XUWGER	.194	.282	.133	16	.009	.021	.004	6
XUWH	.081	.134	.053	0	.005	.015	.002	2

[a]Number of months in experimental period for which the measure exceeds its rejection threshold.

in this time. Seasonal adjustment is therefore inappropriate for either the full or the shortened series.

VIII. Comparison of Measures

In order to examine how the new measures relate to each other and to some of the more conventional measures, correlations between the measures were calculated from their values for the series analyzed here. Two correlation tables are presented within table 8-11. One, with all 31 series, shows the correlations between the sliding-spans measures and the conventional X-11-ARIMA measures. The other, with 14 series (including XU3), contains correlations for those series for which we could calculate the revisions-history measures. While any conclusions drawn from such an analysis should be considered preliminary, we feel that three points should be made. First, there appears to be a strong positive correlation between the sliding-spans measures and the revisions-history measures. These measures apparently capture very similar information. This is reassuring, because for many series only the sliding-spans measures can be computed due to series length. Second, the conventional measures, with the exception of the F test for trading day, display stronger relationships among themselves than with the new measures. Finally, the F test for trading day and the percentage of months flagged for erratic trading-day factors seem to have very little, if any, correlation.

Unlike the conventional diagnostic measures of X-11-ARIMA, the new measures, with the exception of *CONRAT*, are directly interpretable as quantities of interest to many producers of seasonally adjusted data. To the extent that they lead to similar conclusions, which usually happens, they render the decisions suggested by the more traditional diagnostics more intelligible. Even in these situations, they frequently offer valuable supplementary information, as they do in revealing that the series FUASIA, FUOECD, FUWGER, and FUWH while seasonally adjustable, should not be trading-day adjusted by X-11, in contradiction to what is suggested by X-11's F test. Indeed, the results of tables 8-6–8-9 show that this F test has little value for predicting when the trading-day adjustments calculated by X-11 or X-11-ARIMA will be reliable.

The series XULAR, XUOECD, XUOEEC, XUWEUR, and FUWH seem marginal by the standards of X-11-ARIMA and quite adjustable according to the new measures, providing trading-day adjustment is omitted in the case of XUOEEC and FUWH, and perhaps also of XULAR. The greatest disparity occurs with FUOEEC, which is nonseasonal and quite

Table 8-11.   Correlations of Measures Used in Study

A. 31 Series

Series	S(%)	M-M(%)	TD(%)	F ST	F TD	OLDQ
M-M(%)	.884					
TD(%)	.917	.897				
F ST	-.441	-.645	-.453			
F TD	-.086	-.091	-.096	.074		
OLDQ	.579	.670	.542	-.808	-.125	
NEWQ	.602	.697	.575	-.827	-.044	.971

B. 14 Series Analyzed with Revision-History Analysis

Series	S(%)	M-M(%)	TD(%)	CPREV	CONRAT	F ST	F TD	OLDQ
M-M(%)	.856							
TD(%)	.968	.903						
CPREV	.933	.864	.949					
CONRAT	.977	.810	.947	.944				
F ST	-.529	-.766	-.562	-.535	-.478			
F TD	-.427	-.257	-.379	-.445	-.516	-.093		
OLDQ	.792	.869	.762	.763	.741	-.875	-.085	
NEWQ	.719	.850	.703	.695	.668	-.940	-.030	.985

S(%)   : Percentage of months flagged for erratic seasonal factors
M-M(%) : Percentage of months flagged for erratic month-to-month changes in the seasonally adjusted data
TD(%)   : Percentage of months flagged for erratic trading-day factors
CPREV   : Revisions-history measure CPREV
CONRAT : Revisions-history measure CONRAT
F ST   : F statistic for stable seasonality taken from X-11-ARIMA
F TD   : F statistic for trading day taken from X-11-ARIMA
OLDQ   : Conventional Q measure from X-11-ARIMA
NEWQ   : Revised Q measure from X-11-ARIMA

irregular according to X-11-ARIMA and reasonably adjustable for seasonal but not for trading-day variation, as far as the new methods can suggest. In this case, we mildly favor X-11-ARIMA's conclusion. Thus, we do not recommend using only the new measures.

IX. Final Remarks

A subject that needs to be examined further is the effect of trading-day adjustment on estimates of the seasonally adjusted month-to-month change. In our sliding-spans analysis, some series with rather unstable estimates of the month-to-month change in the seasonally adjusted series have stable estimates for the seasonal factors. For example, XUOEEC had only 5 months flagged for erratic seasonal factors, but 61 months flagged for erratic month-to-month changes. When this analysis was repeated without adjusting for trading day, the number of months flagged for erratic month-to-month changes dropped dramatically, despite the fact that XUOEEC had only seven of its months flagged for erratic trading-day factors. Similar occurences in series such as XULAR and XUOECD give the impression that sometimes an apparently good trading-day adjustment can lead to erratic estimates of the month-to-month changes. There is, of course, the possibility that the criterion (equation 8.3) is not sensitive enough to problems with the trading-day adjustment. At present, it seems more likely that there are problems with X-11's approach to trading-day adjustment.

As mentioned before, the revisions-history measures have some limitations. First, these measures cannot be calculated if the series is too short. Shorter start-up periods have been tried, but tend to implausibly inflate the resulting measure. Second, as pointed out by Bell and Hillmer (1984), there are some seasonal adjustment techniques that do not have seasonal factors which converge to a final value in any practical sense. In this case, $CONRAT$ becomes meaningless, as there is no final value to converge to. A possible solution to this might be to pick as a "pseudo-final" value a fixed number of months in the future from the concurrent estimate for each month in an experimental period selected by the user. Third, the values of $CPREV$ and $CONRAT$ sometimes seem to be affected significantly by whether or not the series has been trading-day adjusted. For example, the values of $CPREV$ and $CONRAT$ for XU3 were 0.2851 and 0.0188, respectively. This was from seasonally adjusted data that was also calendar adjusted, because the X-11 F statistic's value of 4.1 suggested the trading-day effect was large enough. If this analysis is done without the calendar adjustment, we obtain $CPREV = 0.18$ and $CONRAT = 0.016$ for XU3. When trading-day adjustment was omitted, such decreases were observed for almost all of the 14 series for which revisions histories were calculated. This suggests that the threshold values for *CPREV* and *CONRAT* presented earlier may not be suitable for series not adjusted for trading-day effects. This phenomenon needs further scrutiny.

Appendix: FOREIGN TRADE SERIES

XUAFR	Exports to Africa
XUANEC	Exports to Asia NEC
XUASIA	Exports to Asia
XUCOME	Exports to Communist Areas in Europe (1/68 to 12/83)
XUCOMEA	Exports to Communist Areas in Europe and Asia (1/68 to 12/83)
XUDEVC	Exports to Developed Countries
XUJAP	Exports to Japan
XULAR	Exports to Latin American Republics
XUOECD	Exports to the members of the Organization for Economic Cooperation and Development
XUOEEC	Exports to members of European Common Market except the United Kingdom and West Germany
XUSASIA	Exports to South Asia
XUUK	Exports to the United Kingdom
XUWEUR	Exports to Western Europe
XUWGER	Exports to West Germany
XUWH	Exports to the Western Hemisphere
FUAFR	Imports from Africa
FUANEC	Imports from Asia NEC
FUASIA	Imports from Asia
FUCACM	Imports from the Central American Common Market
FUCOME	Imports from Communist Areas in Europe
FUDEVC	Imports from Developed Countries (1/71 to 12/83)
FUJAP	Imports from Japan
FULAR	Imports from Latin American Republics (1/71 to 12/83)
FUOECD	Imports from members of the Organization for Economic Cooperation and Development
FUOEEC	Imports from members of European Common Market except the United Kingdom and West Germany
FUSA	Imports from South Asia
FUUK	Imports from the United Kingdom

FUWEUR   Imports from Western Europe
FUWGER   Imports from West Germany
FUWH   Imports from the Western Hemisphere

NOTES:

All series are expressed in terms of hundreds of thousands of dollars. Except as noted, all the export series start in January 1966 and end in December 1983; and all of the import series start in January 1974 and end in December 1983.

The NEC in XUANEC and FUANEC refers to countries not contained in certain subclassifications. Countries whose data are combined to form these two series include Burma, Malasia, Thailand, Campuchia, Korea, and Hong Kong.

Notes

[1] Even if ARIMA forecasts are not used in the adjustment process, X-11-ARIMA uses a modified X-11 procedure which leads to (usually) slightly different seasonally adjusted values than are obtained from Census X-11. For more information on the differences between X-11 and X-11-ARIMA, see Monsell (1984). For specific information about these two procedures, see Shiskin, Young, and Musgrave (1967) for Census X-11 and Dagum (1983) for X-11-ARIMA.

[2] Traditionally, analysts have used mainly the relative contribution of the lag-one percent changes of the irregular series to the sum of squared lag-one percent changes of the original series to measure how much of the irregular component is present in the series. However, an analysis of transfer functions performed by Lothian and Morry (1978) led them to suggest that the third lag provides the best indication of how strong the irregular component is relative to the seasonal component. Values of both measures are given in this chapter.

[3] The SI ratios of a given X-11 (or X-11-ARIMA) seasonal adjustment are the detrended (and, when appropriate, also trading-day-adjusted) values. They are called "ratios" because, in the simple multiplicative model (series = trend × seasonal × irregular), these values are derived by dividing the original data adjusted for extremes by an estimate of the trend. The X-11 procedure obtains its seasonal factors as weighted averages of these SI ratios. For more information, see Shiskin et al. (1967) and Dagum (1983).

[4] While the final version of this chapter was being prepared, an error was discovered in the X-11-ARIMA program affecting the trading-day adjustment of the treatment of leap-year Februaries. The computations listed in this chapter were done using the uncorrected X-11-ARIMA. The number of leap-year Februaries is small enough that different adjustments for them would not affect our conclusions. For more information on this error, contact the authors or Statistics Canada.

[5] Our experience in using the Q measure from X-11-ARIMA has suggested a different strategy for evaluating Q from the one described by Lothian and Morry (1978). A series is to be considered adjustable if Q is less than 0.8. If Q is greater than 1.2, then the series probably should not be adjusted. If Q falls between 0.8 and 1.2, additional diagnostics should be examined before a recommendation is made regarding adjustability.

[6] The statistic in question is based upon the relative contribution of the irregular component to the variance of the series about a fitted mean function. The mean function used in X-11-ARIMA is a straight-line fit to the final trend estimates. The revision uses a linear spline

function rather than a straight line, where each month is a piece of the spline. For more details, see Lothian and Morry (1978) and Monsell and Findley (1984).

[7]These measures should probably be replaced by more robust ones. Being ratios of sums of squares, they can be strongly influenced by outliers, thereby making it difficult to set threshold values for them.

References

Bell, W. R., and Hillmer, S. C. 1984. Issues involved with the seasonal adjustment of time series. *Journal of Business and Economic Statistics* 2:291–320.

Cleveland, W. S. 1983. Seasonal and calendar adjustment. In D. R. Brillinger and P. R. Krishnaiah (Eds.), *Handbook of Statistics Volume 3: Time Series in the Frequency Domain*. Amsterdam: North-Holland. Pp. 39–72.

Cleveland, W. S., and Devlin, S. J. 1980. Calendar effects in monthly time series: Detection by spectrum analysis and graphical methods. *Journal of the American Statistical Association* 75:487–498.

Dagum, E. B. 1983. *The X-11-ARIMA Seasonal Adjustment Method*. Ottawa: Statistics Canada.

Lothian, J., and Morry, M. 1978. A set of quality control statistics for the X-11-ARIMA seasonal adjustment program. Seasonal Adjustment and Time Series Staff, Research Paper. Ottawa: Statistics Canada.

Monsell, B. C. 1984. The substantive changes in the X-11 procedure of X-11-ARIMA. Statistical Research Report No. CENSUS/SRD/RR-84/10. Washington, D.C.: Bureau of the Census.

Monsell, B. C., and Findley, D. F. 1984. Techniques for determining if a seasonal time series can be seasonally adjusted reliably by a given seasonal adjustment methodology. Statistical Research Report No. CENSUS/SRD/RR-84/14. Washington, D.C.: Bureau of the Census.

Morry, M., and Lothian, J. 1978. A test for the presence of identifiable seasonality when using the X-11 program. Seasonal Adjustment and Time Series Staff, Research Paper. Ottawa: Statistics Canada.

Shiskin, J., Young, A. H., and Musgrave, J. C. 1967. The X-11 variant of the Census Method II seasonal adjustment program. Technical Paper 15. Washington, D.C.: Bureau of the Census.

Young, A. H. 1965. Estimating trading-day variation in monthly economic time series. Technical Paper 12. Washington, D.C.: Bureau of the Census.

9 REGIONAL ECONOMETRIC MODELS: THE FORECASTING RECORD

Carl G. Brooking

I. Introduction

The development of regional econometric models has been quite rapid over the past two decades. From the simple theoretical specification offered by Klein (1969), the available models have been developed to include complex multiregional models such as the NRIES model (see Kort, 1983) maintained at the Bureau of Economic Analysis. The vast majority of the literature concerning regional econometric models is concerned with theoretical and structural improvements that can be made to the models. It is appropriate, however, to occasionally pause to reflect on the actual performance of existing models. Such an analysis can provide insight into the strengths and weaknesses of the models as they are actually used, leading to superior models and improved forecasting performance.

This chapter presents an analysis of the actual forecasting record of regional econometric models in six southeastern states. Although it is of necessity a fairly broad look at the record, it offers insight into the accuracy of the models. While actual forecasting accuracy is not the only criterion for a model's usefulness, it is an essential ingredient.

II. Error Measures

The analysis of forecasting errors of econometric models follows a tradition that is quite distinguished. The work of Theil (1966) laid a framework that serves as a standard for most research in the field. McNeese (1976) and Zarnowitz (1978) have compiled and analyzed the record of national forecasts with meticulous detail. More recently Smythe (1983) has analyzed the accuracy of the OECD forecasts for seven countries.

While the history of published forecasts for regional models is quite short (limited primarily to the years since 1972), sufficient data do exist to begin to calculate quantitative measures of forecasting accuracy.[1] The statistics presented here are for six regional models of states in the southeastern United States—Alabama, Florida, Georgia, Kentucky, Mississippi, and Tennessee. While not all of the states have published forecasts for the entire period considered, sufficient data exist to draw general conclusions for the southeastern United States.

The predicted annual percentage change of two variables—personal income and employment—serves as the focal point of the analysis. These forecasts are compared to actual percentage changes, based on the most recently published data revision.[2] Precise definitions of our predicted and actual percentage change date, labeled P_t and A_t respectively, are:

$$P_t = [(p_t - p_{t-1})/p_{t-1}] \times 100$$

$$A_t = [(a_t - a_{t-1})/a_{t-1}] \times 100$$

where

P_t　　= predicted level of variable at time t
p_{t-1} = best guess when forecast is prepared for actual level of variable at time $t - 1$
a_t　　= actual level of variable at time t

The calculation of P_t explicitly recognizes that the correct value of a variable is not always known at the time the forecast for the next year is prepared. The error statistics thus calculated are not biased by this uncertainty. No attempt is made to measure or account for errors resulting from the inaccuracy of the base from which the forecast was prepared.[3].

A number of error measurements are employed in this analysis. The mean absolute error (MAE), perhaps the most common error statistic, is calculated. The root mean square error (RMSE), a measure consistent with the notion of a quadratic loss function, is also presented. Also calculated is Theil's U^2 statistic, a standardized error measurement, which can be interpreted as the ratio of the forecast mean square error to the mean square error of a naive no-change forecast. A zero value for U^2 would represent a perfect forecast; a value of unity would imply that the forecast was equivalent to the naive forecast; a value greater than unity would imply a forecast worse than the naive. Precise definitions of these errors statistics are:

$$\text{MAE} = (\Sigma |P_t - A_t|)/N$$
$$\text{RMSE} = \sqrt{[\Sigma (P_t - A_t)^2]/N}$$
$$U^2 = \Sigma (P_t - A_t)^2 / \Sigma A_t^2$$

In addition to these summary errors, we have also calculated a decomposition of the mean square error along the lines suggested by Theil. The first decomposition is

$$\frac{\Sigma (P_t - A_t)^2}{N} = (\bar{P} - \bar{A})^2 + (S_p - S_A)^2 + 2(1 - r)S_p S_A \qquad (9.1)$$

where

$$\bar{P} = \Sigma P_t / N$$
$$\bar{A} = \Sigma A_t / N$$
$$S_p = [\Sigma (P_t - \bar{P})^2 / N]^{1/2}$$
$$S_A = [\Sigma (A_t - \bar{A})^2 / N]^{1/2}$$
$$r = \Sigma (P_t - \bar{P})(A_t - \bar{A})/NS_p S_A$$

Note that S_p and S_A are the standard deviations of P_t and A_t, respectively, and r is the correlation coefficient between P_t and A_t.

Dividing both sides of equation 9.1 by the mean square error yields

$$1 = \left[\frac{(\bar{P} - \bar{A})^2}{\Sigma (P_t - A_t)^2 / N}\right] + \left[\frac{(S_p - S_A)^2}{\Sigma (P_t - A_t)^2 / N}\right] + \left[2(1 - r)\frac{S_p S_A}{\Sigma (P_t - A_t)^2 / N}\right] \qquad (9.2)$$

or

$$1 = [U^M] + [U^S] + [U^C]$$

where U^M, U^S, and U^C are the respective terms of equation 9.2. U^M will be zero only if no errors of central tendency (bias) occur. U^S will be zero only if the actual and predicted have equal variation. U^C is equal to zero when the actual and predicted are perfectly correlated. Errors due to U^M are most serious, errors due to U^C are the least serious, and errors due to U^S fall between these two extremes.

Theil suggests a second decomposition as follows:

$$1 = \left[\frac{(\bar{P} - \bar{A})^2}{\Sigma(P_t - A_t)^2/N}\right] + \left[\frac{(S_p - rS_A)^2}{\Sigma(P_t - A_t)^2/N}\right] + \left[(1 - r^2)\frac{S_A^2}{\Sigma(P_t - A_t)^2/N}\right]$$

or

$$1 = U^M + U^R + U^D$$

As above, U^M is a measure of bias and ideally should be close to zero. U^R will approach zero as the slope of a regression of P_t and A_t tends toward unity. The U^D term deals with the variance of the regression disturbances and thus is somewhat random and uncontrollable. Thus, forecasts with small U^M and U^R compared to U^D are relatively free from predictable, systematic errors which might be eliminated by the use of a linear correction factor.

III. State Forecast Error

Table 9-1 presents summary error statistics for the six states. In addition, error statistics for a naive forecast assuming that $P_t = A_{t-1}$ are presented for comparative purposes. Table 9-1 indicates that the state forecasts for personal income are superior to the naive forecast by most measures. The Theil U^2 statistics are particularly low, due primarily to the large change over time in this variable. The forecasts for employment are subject to somewhat larger errors, although the Theil U^2 is still well below unity. With the exception of the states of Alabama and Florida, the actual forecast errors are well below those for the naive forecast.[4]

Table 9-2 summarizes the forecast error for all states combined. As one would expect, all three summary measures—mean absolute error, root mean square error, and Theil's U^2 statistic—indicate that model forecasts are superior to the naive forecast. The first decomposition of RMSE for personal income shows no bias, with the bulk of the remaining error due to unequal covariation, the uncontrollable factor. The second decomposition is similar, with 86 percent of the error due to the disturbance term. The first decomposition of the employment variable shows no bias but substantial error due to unequal variation. The second decomposition attributes virtually all of the error to the disturbance term.

The forecasting record of the six states taken as a whole is good. In virtually all cases, the state forecasts outperformed the naive models by a considerable margin. In addition, the decomposition of the error indicated that most of the error fell into the less-important uncontrollable categories.

Another way to analyze the erros of forecasts is to consider a *prediction-*

Table 9-1. Summary of Forecast Error: Individual States

	Personal Income		Employment	
	Model Forecast	Naive Forecast	Model Forecast	Naive Forecast
Alabama (2 observations—1981–1982)				
Mean Absolute Error	3.71	3.96	2.24	0.96
Root Mean Square Error	4.94	4.90	2.31	1.27
Theil's U^2	0.20	0.18	0.50	0.15
Florida (2 observations—1981–1982)				
MAE	4.23	4.51	3.09	2.57
RMSE	4.32	6.11	3.40	2.86
Theil's U^2	0.10	0.21	0.47	0.33
Georgia (4 observations—1975–1978)				
MAE	1.50	3.47	4.26	4.43
RMSE	1.71	3.78	5.04	4.68
Theil's U^2	0.02	0.11	0.70	0.61
Kentucky (5 observations—1974–1978)				
MAE	3.01	1.83	1.57	2.51
RMSE	3.75	2.41	1.78	2.97
Theil's U^2	0.10	0.04	0.22	0.62
Mississippi (9 observations—1974–1982)				
MAE	2.18	3.66	2.66	3.07
RMSE	2.59	4.13	3.18	3.87
Theil's U^2	0.06	0.14	0.71	1.06
Tennessee (7 observations—1976–1982)				
MAE	1.72	2.74	2.07	2.86
RMSE	2.15	3.41	2.34	3.30
Theil's U^2	0.04	0.09	0.49	0.98

Table 9-2. Summary of Forecast Error: All States

	Personal Income		Employment	
	Model Forecast	Naive Forecast	Model Forecast	Naive Forecast
All states (29 observations)				
Mean absolute error	2.37	3.18	2.56	2.93
Root mean square error	3.01	3.79	3.11	3.44
Theil's U^2	0.07	0.11	0.54	0.79
First set of Inequality proportions				
U^M	0.00	N/A	0.00	N/A
U^S	0.16	N/A	0.31	N/A
U^C	0.84	N/A	0.69	N/A
Second set of inequality proportions				
U^M	0.00	N/A	0.00	N/A
U^R	0.14	N/A	0.01	N/A
U^D	0.86	N/A	0.99	N/A

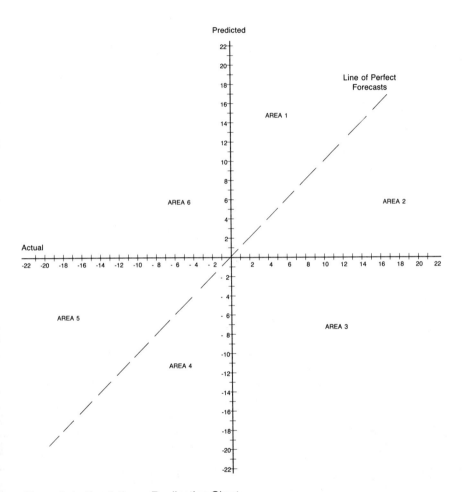

Figure 9-1. Predictions–Realization Chart

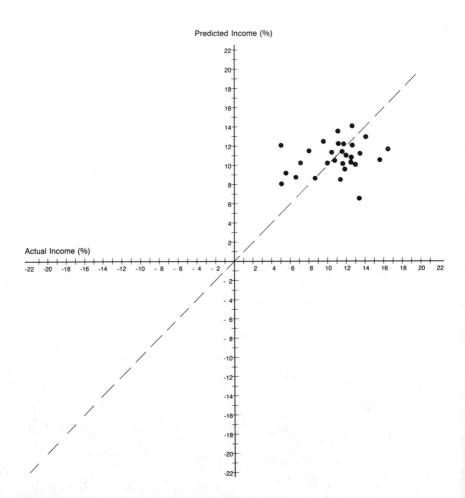

Figure 9-2. Predictions–Realization Chart
All States–Personal Income

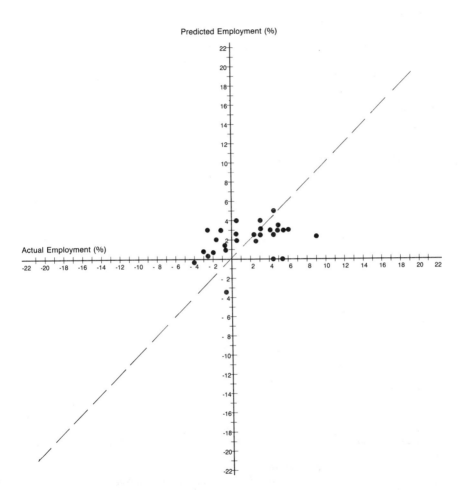

Figure 9-3. Predictions–Realization Chart
All States–Employment

realization chart, a plot of the predicted changes against the actual changes. Perfect forecasts will, of course, lie along the 45-degree line indicated in figure 9-1. In addition, the errors may be classified by area of the chart in which they lie. Areas 3 and 6 represent turning-point error areas, where the direction of change of the predicted and actual do not agree. Area 1 represents an overprediction of positive change, area 2 an underprediction of position change, area 5 represents an overprediction of negative change, and area 4 represents an underprediction of negative change.

Figures 9-2 and 9-3 show the forecasts for the six states. They indicate no turning-point errors for personal income with equal amounts of under- and overprediction. Substantial turning errors exist for the employment forecasts, with only two of the ten downturns forecast correctly. This inability to correctly call negative turns in the regional economy is perhaps the worst problem with forecasting with regional econometric models.

IV. Summary

On balance, the forecasting record in the six states is superior to that which can be achieved using naive models. The average level of error is still quite high—ranging from 2 to 3 percent. The inability of the models to forecast economic downturns is its greatest weakness, a flaw that regional models share with their national counterparts. On the whole, the record is encouraging. Regional econometric models have proved themselves to be useful. Although there is ample room for improvement, there is certainly nothing in the record to indicate that the models should be abandoned.

Notes

[1] See Brooking and Hake (1980) for an earlier effort in this area.

[2] We differ with Eckstein and Warburg [9] on this point. They advocate the use of the first published data, rather than the most recent.

[3] See Su (1978) for such a decomposition.

[4] The Alabama and Florida statistics are based on only a few, very recent forecasts.

References

Brooking, C., and Hake, D. 1980. The impact of the regional econometric model on the policy formation decision process. In F. Adams and N. Glickman (Eds.),

Modeling the Multiregional Economic System. Lexington, MA: Heath (Lexington Books).

Eckstein, O., and Warburg, P. 1978. Discussion. *American Economic Review* 68(3):320–321.

Klein, L. R. 1969. The specification of regional econometric models. *Papers and Proceedings of the Regional Science Association* 23:105–115.

Kort, J. 1983. A multiregional test of the Conway-Howard Housing Construction Model. *Journal of Regional Science* 23(3):413–418.

McNees, S. 1976. The forecasting performance in the early 1970s. *New England Economic Review* (July/August): 1–13.

McNees, S. 1978. The rationality of economic forecasts. *American Economic Review* 68(3):301–305.

Smythe, David J. 1983. Short-run macroeconomic forecasting: The OECD performance. *Journal of Forecasting* (January–March):2(1):37–49.

Su, V. 1978. An error analysis of econometric and noneconometric forecasts. *American Economic Review* 68(3):306–312.

Theil, Henri. 1966. *Applied Economic Forecasting*. Chicago: Rand-McNally.

Zarnowitz, V. 1978. On the accuracy and properties of recent macroeconometric forecasts. *American Economic Review* 68(3):313–319.

About the Authors

Jerald R. Barnard is Professor of Economics and Director of the Institute of Economic Research at the University of Iowa in Iowa City, Iowa. Professor Barnard has an extensive publication record in the areas of urban, regional, and resource economics. He has served as President of the Mid-Continent Regional Science Association and the Missouri Valley Economic Association. In addition to his academic position, Professor Barnard serves as Chairman of the Iowa Economic Forecasting Council.

Richard M. Beemiller is currently a regional economist in the Bureau of Economic Analysis. He has published several papers and has written and presented papers at numerous conferences. He attained his B.S. in Business Administration at the University of Colorado and an M.A. in Economics from the University of Pittsburgh. He has worked as an Account Executive for Merrill Lynch, Pierce, Fenner, and Smith and as Marketing Representative for Philip Morris U.S.A. Beemiller has given numerous public speeches as well as his publications.

Carl G. Brooking is currently Associate Professor at Millsaps College. He received his Ph.D. and M.A. from the University of Pennsylvania in Econometrics and Industrial Organization and Economics, respectively. He has held numerous management and consulting positions and had several publications and reports. He is doing current research on an "Economic Model of Jackson, Mississippi," "Characteristics of Subsidiaries of Electric Utility Holding Companies," and "The Forecasting Record of Regional Econometric Models." His integration of the agricultural sector into the Mississippi Econometric Model was a pioneering development in regional modeling.

Joseph V. Cartwright is currently with the office of The Secretary of Defense. He was formerly a Regional Economist at the Bureau of Economic Analysis, U.S. Department of Commerce. Mr. Cartwright has published a number of monographs and articles on impact analysis with input/output models.

Alberta H. Charney is presently Research Specialist with the Division of Economic and Business Research at the University of Arizona. She received her B.A. in Mathematics from Carnegie-Mellon University, an M.S. in Economics from the University of Illinois, and a Ph.D. in Economics from the University of Illinois. Her areas of research include regional modeling, transportation economics, and consumer demand.

David F. Findley is currently a Mathematical Statistician/Time Series Analyst for the Bureau of the Census in Washington D.C. He attained his B.S. and M.A. in Mathematics from the University of Cincinnati and Dr. Phil. Nat. in Applied Mathematics from the University of Frankfurt where he was Magna Cum Laude. He received the U.S. Department of Commerce Bronze Medal in 1983. Dr. Findley has published numerous seminal writings and is presently Vice Chairman of the Time Series Interaction Committee.

James E. Kennedy is an economist at the Division of Research and Statistics, Board of Governors of the Federal Reserve System in Washington, D.C. He was previously affiliated with the Institute of Economic Research at the University of Iowa where he participated in the construction and management of a large-scale econometric model of the state of Iowa. Dr. Kennedy's research interests include labor and production economics as well as regional econometric models.

John R. Kort is currently employed with the U.S. Department of Commerce as a regional economist and is director of the National-Regional Impact Evaluation System. Dr. Kort is the author of a number of professional publications, including articles, monographs, and professional reports. He holds a B.A. from Indiana University of Pennsylvania and a M.A. and Ph.D. from the University of Tennessee. His research interests include regional economics, econometric modeling, computer programming, and international economics.

Brian C. Monsell received his Master of Science degree in Statistics from Florida State University in 1982. Since then, he has served as a mathematical statistician for the Statistical Research Division of the Bureau of the Census, where he carries out research in time series methodology. Mr. Monsell has written a number of technical papers on seasonal and calendar adjustment techniques during his tenure at the Bureau of the Census, and consults with clients both in and out of the Bureau of the Census on topics dealing with seasonal adjustment.

M. Ray Perryman is Herman Brown Professor of Economics and Director of the Center for the Advancement of Economic Analysis, Baylor University. Additionally, he serves as Director of Baylor University Forecasting Service and is the architect of the Texas Econometric Model. He holds a B.S. in Mathematics from Baylor and a Ph.D. in Economics from Rice University. Dr. Perryman is an internationally respected scholar, having published hundreds of scholarly papers and books on a wide range of topics. He has received numerous research awards and holds offices in a number of international academic societies. Dr. Perryman is the author of the *Texas Economic Forecast: The Perryman Report*, a subscription service providing detailed projections from the Texas econometric model.

Nancy S. Perryman is Assistant Director for Research at the Center for the Advancement of Economic Analysis, Baylor University. She holds a B.S. in Mathematics Education from the University of Houston and an M.S. in Economics from Baylor. She has extensive experience in data base design, econometric model simulation, and data construction.

James R. Schmidt is Associate Professor of Economics at the University of Nebraska-Lincoln. Professor Schmidt has published articles in a variety of fields within economics including econometrics, monetary economics, regional economics, and social insurance. In the field of regional economics, Professor Schmidt's research efforts and writings have involved tax base forecasting, local tax issues, economic activity accounts, energy production, and state econometric models.

Carol A. Taylor is currently Associate Professor of Economics and Program Director for Forecasting in the Bureau of Economic and Business Research at the University of Florida. She attended Harvard University where she received her B.A. in Economics. Dr. Taylor received her Ph.D. from the University of Michigan. She has numerous publications in the areas of regional modeling, mineral economics, and applied microeconomic theory. Dr. Taylor also has several research projects in progress and participates in several professional associations. She was formerly associated with the University of Arizona.

Jan Tinbergen received a Ph.D. in Physics from Leiden University in 1929. He did business cycle research at the Dutch Central Statistical Bureau from 1928–1945. During a two-year period (1936–1938) he combined this with similar research at the League of Nations Secretariat Geneva. He was director of the Dutch Central Planning Bureau from 1945–1959 and also worked full time as a Professor from 1956–1973. During that time he also acted as expert to the World Bank and a number of governments of developing countries. He received the Alfred Nobel Memorial Prize for Economic Science in 1967. He is presently emeritus professor at Erasmus University, Rotterdam.

Richard E. Weber is currently an associate professor of economics and finance at Monmouth College in New Jersey. He has published more than twenty monographs and articles in numerous journals. He works in the general area of economic development of New Jersey. He has held management and engineering positions and has memberships in several economic organizations.

Index

DATE DUE